Dag Hammarskjold's United Nations

NUMBER SEVEN

Columbia University Studies in International Organization

EDITORS

Leland M. Goodrich
William T. R. Fox

Dag Hammarskjold's United Nations

Mark W. Zacher

Columbia University Press
New York and London
1970

Mark W. Zacher is Associate Professor of Political Science, University of British Columbia, Vancouver

Copyright © 1970 Columbia University Press
SBN: 231-03275-7
Library of Congress Catalog Card Number: 71-101593
Printed in the United States of America

To My Mother and Father

Columbia University Studies in International Organization

This series of monographs was initiated to provide for the publication under University auspices of studies in the field of international organization undertaken and carried out, in whole or in part, by members of Columbia Faculties or with the assistance of funds made available under research programs of the University. Work in this field has been substantially assisted by grants from the Rockefeller and Ford Foundations.

The series is not intended to provide a systematic coverage of the field of international organization nor is it anticipated that volumes will appear with any set regularity. The value of the contribution which the monograph makes to knowledge and understanding of the role of international organization and its functioning in the world in which we live will be the dominant consideration in determining inclusion. The series is published under the joint editorship of Leland M. Goodrich and William T. R. Fox, with Andrew W. Cordier and Louis Hankin acting in an advisory capacity.

The other books in this series are *Controls for Outer Space*, by Phillip C. Jessup and Howard J. Taubenfeld, *The United Nations Emergency Force*, by Gabriella Rosner, *UN Administration of Economic and Social Programs*, edited by Gerard J. Mangone, *The UN Secretary-General and the Maintenance of Peace*, by Leon Gordenker, *The United Nations Economic and Social Council*, by Walter R. Sharp, and *Legal Effects of United Nations Resolutions*, by Jorge Castañeda (translated by Alba Amoia).

Acknowledgments

In the writing of this study many books and articles have served as valuable aids, but I wish to cite two books which have proved to be of exceptional assistance. They are Wilder Foote's excellent and quite comprehensive collection of Hammarskjold speeches and writings, *Servant of Peace: A Selection of Speeches and Statements of Dag Hammarskjold* (Harper and Row, 1962) and Joseph Lash's political biography of the late Secretary-General entitled *Dag Hammarskjold: Custodian of the Brush-Fire Peace* (Doubleday, 1961). Although the latter book is journalistic in format, it contains a great deal of valuable information and many interesting insights. I also wish to cite one book which has been of considerable assistance in organizing this study, Myres S. McDougal's and Florentino P. Feliciano's *Law and Minimum World Public Order* (Yale University Press, 1961; especially Chapter IV).

During the course of writing this study I interviewed twenty-two individuals who knew Dag Hammarskjold and who had contact with him in his capacity as Secretary-General. Because many of these people still occupy positions in the United Nations Secretariat or in national governments or because they did not want information attributed to them, I have been unable to cite them in my bibliography and footnotes. To all of these people I express my sincere thanks for their time and courtesy.

Throughout the preparation of this study I benefited from the comments of a number of people. From Columbia University I wish to thank René Albrecht-Carrie, Percy E. Corbett, Andrew W. Cordier, Leland M. Goodrich, Henry F. Graff, and Oliver J. Lisitzyn. To friends and colleagues, Yale Ferguson, K. J. Holsti, Ole R. Holsti, and David A. Kay, I also express my appreciation. My

Acknowledgments

most profound intellectual debt throughout the writing of this study has been to Professor Goodrich. He strongly influenced the choice of the topic, and during its writing he was very generous with his time and suggestions. My work in the field of international organization in graduate school was significantly due to his guidance and interest. I also want to offer special thanks to President Andrew W. Cordier for having given me some of his vast and intimate knowledge about Dag Hammarskjold's work as Secretary-General and for having read and commented upon several drafts of this study. I am especially grateful to President Cordier since he did these things amidst his own very demanding schedule.

I am indebted to two sources for financial assistance in the writing of this study. The Woodrow Wilson Foundation supported me generously during my dissertation work, and while at the University of British Columbia I have been assisted by the Dean's Committee on Research (Faculty of Graduate Studies), which has paid for all typing and travel expenses associated with the rewriting of the dissertation. During the process of preparing this manuscript for publication, I have greatly benefited from the cooperation and criticism of Frederick Nicklaus and Robert J. Tilley of the Columbia University Press, and I wish to express my gratitude to them.

Throughout the initial writing of this study in graduate school, as throughout all previous stages of my formal education, my parents have been as helpful and encouraging as parents could possibly be. I want to thank my father especially for having given me many valuable suggestions on improving the style of my first draft. Finally, I want to thank my wife, Carol, for having typed several drafts of this study and for having provided a pleasant atmosphere in which to work.

Mark W. Zacher

Vancouver, B.C., Canada
June 1969

Contents

Dag Hammarskjold's
United Nations

Introduction

No international institution has been so shrouded in myths and inaccurate criticism and praise as has the United Nations. The reason for this lies partially in the contrast between the initial hopes for the Organization and its more modest accomplishments, partially in its unique supranational aspects in our present world system of sovereign states, and partially in the tendency of both statesmen and laymen to discuss it in a symbolic rather than an analytical manner. One often hears such statements as: "The foreign policy of our nation is based first and foremost on its participation in and adherence to the United Nations"; and "The United Nations represents the last and best hope for mankind." In such statements the United Nations is used as a symbol of justice and morality with which statesmen and laymen like to associate their nations or as a symbol of moral redemption for a conflict-ridden world. While such remarks may have the purposes of setting forth lofty, although usually somewhat misleading, goals of national foreign policies and of trying to prod nations into greater international cooperation, they do not reflect the real role which the United Nations plays in international politics.

At the time of its creation in 1945 there were great hopes that by working through the United Nations the Member States, and especially the Great Powers, would be able to secure international peace. With the coming of the Cold War these hopes were crushed, and many people viewed the Organization as a "debating society" with little or no influence on the behavior of states. The United Nations during the first several years of its existence did have some influence on the conflicts concerning Indonesia, Palestine, the former Italian colonies, and Kashmir, but its role was such a far cry from the initial hopes for the Organization that there was little analysis at that time concerning the nature of its influence. There were during the late 1940s people who still cried for humanity to rally to its cause and statesmen who declared that it was the strongest pillar of their nations' foreign policies, but its popular image was that of an impotent debating society. For a short while, the United Nations' support for the resistance to the North Korean attack on the Republic of Korea and the provision of troops and supplies by a number of United Nations Members to the Republic of Korea renewed the hope of many that it would become a powerful force for resisting aggression; but that image was soon weakened when it was recognized that the military power and the political direction for the United Nations Force were coming primarily from the United States. By the time that the first Secretary-General, Trygve Lie, left his post in 1953, the United Nations had been the victim of exalted and unrealistic hopes on the one hand and despair and cynicism on the other. A study of the Organization's activities during the years 1946–1953 reveals that its political influence was slight and was confined primarily to the problems surrounding decolonization processes in Indonesia, Palestine, the Indian subcontinent, and the former Italian colonies.

During the eight-and-one-half years that Dag Hammarskjold served as Secretary-General of the United Nations, from 1953 to 1961, it was obvious to observers of the international scene that the political role of the United Nations underwent a rapid evolution. The diplomatic activity concerning many of the major international crises of the period, such as those concerning the Communist Chinese imprisonment of American fliers under the United Nations Command in Korea, the nationalization of the Suez Canal, the Israeli and Anglo-French invasions of Egypt, the Middle East conflict of 1958, and the disorders in the Congo, was centered in the United Nations. This activity was not confined only to discussions among the Members, but also involved the delegation of different kinds of diplomatic and operational responsibility to the Secretary-General and bodies under him. Although many people were aware that all of these activities signified a new and more influential role for the United Nations, there was little understanding of the nature of this new role and the factors upon which it rested. It was obvious that an evolution had taken place, but exactly what it was and where it was going were unclear to most people.

The one individual who influenced this development more than any other person, who commented on it more than any other, and who was in a position to understand it better than any other was Secretary-General Dag Hammarskjold. During his term of office he stepped into the relatively new area of international organization and became an important force in changing its character. He did this mainly by providing the Member States with a resourceful instrument for direct action in the Secretary-General and his staff and by providing advice and leadership regarding the utilization of different United Nations means of action in international politics. With an exceptional understanding of international politics and an unusual diplomatic finesse, he helped to mold a new political role for the United Nations. During this very creative period of activity Hammarskjold left a record in words and actions which reflects his ideas regarding the political role of the United Nations, or what Michel Virally has described as his "doctrine of the United Nations." [1]

It is precisely this conception or doctrine of the United Nations which Hammarskjold developed which will be the primary focus of this study. A conception or doctrine of a political organization such as the United Nations generally encompasses views on particular traits which the Organization does and/or should possess and certain courses of action which it does and/or should pursue; and it often includes predictions of what is likely to develop. The particular traits of the Organization in respect to which Hammarskjold's views will be examined are its goals and bases of power, and the particular courses of action are its strategies and tactics. Most of these concepts have been borrowed from the writings of Myres S. McDougal and Harold D. Lasswell, and the general structure of the study has been strongly influenced by their policy-oriented approach to the study of politics. [2] At the same time a new concept (that is, tactics) has been added to their lexicon. Also, their definitions have been modified. *Bases of power* refer to all resources or bases values—material and non-material—which can be used to influence events. *Strategies* are policies which indicate *where* or *in what contexts* certain actors should employ certain means of action within a political system—in our case, the international system—in order to promote certain goals. Strategies are thus courses of action which are oriented to a particular structure of relationships in a political system and particular issues in that system. In explaining why a strategy has been prescribed, it is necessary to set forth why certain actors or groups of actors are likely to support the activities of a political organization in certain contexts and why their support and the resources of the organization may or are likely to assure their success. *Tactics* are policies which indicate *how* certain actors should act in the processes of initiating, utilizing, and directing specific means of action. They thus indicate *how* different actors should go about creating or using certain means of action rather than *where* or *in what systemic contexts* they should be used. They are generally applicable to action in any kind of situation rather than action in specific types of situations. In explaining why a certain tactic should be adopted, it is necessary to state why specific policies by the actors in creating certain means of action or in directing them along specific courses of action are likely to engender greater cooperation or compliance by various parties.

A criticism may be raised by some readers of this study that the author has pushed Hammarskjold's attitudes into a framework which was not Hammarskjold's and which thus distorts his views. Concerning such a criticism it should be noted that any study which aspires to analytical coherence must adopt a framework which breaks down the reality which it is examining. The value of the framework rests on the clarity of the analysis, and it is hoped that the following study will justify the framework which has been employed. Another point which should be raised in respect to this possible criticism is that the structure of Hammarskjold's last major analysis of the United Nations' role in world politics bears a striking resemblance to the general organization of this study.[3]

Another objection which may be raised by some readers and which is closely related to the previous possible criticism is that the spelling out of his strategies and tactics imposes on Hammarskjold's thought and activities a greater rationality and coherence than existed in fact. Regarding such a critique the author would point out that wherever possible the study has based its interpretations on Hammarskjold's own statements (of which there were many), and where these were not available or were not thorough, the author has consulted a number of people who worked with Hammarskjold to determine whether his interpretations of Hammarskjold's intentions and calculations were correct. The author has also benefited from a number of other studies on Hammarskjold's activities and views and on United Nations politics during Hammarskjold's years as Secretary-General. The information on which each of the strategies and tactics is based is set forth quite clearly in the discussion of each strategy and tactic, and the author believes that in very few cases are there any very risky judgments. It is possible that Hammarskjold followed certain strategies and tactics which have not been articulated in this study. While the author has sought to be as thorough as possible in studying existing information, it has been impossible to obtain all relevant information since Hammarskjold's private papers have not been made public and since the death of the Secretary-General has precluded firsthand interviews.

While the primary focus of this study is a presentation of Hammarskjold's conception of the United Nations, a subsidiary focus is to present a partial record of Hammarskjold's diplomatic activities as Secretary-General. As a result of having this subsidiary focus, the study has given more examples of the application of the strategies and tactics and has gone into greater detail on these examples than perhaps would have been necessary if a presentation of Hammarskjold's conception of the Organization was its only objective.

Before proceeding with the body of this study, its organization will first be outlined. The first chapter is devoted to a short description of Hammarskjold's background and a presentation of the political attitudes which he possessed when he came to the United Nations. Since these attitudes are one set of variables which influenced his conception or doctrine of the Organization, they are set forth at the beginning of the book. The second chapter presents Hammarskjold's views on the goals of the United Nations and its permanent bases of power. His views on these aspects of the Organization have both a descriptive and prescriptive character. In some cases what he felt existed and what he felt should exist coincided, but in some cases his views on what existed and what should exist differed. It should also be mentioned that his views were sometimes predictive in that they concerned the conditions which would encourage certain attributes of the United Nations and the likelihood of their emergence.

The following four chapters (Chapters III–VI) are devoted to Hammarskjold's strategies and tactics for promoting the major goals of the United Nations. All of his strategies for promoting a particular goal are set forth separately in the first part of each chapter, and then his tactics are listed in the second part. Under each strategy and tactic there is an analysis of why he prescribed it and a description of his and/or the United Nations representative organs' applications of it during the years 1953–1961. The analyses of why he prescribed each strategy and tactic are based on his views of the existence of certain conditions and certain causal relationships in international politics. While Hammarskjold's views on different strategies and tactics were primarily prescriptive in character, many did tend to have a predictive character also in that they involved some ideas on what conditions would have to emerge in order to permit their success in the future and what the likelihood of their emergence was.

While this study does not try to be a critique of Hammarskjold's conception of the Organization, a number of the author's judgments on Hammarskjold's views and activities do appear in the study. When such defenses of some aspects of his conception of the Organization do appear, they are generally expressed in order to rebut some existing interpretations about these aspects of his conception. The only section of the study which has as a primary purpose an evaluation of Hammarskjold's conception is the conclusion, and then only the most prominent aspects of his conception are discussed.

In concluding this introduction, it should be stated that although Hammarskjold's conception of the Organization developed in response to the character of the Organization and the international environment during a particular period of time, namely the years 1953–1961, they have a great deal of relevance to the United

Nations' present and future position in international politics. The bases of power which Hammarskjold analyzed have not changed substantially since his death, and they are unlikely to undergo any marked changes in the near future. Also, his views regarding the likelihood of their development and the conditions under which they are likely to develop constitute interesting theoretical insights which can be evaluated and checked against future trends. The strategies and tactics which he prescribed for the Organization are also very relevant to the present and future activities of the Organization. Since there are still a number of similarities between the international system during the period 1953–1961 and the present international system, a number of the strategies which Hammarskjold prescribed for the Organization may also have a great deal of relevance to present and future activities of the Organization. Even if the international system has so changed that some of these strategies have little relevance to the present and future, it is hoped that a study of Hammarskjold's strategies will assist the reader in understanding the political role of the Organization during a past period and will guide his attention to those types of conditions in the United Nations and the international environment which affect the activities of the United Nations. In respect to Hammarskjold's tactics, which are not tied as closely to a particular structure of relations among the states in the world, it is posited that they still should have as much relevance for the United Nations as they had during Hamarskjold's tenure.

The accuracy and desirability of various aspects of Hammarskjold's conception of the Organization both during his tenure as Secretary-General and during the present and future will have to be judged by every student of the United Nations for himself. However, in order to understand the development and activities of the Organization during his years as Secretary-General and in order to make sound and rational prescriptions for the future, it is very important—if not crucial—to grasp Hammarskjold's legacy.

Chapter One

Dag Hammarskjold: Background and Political Attitudes

Background

Dag Hammarskjold was born on July 29, 1905 in south-central Sweden in the town of Jonkoping. He belonged to an aristocratic family which traced its origins back to the seventeenth century.[1] His father, Hjalmar Hammarskjold, was a well-known public figure in Sweden who held positions of professor of law, civil servant in the Ministry of Justice, Prime Minister (throughout most of World War I), and Governor of the Province of Uppsala. In addition, he took part in a number of international arbitrations and was Chairman of the Committee of Experts for the Progressive Codification of International Law of the League of Nations.

In 1924 Dag Hammarskjold graduated from secondary school at the top of his class and enrolled at the University of Uppsala where he studied political economy, philosophy, literature, and French. Two years later he was awarded a Bachelor of Arts degree and again was at the top of his class. Continuing at the University of Uppsala, he earned both a Master of Arts degree in political economy and a Bachelor of Law degree between 1926–1930. In 1930 he enrolled at the University of Stockholm for a doctorate in economics, and four years later he obtained his degree. During this period he also held a position as Secretary of the Government's Committee on Unemployment and in this capacity distinguished himself as a brilliant young economist.

In 1935 Hammarskjold became Secretary of the National Bank

of Sweden, and in 1936, at the age of thirty-one, he was appointed Under-Secretary of Finance by the Finance Minister, Ernst Wigforss, who had worked closely with him while he was Secretary of the Committee on Unemployment. Wigforss has recorded that there was opposition to Hammarskjold's appointment because of his age but that this was overcome because of his reputation as a brilliant scholar.[2] The appointment was under the Social Democratic Government which was laying the foundations of the Swedish welfare state. Hammarskjold was not a member of the party at the time nor did he join it later. In 1941 he was appointed Chairman of the Board of the Swedish National Bank in addition to his duties as Under-Secretary in the Finance Ministry.

At the end of World War II Dag Hammarskjold became adviser to the cabinet on international economic problems arising out of the war and concentrated on Sweden's trade policies. In 1947 he moved into the Foreign Affairs Ministry as Under-Secretary and then as Secretary-General of the Foreign Office. In these capacities he became a leading figure in the framing of Sweden's international economic policies. In 1948 he relinquished his position as Chairman of the Board of the Swedish National Bank in order to devote all his time to international matters. In the same year he became head of Sweden's delegation to the Organization for European Economic Cooperation and vice-chairman of the OEEC's Executive Committee. As a result of the respect which he gained among other diplomats in this context, he was nominated for the position of Secretary-General of the United Nations in 1953. Paul G. Hoffman, who was the Administrator in Europe for the United States Economic Cooperation Administration and who in this capacity worked closely with the delegations to the OEEC, has remarked that Hammarskjold and the Frenchman, Robert Marjolin, were the two most capable delegates to the OEEC.[3] Hoffman has noted too that Hammarskjold was never flamboyant, had a great ability to master very complicated and technical problems, and was able often to find compromises upon which disputing parties could agree.[4]

The last position which Hammarskjold held in Sweden prior to his election as Secretary-General of the United Nations was that of Deputy Foreign Minister which he assumed in 1951. He also became a Minister without portfolio in the Swedish cabinet. In his new office in the Foreign Ministry he dealt primarily with Sweden's foreign economic relations. It should be stressed that in all his assignments he was considered to be primarily an economic expert and a technician rather than a politican. His ability to bring parties together either within the Swedish government or in the OEEC was viewed as a function of his great economic expertise rather than any great political skill. Rikard Sandler, a former Prime Minister and Foreign Minister of Sweden, who was head of the foreign relations committee of the Swedish parliament during Hammarskjold's years in the Foreign Ministry, has remarked that neither he nor most of his colleagues had any idea that Hammarskjold possessed the great political skills demonstrated later in his work at the United Nations. It was his impression that Hammarskjold actually tended to shun publicity and political involvement.[5]

Political Attitudes

Prior to becoming Secretary-General in 1953 Hammarskjold had developed a number of distinct political attitudes. One can find these attitudes expressed in articles which he wrote prior to 1953 as well as in several of his statements after 1953 in which he reflected on his background and beliefs. These convictions had a distinct influence on his thought about the United Nations, and one can recognize their impact throughout his statements concerning the Organization. A cursory description of their influence on his conception of the United Nations will be presented in this section, but their influence can also be detected throughout the body of this study.

WESTERN LIBERAL DEMOCRACY

Dag Hammarskjold was culturally and politically a Westerner and a European. His own adherence to the values of the West had a deep foundation in his Christian religion and his study of Western history and philosophy, and he found them best expressed in the contemporary world in Albert Schweitzer's philosophy of "reverence for life." He once wrote that "the political reactions" of a person who adheres to this approach to life

will be guided by a respect for the individual out of which can be deduced a demand for the greatest possible freedom for the individual to live
as he sees fit, on the one hand, and the demand for social justice in the
form of equal rights and equal possibilities for all, on the other.[6]

It is interesting to note that Hammarskjold believed that one could
not claim these Western values of intellectual liberty and social
justice for oneself and one's own group without advocating them
for all people and all groups. He remarked in the same article quoted
above that

the ethic which Schweitzer has formulated is exemplified by the self-
evident subordination of one's own interests to those of the whole—with
a morally-determined loyalty toward society as represented in the nation,
on the one hand, and toward a larger social viewpoint represented by
internationalism on the other.[7]

Hammarskjold also implicitly pointed out the universal nature of
Western or European values in a speech before the Swedish Academy on the Swedish naturalist Linnaeus when he remarked that
Linnaeus "knew no national frontiers. He was a European and, as a
European, a citizen of the world." [8] Prior to his coming to the
United Nations Hammarskjold already considered himself philo-
sophically to be a citizen of the world as a result of his adherence to
the values of Western civilization. Therefore, the transition to the
position of an international civil servant who served the international community did not require a radical change in perspective for
him. In fact, it gave him the opportunity to realize the values in
which he had already come to believe.

Hammarskjold's belief in the equality of all men and the ethical
desirability of social justice were deeply rooted in his total outlook
on life. In a short statement in 1953 he declared that the tradition of
service to one's fellow men and an acceptance of the values of
Christianity, which he had inherited respectively from his father
and mother, were the bases of his outlook on life. He said at that
time:

From generations of soldiers and government officials on my father's side
I inherited a belief that no life was more satisfactory than one of selfless
service to your country—humanity. This service required a sacrifice of
all personal interest, but likewise the courage to stand up unflinchingly
for your convictions.

From scholars and clergymen on my mother's side I inherited a belief that, in the very radical sense of the Gospels, all men were equals as children of God, and should be met and treated by us as our masters in God.[9]

The religious roots of Hammarskjold's belief in social justice were probably strengthened also by the movement in the Swedish Lutheran Church during his youth which brought the teachings of the church to bear on the social, economic, and industrial problems of society. The leader of this movement, Archbishop Nathan Soderblom, was a very close friend of the Hammarskjold family,[10] and the young Dag Hammarskjold sometimes had the opportunity to discuss the problems of modern society with him.

While Hammarskjold was very concerned with the problem of social justice and worked for the Social Democratic governments in Sweden which created the modern Swedish welfare state, he never associated himself with the Social Democratic Party. One reason for his political disengagement was his dedication to the role of a civil servant who serves the state and not any group or party within it. Another reason was his opposition to the predilections of the socialists for constructing neat plans for solving problems along the lines of socialist theory. While Hammarskjold was interested in achieving the same goals as the Social Democrats, he was more pragmatic and nondoctrinaire in choosing the means. The Swedish Finance Minister Ernst Wigforss, under whom he worked for many years, has called him a "Tory Democrat." [11] Wigforss thought that he differed from the Social Democrats in his conservative rationale for state intervention in social and economic matters and in his opposition to the doctrinaire plans of the socialists. Wigforss wrote in his memoirs:

His emotional attitude towards men and class differences between human beings did not seem very far removed from my own and a policy of democratic levelling. He seemed to consider it a matter of course. His view of the role of the government was colored by an older conservatism, to which the state was a highly developed form of human coexistence, the custodian of common values against private interests. A liberal suspicion of the state, which has gradually put its stamp on political conservatism, was in fact not very compatible with the view of the tasks of the state in economic life which placed Hammarskjold more decisively among the planners than among the economic liberals. But the difference both in tradition and in generation drew a dividing line against the social-ism which was alive within the Socialist Democratic Party. What role the family traditions of civil service played I dare not guess. But he be-longed to a younger tradition with greater fear of neat constructions concerning social problems and other problems of life. . . .[12]

Throughout Hammarskjold's work for the United Nations he was to show this same pragmatism in combination with a strong com-mitment to the ethical principles of the Organization. This absence of any preconceived notions regarding how problems should be solved helped him play a constructive role in negotiations among conflicting parties, and it usually helped him avoid alienating the parties with whom he was working.

AN IMPARTIAL CIVIL SERVICE

In his address to the United Nations on April 10, 1953, Ham-marskjold remarked: "My background is, as you know, the civil service of my country—a civil service strengthened by a long tradi-tion and firmly founded on law." [13] This tradition in Ham-marskjold's own family dated back to the beginning of the seven-teenth century,[14] and it was a tradition in which he believed very deeply. In an article entitled "The Civil Servant and Society," which he wrote in 1951, he elaborated on the importance of impar-tial civil servants whose tasks are to serve the state rather than any particular groups within it and to provide impartial advice to the government. He wrote about the civil servant:

The principal and obvious aspect of the civil servant's political ethic is that he serves society and not any group, party or special interest. This does not imply by any means that he may be—or even that it is desirable that he be—politically indifferent. But it does imply that no matter how deeply he may be politically committed, he may not as a civil servant—that is, as the representative of the state and the implementor of its decisions—work for his political ideals *because they are his* . . . .[15]

Hammarskjold recognized that the moral obligation of a civil ser-vant to society as a whole might come into conflict with his own ideas concerning the policies which society should follow, but he thought that the commitment to serve society as a whole must be "the decisive basis for his actions." [16] He remarked that a public servant cannot refuse to implement a particular objective sanctioned by society because it represents, or he thinks it represents, a group interest which is foreign to him personally. Nor can he maintain that such a group interest is incompatible with or directly injurious to the interest of society at large which it is his task to serve.[17]

While Hammarskjold believed that civil servants were bound to implement the policies of authoritative political organs within the state, he by no means thought that they lacked influence in formulating these policies. In fact, he felt that their freedom from any ties to specific groups within the society allowed them to think and speak more freely than the politicians regarding the problems facing the society. On this matter he wrote:

As one of its basic principles, modern democracy has a healthy and strong party structure, but that does not prevent the democracy's need to have groups and individuals whose political interests find expression other than through political parties. For example, there is the . . . kind of person who in his political work has the individualist's need to examine without prejudgment, all questions and suggestions "on their merit" and attempts to find expression for his societal interests—without being bound by any special interest—in public service rather than through party channels.[18]

During Hammarskjold's years in the Swedish government he lived by the norms of this "civil service ideology." [19] He abjured all public controversy and served as a private adviser to the Social Democratic government from 1934 to 1953.

Hammarskjold's belief in the desirability and the possibility of an impartial civil service manifested itself in several ways in his work for the United Nations. In his first years at the United Nations he strove very hard to persuade the members to respect the impartiality and "international character" of the personnel in the Secretariat in order to permit these international civil servants to serve effectively these states and the cause of peace. He also entered many negotiations with national diplomats and statesmen at the United Nations and abroad in order to impress upon them his own impartiality and objectivity. Another manifestation of his civil service background during his tenure as Secretary-General was his own preference for private negotiations rather than public statements in seeking to persuade states to settle their disputes peacefully. He once, in fact, commented to a friend that his preference for private diplomacy and his predecessor Trygve Lie's preference for public diplomacy could be attributed to the fact that he had previously been a civil servant and Lie had been a politician.[20]

THE POSITION OF SMALL STATES
IN INTERNATIONAL POLITICS

Hammarskjold's strong association with his native Sweden and his service to that country no doubt left strong predispositions in his own mind regarding both the importance of protecting the independence of small states and the positive role which they could play in international politics. Ever since 1814 Sweden has successfully preserved its own independence by pursuing a policy of neutrality, and this was a policy to which Hammarskjold adhered strongly. In his Inaugural Address to the Swedish Academy in 1954 he defended his father's decision as Prime Minister to keep Sweden out of World War I as "the best possible protection of Swedish interest"—a decision which his father had called "Swedish and nothing but Swedish." [21] This predisposition in favor of the right of small states to pursue their interests independently and to remain neutral in Great Power political struggles surely must have influenced the way in which as Secretary-General he viewed the policies of nonalignment and neutralism of the African and Asian states which during the 1950s were under question—if not reprobation—from several corners of the world.

Apart from his belief in the right of the small states to pursue independent policies, he also believed that they could play an influential role in preserving peace. Per Lind, one of Hammarskjold's closest friends and a colleague of his in both the Swedish Foreign Ministry and the United Nations, remarked that Hammarskjold always believed that the ability of small states to examine issues on their own merit in international councils could often moderate a conflict among the Great Powers by interjecting a voice of reason and calmness into their dialogue.[22] One of the defenses of his father's policy in keeping Sweden out of war in 1915 was that his father had hoped that its neutrality would allow it to be an impartial participant in the process of building a new international legal order after the war. On this point he remarked that his father hoped that ". . . when the work of developing an international order of law as a framework for Western life was later to be resumed, Sweden ought to be present as a participant who had not—without the excuses the belligerents were able to invoke—sacrificed its loyalty to such an order on the altar of opportunism." [23] During his efforts as Secretary-General, Hammarskjold often relied heavily on small states or non-Great Powers to put pressure on the Great Powers and any other states that might be involved in a conflict to act in a peaceful or compromising manner. How much his Swedish background influenced such strategies is difficult to say, but it surely had some influence. It is also possible to conjecture that Hammarskjold's belief that small states could have an impact on the behavior of the Great Powers by representing the interests of reason and morality led him to think positively about a possible influence for the United Nations and the office of the Secretary-General in international politics.

INTERNATIONAL LAW

In Hammarskjold's estimation the rule of law was an integral part of Western civilization in that it assured order and excluded the rule of caprice on the part of the leaders of a society. In 1952 he wrote:

In lofty speeches Jerusalem, Athens and Rome are generally apostrophized as being the holy cities of European culture. And every school child is taught the meaning of those names. Let me express this in my own words: the equality of every person, the unlimited freedom of thought and the law as the foundation of the community.[24]

Apart from his philosophic predispositions to the law he also came from both a national and a family background in which both municipal and international law were regarded very highly. Regarding the importance of law in Swedish political life, Professor Dankwart Rustow has written that an "important legacy of the past is the traditional, at times, perhaps over-meticulous, regard for law and legal procedure." [25] Within his own family Hammarskjold's father and his brother Ake had been educated primarily in the law, and his father was a professor of law prior to his entry into government.

Hammarskjold himself also had obtained a law degree prior to earning a doctorate in economics. Oscar Schachter, the director of the General Legal Division of the United Nations, has remarked that Hammarskjold had "a strong sentimental feeling for law" [26] as a result of his family and educational backgrounds, and he noted that this was reinforced by "his intellectual delight in the subleties of legal analysis." [27]

Apart from his general interest in and dedication to law, Hammarskjold also had a particular interest in international law. His father had been the chairman of the Committee of Experts for Progressive Codification of International Law of the League of Nations and a president of the International Law Association, and his brother Ake was the Registrar of the Permanent Count of International Justice from 1922 to 1936 and a Judge on the Court from 1936 to 1937. Some of his most penetrating comments on the role of international law occurred in his Inaugural Address to the Swedish Academy which was on the topic of his father's life. In that speech he said that his father's policies in World War I were directed toward leaving Sweden free to defend international law, and he then went on to explain his father's, and probably his own, feelings regarding the importance of international law for a small state. He remarked:

What the critics have not realised, he said once, is that for a small country, international law, in the final analysis, is the only remaining argument, and that its defense is therefore worth sacrifices even in the egotistical interest of the country itself. It seems to me that this is the background against which it is necessary to view Hjalmar Hammarskjold, when he invoked the 'obligations' of the neutrals as grounds for demanding considerate treatment by the belligerents, and when at the same time he found it necessary to widen the application of the principles of neutrality to trade policy.[28]

The Swedish roots of Hammarskjold's concern with international law have also been pointed out by Joseph Lash in his political biography of Hammarskjold. In it Lash wrote:

Sweden has not had to claim a right that meant going against international law. Its vital interests have been best served by the development of international law, and with the oldest written constitution in Europe it was temperamentally disposed toward such a development. When international disputes do arise, it is part of the Swedish tradition to look first for a solution by isolating the legal factors.[29]

Throughout Hammarskjold's tenure as Secretary-General the desire to further the development of international law was a strong theme in his policies. The centrality of the law to his policies for the United Nations was pointed out by Walter Lippmann, who wrote following Hammarskjold's death:

Hammarskjold was in fact the embodiment of the noblest Western achievement—that laws can be administered by judges and civil servants who have their first allegiance to the laws, and not to their personal, their class, or even their national, interest.[30]

Andrew W. Cordier, who worked very closely with the Secretary-General at the United Nations as his Executive Assistant, has also remarked that Hammarskjold's training in the law led him to be very concerned with how results were achieved and what impact actions would have on the legal development of the United Nations.[31] Hammarskjold's ideal of a rule of law and his concern for the legal correctness and the legal implications of his actions were no doubt strongly influenced by the loyalty to the law which he developed as a young man in Sweden.

A REJECTION OF MARXISM AND ITS THEORY OF IMPERIALISM

Shortly prior to becoming Secretary-General, Hammarskjold wrote an article [32] in which he rejected both the need for complete socialization of the means of production in order to achieve economic democracy and the Marxist thesis that capitalistic countries are necessarily imperialistic as a result of their need to export the capital which they have denied their workers. Although his actions within the Swedish government showed clearly that he did not sympathize with a completely socialistic organization of Sweden's economy, this was his only explicit statement regarding the Marxist theory of international politics. In the article he noted that not only were the European countries themselves in need of outside capital investment but also that there was "probably neither the need nor the possibility for capitalistic expansion." [33] Although he did not state so precisely, he probably thought that there was no "need" for the export of capital because of the present systems of economic democracy in Europe which bestow a greater percentage of the profits of production on the workers and because of the internal needs for capital investment. When he spoke of the lack of a "possibility" of imperialism by capital expansion, he was referring to the accelerating process of de-colonization in Africa and Asia and the growing desire for independence and equality by the peoples in these areas. Hammarskjold concluded in his article that the Marxist theory of imperialism "has shared the same fate as many other economic doctrines: to be exposed by subsequent developments as a generalization *in absurdum* of the experience of one special point and during a limited period of time. . . ." [34]

While it would be very difficult to point to any of Hammarskjold's specific policies as Secretary-General which one could say were influenced by this political attitude, the fact that he was not a Marxist surely meant that he did not view the existence of the Western capitalist states as an impediment to international peace. It was to this problem that Premier Khrushchev addressed himself when he declared that no man could be neutral in the modern world at the time that the Soviet Union was seeking Hammarskjold's resignation and a "troika" in the Secretariat. [35]

THE INFLUENCE OF MORAL VALUES
ON FOREIGN POLICIES

It is an interesting fact that less than half a year before Hammarskjold became Secretary-General, he wrote an article in which he examined the influence which moral values have on foreign policies and the effect which greater international cooperation through international organizations was having on this influence. In the article he noted that the influence of ethical values on the foreign policies of states is less than on the actions of individuals in a society but that it would be wrong to say that such values are without influence in the international sphere. On this point he remarked:

Background and Political Attitudes

In a foreign policy context the situation can appear quite different. There the nation has been built into the ideology in such a fashion as to allow it to obscure the goals the ideology otherwise has indicated. The nature of the consideration by which the individual may feel bound within his own country when he propagates the interests of his own group at the cost of others does not make itself felt when he considers the demands of his own country in an international context.[36]

He continued:

If the practitioner of realpolitik in this case is more independent with regard to group ideology in his conduct of foreign policy than he is in domestic politics, he still is far from free. He must reckon with it as a serious weakness in his case if opinion at home is disturbed in its feelings for what is considered right in an ideological sense. And he has to reckon with even greater risks in connection with the reaction within other countries.[37]

In terms of his later work for the United Nations the most interesting point which he made regarding the influence of moral values on foreign policies was that it was likely to increase as a result of greater international cooperation in international organizations like the United Nations. With increased cooperation he envisaged the emergence of common values among nations and a greater responsiveness of governments to the opinions of other nations. In the article he wrote:

There exists here an interdependent effect between outer criticism and inner insecurity which grows in strength with the intensity of international collaboration and the degree of uniformity in fundamental ideological reactions between nations. One cannot exaggerate the importance in this context of the emergence of a new international solidarity on a European ideological basis within the Western world and within the United Nations and its organs as a universal forum. We have come a long way from Machiavelli when today even the actions of "Princes" are judged by national and international opinion—regardless of the "result" and even if they are not brought before a court of law.[38]

During the eight-and-one-half years that he was Secretary-General, Hammarskjold sought to increase the influence of United Nations decisions and the moral values which are stated in the Principles and Purposes of the Charter in international relations. One of the major ways in which he did this was by broadening the forms of international cooperation. He hoped that through such cooperation the governments and populations of states would become responsive to the value judgments of foreign peoples as they were expressed in United Nations organs and would realize that they shared common interests and common ideals with these foreign groups.

Chapter Two

Hammarskjold's Conception of the United Nations' Objectives and Bases of Power

The Objectives of the United Nations

Hammarskjold's best statement concerning the objectives of the United Nations was contained in the Introduction to his 1961 Annual Report. In that document he recalled that the end goal of the Organization was "to save succeeding generations from the scourge of war," [1] but he noted that its ability to realize this goal of peace was dependent upon its ability to promote five principles or objectives which are contained in the Purposes and Principles of the Charter. He defined these objectives as the prevention of armed conflict through negotiation, the prohibition of the use of force "save in the common interest," equal economic opportunity, political equality, and the rule of law or justice.[2]

He made it quite clear that these principles are interdependent principles of a total approach to the relationship of human beings—whether between individuals in a state or between peoples grouped into states. He viewed the attempt on the part of the international community to establish its relations along the lines of these principles as an extension of a movement which had been taking place for centuries to realize the principles of Western civilization in the world. Politically, they were the standards of liberal democracy which had been gaining ascendancy within many states over the past several centuries. He viewed their adoption by the United Nations as "the first step toward the establishment of an international democracy of peoples, bringing all nations—irrespective of history, size or wealth—together on an equal basis as partners in the vast venture of creating a true world community." [3]

To a large extent, the rules reflect standards accepted as binding for life within States. Thus, they appear, in the main, as a projection into the international arena and the international community of purposes and principles already accepted as being of national validity. In this sense, the Charter takes a first step in the direction of an organized international community. . . .[4]

Hammarskjold went beyond stating that the objectives were the same as those pursued in most states to a view that the United Nations could realize them only by taking on executive and administration responsibilities such as states possess. He noted that it might be possible for the Organization to realize the objective of the peaceful settlement of disputes while being merely a conference organ, but that in the case of the other four objectives executive actions were a prerequisite for their realization.[5]

Hammarskjold's attachment to these objectives went beyond a mere existential preference for them as a basis for human relationships. They were also a part of his total philosophical outlook on life. This aspect of his thought was pointed up by a remark of Andrew W. Cordier, the former Executive Assistant to the Secretary-General, that Hammarskjold "had almost a religious respect for the Charter" [6] and by a statement of his own that the United Nations represented "a secular 'church' of ideals and principles in international affairs." [7] These attributions of a certain "religious" character to United Nations principles reveal in an indirect manner that Hammarskjold saw the normative bases of the United Nations as an extension of his own philosophical principles into international affairs. The United Nations in the secular international world was supposed to challenge and exhort states to realize their best moral potentialities in a manner similar to what churches do on interpersonal and more limited societal levels. The main difference in the analogy between the United Nations and the church from Hammarskjold's point of view was, as will be pointed out, that the United Nations has the potential of organizing more effective sanctions on behalf of its principles than do churches. In this respect the United Nations is more analogous to a modern state which has tried to establish liberal democratic principles within its own societal jurisdiction.

While Hammarskjold's understandings of these principles and his policies for realizing them will be presented in detail in the chapters on his strategies and tactics for the United Nations, a short description of their operational meanings is presented here. The principle of preventing armed conflict through negotiations is related to attempts on the part of the Organization to bring about the peaceful settlement of disputes which have not erupted in physical conflict. The principle of prohibiting the use of force except in the common interest concerns a number of forms of activities. They include the deterrence of conflicts through the interposition of U.N. personnel and/or the threat of sanctions against aggressors, the termination of conflicts through the initiation of sanctions and/or the mounting of diplomatic pressures, and the reconstruction of situations which seriously threaten international peace. Hammarskjold's strategies and tactics for achieving the above-two objectives will be discussed in three chapters (Chapters III–V). A single chapter will be devoted to the peaceful settlement of disputes, and two chapters will concern the prohibition or control of the use of force. Of the latter two chapters the initial one will deal with efforts to control the use of force in conflicts in specific geographical settings, and the second one will deal with the control of the general military environment through arms control and disarmamant measures.

Whereas the previously mentioned objectives are concerned primarily with immediate threats to or breaches of the peace, Hammarskjold's other three goals of equal economic opportunity, political equality, and the rule of law are directed at removing the underlying causes of international conflict and at building a more peaceful world order. Their realization is sought *inter alia* in order to help eliminate the occurrence of international disputes and violence and hence the need for employing means of easing tensions, settling disputes, and controlling the use of force. The operational meanings of these three principles are quite clear in that their respective purposes are: (1) to promote greater equality in economic standards among the peoples of the world; (2) to secure a voice for all nations in international decisionmaking in addition to protecting the political independence of all nations; and (3) to expand the number of questions of international concern which are covered by international agreements and to promote the settlement of disputes and the creation of cooperative endeavors in accordance with legal procedures and substantive law. This definition of the rule of law implies the added goal of furthering the constitutional development and political integration of international society. Because of the common underlying theme of the above three objectives—namely, building a more peaceful world order—and because of the limited amount of material on each, Hammarskjold's strategies and tactics for them will be discussed in a single chapter (Chapter VI).

The Bases of Power of the United Nations

The *permanent* bases of power which the United Nations has at its disposal can be classified into several categories: (1) its legal authority flowing from the Charter (the legal responsibilities of its Members and the legal powers of its organs); (2) the loyalty, skills, and reputation of Secretariat personnel; (3) its diplomatic facilities; (4) the character of its membership; and (5) the economic resources to finance its Secretariat and its technical aid program.[8] As will be made clear in the rest of this chapter, there is a great disparity between its permanent bases of power and the bases of power which it needs to influence most situations in international politics. The United Nations must therefore presently be viewed basically as an organization in which states voluntarily concert power to influence international situations. At the same time the Organization's permanent bases of power do allow the Members and the Secretariat to influence international problems in a way that would not be possible if the United Nations did not exist, and this influence is often crucial. During his tenure Hammarskjold had a clear conception of the nature of the United Nations' bases of power, and it included not only his ideas on what the bases of power were during his tenure but also on how they should and might develop in the future.

Objectives and Bases of Power

THE RESPONSIBILITIES OF
UNITED NATIONS MEMBERS

The responsibilities which the Charter requires of the Member States are bases of power of the Organization in that, as obligations, they can be invoked by the Members or one of the principal organs to induce a certain Member to conform to a certain line of action. The most basic responsibility which Hammarskjold believed was incumbent upon the Members was that they act in accordance with the Principles and Purposes of the Charter, which he called "some basic rules of international ethics." [9] He reasoned that only as the Members perceived that their own security and economic and social well-being depended upon adherence to these principles could the United Nations and peace be strengthened. The extent to which he thought of their acceptance as the foundation upon which the Organization and international peace rested was reflected in a 1956 statement to the Security Council: "The principles of the Charter are, by far, greater than the Organization in which they are embodied. . . ." [10]

Another responsibility which he believed was incumbent upon all Members was that they comply with those decisions of United Nations organs which were meant to be binding in the Charter and that they give serious consideration to those decisions which were only recommendations.[11] He recognized that the practice of the Members fell far short of the intended legal norms of the Charter, and he urged "that Member nations jointly should increase their efforts to make political realities gradually come closer to the pattern established by the Charter." [12] He also explicitly requested that the Members give "increasing respect" to the nonbinding decisions of the organs, and he expressed the hope that they would someday feel a responsibility to abide by all United Nations decisions.[13]

A responsibility which Hammarskjold believed that states assumed in adhering to the Charter was to submit conflicts and tensions to the Organization for solution, sometimes even when there were alternative methods available for solving them. Although he once wrote that "the United Nations is not intended to be a substitute for normal procedures of reconciliation and mediation but rather an added instrument providing, within the limits of its competence, a further or ultimate support for the maintenance of peace and security," [14] he thought that states had an obligation to use it as much as possible in order to strengthen its effectiveness. As he once wrote:

To fail to use the United Nations machinery on those occasions when the Charter plainly means that it should be used, to improvise other arrangements without overriding practical and political reasons—this may tend to weaken the position of the Organization and reduce its influence and effectiveness, even when the ultimate purpose is a United Nations purpose.[15]

At another time he said that there was an "interest of the Member Governments in strengthening the institutions which they have endowed with a primary responsibility for world peace. . . ." [16] By taking this position Hammarskjold was assuming that the Members had committed themselves to solve by United Nations procedures not only those disputes which traditional diplomatic methods had not been able to solve but also those which might be solved outside of the United Nations. This was because such activities strengthened the weight of the Organization's influence in such conflicts and often led to an increase in the means of action at its disposal. Hammarskjold was clearly of the opinion that the bypassing of the Organization by the Members would lead to a gradual atrophy of and loss of respect for the United Nations as an instrument for cooperation and peace. Use of the Organization was necessary both to prove its utility and to increase the weight which its actions might bring to bear on the behavior of states, and he thought that the Members had obligated themselves to this course of action.

THE LEGAL POWERS OF THE PRINCIPAL ORGANS OF THE UNITED NATIONS

In regard to the powers of the Security Council, Hammarskjold reflected the commonly accepted position that it was the only organ with the power to order enforcement action against a state or states. He expressed this understanding when he once remarked:

in 1945 the governments were unwilling to give to the United Nations any sovereign powers with the sole exception of the Security Council's power to order enforcement action to prevent or suppress armed aggression when—and only when—the five Great Powers agreed unanimously to do so. In every other respect, the United Nations was always intended to rely for the accomplishment of its purposes upon the moral power of the undertakings of the Charter and upon the influence which its recommendations could exert upon the policies of its Members.[17]

While Hammarskjold always recognized the role of the Security Council in determining any enforcement action by the Organization, he did not attribute to the five Gerat Powers and the Security Council any sacrosanct responsibility for peace and security outside of the enforcement field. He held that in keeping with Articles 12 and 24 of the Charter the Security Council possessed the legal power to consider any threats to the peace when they were initially brought to the United Nations. But he believed that upon its failure to act the General Assembly could and should debate them and make recommendations for their solution. He expressed his thinking upon the primary but not sole responsibility of the Security Council for maintaining international peace when he wrote:

There are in the Charter elements of a thinking which, I believe, belongs to an earlier period in the development of the world community. I have in mind especially the concept that the permanent members of the Security Council should not only, as is natural, be recognized as carrying special responsibility for peace and security, but that, further, these permanent members, working together, should represent a kind of "built-in" directing group for the world community as organized in the United Nations.[18]

While Hammarskjold opposed the idea that the Members of the Security Council, especially the Great Powers, constituted anything like a ruling clique in the Organization, it should be stressed that he supported their central role in the United Nations system and their power, in accordance with Article 12, to consider a dispute before the General Assembly might make any recommendations regarding it. Apart from his respect for the law of the Charter, he possessed a realistic appreciation of the need for Great Power support if United Nations enterprises were to succeed. In fact, after the Suez and Hungarian crises of 1956, in which the General Assembly had played predominant roles, he took steps to urge that the Security Council's role as the organ with primary responsibility for the maintenance of peace be revitalized within the United Nations diplomatic process. In 1957 he urged that in conformity with Article 28, paragraph 2 of the Charter the Security Council hold periodic meetings to discuss existing threats to international peace,[19] and then in 1959 he suggested that it meet periodically in executive session to discuss "any aspect of concern to the Council because of its responsibilities under the Charter." [20] His general satisfaction with the post-Suez increase in the Security Council's activity was voiced in the summer of 1960 when he noted the significant roles it had played in conflicts during the past three years.[21]

Hammarskjold's best statement concerning the authority of Security Council resolutions is found in his last Introduction which was issued in August 1961. In it he wrote that all decisions of the Security Council, unless explicitly specified as recommendations, are legally binding on the Members of the Organization under Article 25 of the Charter.[22] At the same time he noted that "the experience of the Organization, as regards the implementation of the Council decisions, is uneven and does not indicate full acceptance in practice of Article 25." [23] He also remarked that this failure to give the resolutions of the Security Council "the intended legal weight" of the Charter had arisen in cases where the Members had refused to shoulder the financial consequences of Council decisions establishing operational actions.[24] In conclusion, Hammarskjold urged the Members to bring their actions in line with the law of the Charter, and noted that it was upon such a policy that the development of the Organization into an "increasingly effective instrument" depended.[25]

Another legal power of the Security Council which Hammarskjold discussed was its authority to consider and debate any threats to the independence and territorial integrity of Member States regardless of whether any other security organization to which the threatened Member belonged was considering it. This point was established very early in Hammarskjold's tenure as Secretary-General when in 1954 Guatemala asked the Security Council to consider its complaint that it was being invaded by troops from Nicaragua. At that time Ambassador Lodge of the United States claimed that it could not be considered by the Security Council because the Organization of American States had primary responsibility for threats to the peace in the Western Hemisphere and that the United States would never have signed the United Nations Charter if this understanding had not been accepted.[26] Hammarskjold did not publicly voice his judgment on the United States position at that time, though he voiced his disapproval of it in conversations with his colleagues in the Secretariat [27] and in his 1954 Introduction which was issued within the month following the Guatemalan crisis. He wrote:

in those cases where resort to such arrangements [regional organizations] is chosen in the first instance, that choice should not be permitted to cast any doubt on the ultimate responsibility of the United Nations. Similarly, a policy giving full scope to the proper role of regional agencies can and should at the same time fully preserve the right of a member nation to a hearing under the Charter.[28]

As well as asserting the power of the United Nations to consider a plea from any Member which thought its security endangered, Hammarskjold held that the Organization possessed the formal power to consider and make its voice heard on any conflicts between states where there were "legitimate third party interests" at stake, even if the conflict were under consideration by the parties involved.[29] These legitimate third party interests in his estimate arose where it appeared that a conflict was likely to lead to armed violence. His ideas on this matter were clearly revealed in his attitude regarding the United Nations' relation to the Berlin question, which was always a point of friction between the Cold War blocs. In 1961 he wrote:

The United Nations, with its wide membership, is not, and can, perhaps, not aspire to be a focal point in the debate on an issue such as the Berlin question, or in the efforts to solve it, but the Organization cannot, for that reason, be considered as an outside party which has no right to make its voice heard should a situation develop which would threaten those very interests which the United Nations is to safeguard and for the defense of which it was intended to provide all Member nations with an instrument and a forum.[30]

In this statement he was pointing out that states—especially the Great Powers—should generally be allowed to pursue negotiations concerning their conflicts outside of the United Nations framework, but that if their conflicts attained such intensity that they seriously threatened international peace, then the United Nations had a legitimate claim to make its voice heard on their solution.

Regarding the powers of the General Assembly, it has already been mentioned that Hammarskjold believed that the General Assembly possessed the authority to consider threats to the peace only if the Security Council had discussed them and had been unable to act on them. During the Suez and Hungarian crises his actions revealed that he thought that the General Assembly need not wait to take up a threat to the peace after an impasse appeared in the Security Council. On October 31, 1956, after the Suez question had been before the Security Council for less than two days, he privately supported the Yugoslav resolution to refer the question immediately to an emergency session of the General Assembly.[31]

Hammarskjold's ideas concerning the powers of the General Assembly to take different forms of action were most clearly and elaborately set forth in his 1957 Introduction, which to a significant extent was an explanation of why the United Nations had acted as it had during the Suez and Hungarian crises of October and November 1956. He summed up the General Assembly's powers to act in that report when he wrote:

The Assembly may recommend, it may investigate, it may pronounce judgment, but it does not have the power to compel compliance with its decisions. Under the Charter, only the Security Council has the power to order the use of force . . . .[32]

In keeping with his support for the general recommendatory power of the General Assembly and for its power to consider any threat to the peace following the failure of the Security Council to act on it, Hammarskjold defended the controversial "Uniting for Peace" Resolution of 1950.[33] This resolution provided procedures for transferring an issue from the Security Council to the General Assembly and stated that the General Assembly could recommend collective measures in situations where peace was threatened or had been breached. In the 1957 Introduction he explained its legality when he wrote:

it is worth recalling that the "Uniting-for-Peace" resolution, in establishing a procedure intended to safeguard the application of the relevant

provisions of the Charter—Articles 10, 11 and 51—in support of the maintenance of peace, did not constitutionally transfer to the General Assembly any of the enforcement powers reserved to the Security Council by
the Charter.[34]

While Hammarskjold always supported the power of the General
Assembly to recommend measures in the peace and security field, it
should again be stressed that he did not encourage its activity at the
expense of the primary responsibility of the Security Council.

Concerning the legal weight of General Assembly resolutions
on matters of peace and security, he noted that they were "legally
only recommendations" and that their effect had been "very close
to the restrictive Charter formula." [35] At the same time he held that
the resolutions often influenced the settlement of conflicts because
they "introduce [d] an important element by expressing a majority
consensus on the issue under consideration." [36] He also believed
that the legal weight of the recommendations was likely to increase
as the Organization assumed a more central and influential role in
international politics and as it passed from what he called "institutional systems of co-existence" to "constitutional systems of cooperation." [37] Concerning the Charter formula and its future development he wrote:

such a formula leaves scope for a gradual development in practice of the
weight of the decisions. To the extent that more respect, in fact, is shown
to General Assembly recommendations by the Member States, they may
come more and more close to being recognized as decisions having a
binding effect on those concerned, particularly when they involve the
application of the binding principles of the Charter and of international
law.[38]

Throughout Hammarskjold's tenure as Secretary-General he had
observed that General Assembly resolutions often had an important
impact on the settlement of different crises, and he hoped that the
influence of such decisions of the international community would
obtain "increasing respect" in the future.[39]

The one kind of General Assembly resolution which Hammarskjold did think binding was a financial assessment of the Members under Article 17, paragraph 2 of the United Nations Charter.
He believed that the binding quality of these resolutions covered

not only the annual expenses for the administration of the Organization but in principle also the expenses for United Nations peacekeeping operations. Following the creation of the United Nations Emergency Force in the Middle East in November, 1956, he initially suggested that the expenses be levied on the same scale as the regular assessments,[40] but later agreed to the establishment of a voluntary fund **to** pay these expenses. He supported the same *ad hoc* policy for the United Nations Operation in the Congo and the subsequent reductions which were granted to the states with low national incomes; but he always upheld the binding character of the General Assembly's financial assessments and the political desirability of collective financial responsibility in the peacekeeping field. During the Congo crisis he stressed the General Assembly's legal power to determine the financing of those operations which were created by the Security Council. In a speech to the General Assembly on April 5, 1961, he pointed out the political meaning of this authority for the United Nations' role in international politics when he said:

once the Council has taken a valid decision which imposes responsibilities on the Organization and requires implementation by the Secretary-General, then the costs which are involved are clearly "expenses of the Organization" within the meaning of Article 17, paragraph 2 of the Charter and therefore must be apportioned by the General Assembly. True the Council retains the right to revoke or change its decisions, but as long as the decisions require expenditures by the Organization then Article 17, paragraph 2 must be considered applicable.

If this provision of the Charter were to be disregarded and the apportionment of expenses left to the Security Council, this would obviously involve an extension of the unanimity rule in that the approval of all the Permanent Members would be required for the continued financing of peace and security operations. In short, each Permanent Member would then have a continuing veto over the implementation decided on by the Council.[41]

Hammarskjold apparently thought that to deprive the General Assembly of its responsibility over the financing of United Nations peacekeeping operations and to place it within the Security Council, as the Soviet Union proposed, would have approached what the Soviet proposal for a "troika" in the Secretariat would have done.

Instead of requiring the assent of three individuals for any decision on behalf of any United Nations operational action, it would in fact have required the approval of the five Great Powers. In Hammarskjold's estimation this arrangement would have saddled the United Nations with a five-headed Hydra-like monster which would have stymied the Organization in establishing any operational actions and in encouraging higher forms of internation cooperation.

Throughout his term in office Hammarskjold reflected a great deal on the legal powers of the Secretary-General which are based on Articles 98 and 99 of the Charter. Many of his statements regarding these powers were reflections on or justifications of the many new kinds of activities which he undertook during his eight-and-one-half years at the United Nations. His most extensive statements actually came in response to the attacks by the Communist states against his management of the United Nations Operation in the Congo and their proposal that a three-man executive (a "troika") be created in the Secretariat.

Article 98 of the Charter states that the Secretary-General will perform those functions which are entrusted to him by the representative organs of the United Nations. Prior to Hammarskjold's accession to the office of Secretary-General in 1953, the functions which had been entrusted to the Secretary-General were in the main, but not exclusively, responsibilities in the administrative and economic fields; but this changed quite radically during the years 1953–1961. During those years the Security Council and General Assembly entrusted many important diplomatic responsibilities to Hammarskjold, and they empowered him to direct several peacekeeping operations. Until the Congo crisis and the Communist states' criticisms of his interpretation of the United Nations mandates, Hammarskjold did not feel any need to comment on the Secretary-General's powers under Article 98; but the disagreements which developed over the meaning of the imprecise Congo mandates and over the Security Council's and the General Assembly's attempts to reformulate those mandates forced him to speak out on the powers of the Secretary-General to direct peacekeeping forces when such differences among the Members did develop. In a speech at Oxford University in May 1961, he said regarding the powers of the Secretary-General in such circumstances:

non-action—may be tempting; it enables him to avoid criticism by refusing to act until other political organs resolve the dilemma. An easy refuge may thus appear to be available. But would such refuge be compatible with the responsibility placed upon the Secretary-General by the Charter? Is he entitled to refuse to carry out the decision properly reached by the organs, on the ground that the specific implementation would be opposed to positions some Member States might wish to take, as indicated perhaps, by an earlier minority vote? Of course the political organs may always instruct him to discontinue the implementation of a resolution, but when they do not so instruct him and the resolution remains in effect, is the Secretary-General legally and morally free to take no action, particularly in a matter considered to affect international peace and security? . . .

The answers seem clear enough in law; the responsibilities of the Secretary-General under the Charter cannot be laid aside merely because the execution of decisions by him is likely to be politically controversial. The Secretary-General remains under the obligation to carry out the policies as adopted by the organs; the essential requirement is that he does this on the basis of his exclusively international responsibility and not in the interest of any particular State or groups of States.[42]

Hammarskjold's interpretation of the legal power of the Secretary-General in these circumstances was that unless he received a specific mandate to cease applying a particular mandate, he possessed the power and the obligation to continue to act in accordance with it. He realized that there were risks for the Secretary-General in executing mandates concerning which the members had different interpretations, but he believed that his degree of discretionary authority could be minimized through a variety of consultative techniques. He also thought that a refusal to continue a peacekeeping force under past mandates, if the crisis remained or was likely to recur, would have the effect of undermining seriously both the United Nations and international peace.

The other article which bestowed legal authority on the Secretary-General, Article 99, is less precise and more controversial in what powers it confers on the Secretary-General. It states: "The Secretary-General may bring to the attention of the Security Council any matter which in his opinion may threaten the maintenance of international peace and security." Hammarskjold's own judgment of the importance of this article was set forth in his Oxford University speech when he said:

> It was Article 99 more than any other which was considered by the drafters of the Charter to have transformed the Secretary-General of the United Nations from a purely administrative official to one with an explicit political responsibility.[43]

Aside from the obvious meaning of the article which allows the Secretary-General to call the Security Council into session so as to bring before it matters which in his judgment seriously threaten international peace, Hammarskjold noted that legal scholars have interpreted it as bestowing upon the Secretary-General "a broad discretion to conduct inquiries and to engage in informal diplomatic activity." [44] One of these scholars, Michel Virally, whose analysis of the political role of the Secretary-General Hammarskjold particularly respected, has written about the powers implicit in Article 99:

> Very evidently, if the Secretary-General estimates that international peace and security are threatened, he ought to be able to say why, which implies for him the right to make some declarations to the Security Council each time that he judges it useful and to take a position in face of what seems to him dangerous for international peace or, on the contrary, susceptible to consolidate it. We think even that his responsibilities imply that he can make, eventually, some proposals on appropriate means to push back the dangers which challenge international peace and security.[45]

It was contrary to Hammarskjold's basic outlook on his office and the development of the Organization to try to define in very precise terms exactly what the Secretary-General's "broad discretion to conduct inquiries and to engage in informal diplomatic activity" meant. One of his best statements on this rather flexible approach to the powers which the Secretary-General could utilize was made in a press conference in May 1953 when he said:

> I think the right of initiative in a certain sense, informally, of the Secretary-General goes far beyond what is described in the Charter, provided that he observes the proper forms, chooses his approaches with tact and avoids acting in such a way as to say, counteract his own purpose—

this is to say, by his own initiative further the development but at the same time not introducing unnecessary complications.[46]

By this statement he was saying that the Secretary-General is allowed to try to further peaceful relations among states in any way that is politically realistic and which does not violate any specific provisions of the Charter. Underlying this was a conviction that he would politically imperil the utility of the office of the Secretary-General in the future if he did not follow certain norms of political propriety.

While he did not try to specify all of the powers of the Secretary-General which were derived from Article 99, a number which emerged in practice can be delineated. They are the ability to conduct investigations of problems with government officials either at the United Nations or abroad, the right to offer his services in a good offices or mediatory capacity, the power to assume such third party roles, and the prerogative to voice his own views on a crisis either privately or publicly.

Apart from Hammarskjold's ideas regarding specific powers of the Secretary-General, he also made a statement of a more general nature concerning the Secretary-General's role within the United Nations' security system following his election to a second term as Secretary-General in September 1957 which appears quite radical at first glance. At that time he said:

I do not believe that the Secretary-General should be asked to act, by the Member States, if no guidance for his action is to be found either in the Charter or in the decisions of the main organs of the United Nations; within the limits thus set, however, I believe it to be his duty to use his office, and indeed, the machinery of the Organization to its utmost capacity and to the full extent permitted at each stage by practical circumstances.

On the other hand, I believe that it is in keeping with the philosophy of the Charter that the Secretary-General should be expected to act also without such guidance, should this appear to him necessary in order to help in filling any vacuum that may appear in the systems which the Charter and traditional diplomacy provide for the safeguarding of peace and security.[47]

This statement, that the Secretary-General should personally try to solve conflicts of a serious nature upon the failure of the Security

Council and the General Assembly to do so, may seem out of keeping with Hammarskjold's political discretion and his respect for the legal provisions of the Charter. In fact, this "vacuum theory," as it came to be called, was regarded by most Members as desirable in filling a void in the instrumentalities for coping with threats to the peace and as an appropriate legal interpretation of the Secretary-General's independent powers under the Charter. At the same time it should be pointed out that this general acceptance of independent prerogatives for the Secretary-General was predicated on the Members' realization that Hammarskjold would not stray from what was acceptable to the great majority of them and that he would always be an impartial and discreet diplomat. Following the Israeli and Franco-British actions in Egypt in October 1956, Hammarskjold made a statement similar to that of September 1957 when he stated that the Secretary-General was "the servant of the Charter" [48] and that as such he could serve in that position only if he could publicly judge when the Organization's principles were being seriously violated.[49] Such statements bestowed upon his views and actions greater acceptability and authority in the eyes of the United Nations Members and strengthened the consensus regarding the Secretary-General's powers for implementing the Purposes and Principles of the Charter.

To conclude this section on the powers of the Security Council, the General Assembly, and the Secretary-General, Hammarskjold's general thinking regarding the legal power of these organs to initiate and promote various means of action will be presented. His approach was based on a very liberal legal interpretation of the Charter. He thought that it was neither necessary nor even desirable to find a specific provision in the Charter for certain types of action which the Members or the Secretary-General might find useful for solving a conflict or a dispute. As long as a means of action did not violate any specific provisions of the Charter, and as long as it was in consonance with the Purposes and Principles of the Organization, it was legal and appropriate. On this question he wrote in his 1959 Introduction:

the Charter as an international treaty establishes certain goals for international cooperation and creates certain organs which the Member States may use in their cooperation towards these goals. The statement of objectives in the Charter is binding and so are the rules concerning the various organs and their competence, but it is not necessary to regard the working methods as indicated in the Charter as limitative in purpose. Thus, they may be supplemented by others under the pressure of circumstances and in the light of experience if these additional procedures are not in conflict with what is prescribed.[50]

Hammarskjold viewed the Charter as a procedural and normative framework within which the Members and the Secretary-General could create new "working methods" or means of action for promoting the goals of the Organization. He held that each means of action had to be fitted to the particular circumstances of the situation that it was trying to influence, and he took a great interest in expanding the variety of these tools and in impressing upon the Members the flexibility and the utility of the United Nations as an instrument of peace. The period of his tenure as Secretary-General was an exceptionally creative one in terms of the creation of numerous new diplomatic and operational forms of action, and this movement can be significantly attributed to the diplomacy of Hammarskjold and his conception of the Organization.

THE CHARACTER OF THE
INTERNATIONAL CIVIL SERVICE

Throughout his tenure Hammarskjold was very concerned with the impact of the Secretariat's character on the Organization's activities and influence in international politics. Those aspects of its character with which he was particularly concerned are those which are specifically mentioned in the United Nations Charter. These are its international impartiality (Article 100), the unitary character of its executive office (Article 97), and the high level of skill of its personnel (Article 101).

In his 1953 Introduction Hammarskjold remarked that the establishment of "a truly international civil service, free from all national pressures and influences . . . not only in words but in deeds" was one of the "fundamental principles" upon which the Organization's influence and growth depended.[51] At that time the impartiality of the United Nations Secretariat was under attack from small but vocal elements in the United States who were claiming that there were some United States citizens in the Secretariat who were Communists and who therefore were consciously opposed to the policies of the United States.[52] Also, the international impartiality of the Secretary-General had been under fire by the Soviet bloc over the past three years as a result of their opposition to the position which Secretary-General Trygve Lie had taken toward the Korean conflict since 1950. Ernest Gross, who was legal counsel to the United Nations on personnel matters from 1953–1956, wrote that the personnel situation was of "first priority" for Hammarskjold during his first year as Secretary-General. He said that Hammarskjold was deeply concerned with obtaining from certain nations, especially the United States at that time, greater respect for the international status and impartiality of the Secretariat.[53] In those initial years he established the Secretary-General's power to resist Members' demands for dismissal of certain Secretariat officials whom these Members claimed were not impartial in their work.[54] After 1954 there was very little criticism by the Members of the Secretariat's hiring policies. Hammarskjold had established the power of the Secretary-General over the Secretariat's personnel policies, and this was a significant indication that most of the Members were prepared to accept the independence and impartiality of the Secretariat's personnel.

During Hammarskjold's tenure there was also a challenge to the impartiality and international status of the personnel of the United Nation's Specialized Agencies. In 1956 President Nasser of Egypt tried to obtain dossiers on all Egyptians who worked for Specialized Agencies in Egypt so that the Egyptian government could have them fired if it did not approve of them.[55] Hammarskjold persuaded Nasser to abandon this policy since it would have compromised the international status of the personnel in the United Nations family of agencies. Hammarskjold believed that a recognition on the part of states of the international impartiality and loyalty of United Nations personnel was necessary if the states were going to seek and respect their advice and to entrust them with important political and economic responsibilities. He also apparently believed that without the willingness of states to delegate responsibilities to the international civil service, the United Nations and the Specialized Agencies would be reduced to forums of discussion which could only have a very minor impact on the behavior of states. With the Members' delegation of operational responsibilities he thought that the United Nations and its Specialized Agencies would assume much more influential roles in international politics.

Throughout his tenure as Secretary-General, Hammarskjold sought scrupulously to be impartial and tactful in his communications with national officials since he felt that the possession of such qualities was important to his own and the Organization's influence. He realized that the willingness of the Members to create operations which required direction or mediation by the Secretariat was dependent on their respect for his skill and impartiality since he was the major negotiator and ultimate decisionmaker within the Secretariat.[56] A statement by Dr. Conor Cruise O'Brien, who himself had certain reservations about the impartiality of Secretariat officials in regard to the national interests of the Members, revealed that Hammarskjold enjoyed considerable success in establishing his own loyalty to the Organization and his lack of national biases. He wrote: "Hammarskjold more than anyone had given the United Nations a focus of moral authority which would attract an international loyalty, and use it in the cause of peace and justice." [57]

Hammarskjold's most articulate defense of the possibility for international civil servants to assume a position of impartiality toward all states and a primary loyalty to the United Nations came in response to the Soviet bloc's charge during the Congo crisis of 1960–1961 that no individual could be neutral in today's world.[58] In his 1961 Introduction he refuted the Soviet claim when he stated:

Anyone of integrity, not subjected to undue pressures, can, regardless of his own views, readily act in an 'exclusively international' spirit and can be guided in his action on behalf of the Organization solely by its interests and principles, and by the instructions of the organs.[59]

During the same year in a speech at Oxford University he discussed at length the possibility of the Secretary-General's acting in an impartial manner when he had to apply an imprecise mandate or mandates on whose meaning the Members disagreed. He noted that in such circumstances there were a number of sources from which the

Secretary-General could seek guidance which strengthened his ability to make impartial decisions. He described these sources of guidance as the Principles and Purposes of the Charter, the body of United Nations legal doctrine which has accrued since the founding of the Organization, and the policy preferences of the Members as they were expressed in special advisory committees and private diplomatic exchanges.[60] Apart from Hammarskjold's own statements on the possibility and importance of impartial decisionmaking by international civil servants, several of his colleagues have also attested to his beliefs on his matter. One of Hammarskjold's closest associates, Under-Secretary Ralph Bunche, has remarked:

> It was his firm conviction that it was not only possible to conceive of but that there actually had been built up at the United Nations—at the very heart of world events—a body of thoroughly objective, if not "neutral" international officers who, under his leadership, when given opportunity and resources and the confidence of enough governments, could play a vital and at times even decisive role in averting conflict.[61]

Another of Hammarskjold's associates felt that Hammarskjold's attitudes regarding the Soviet Union's attack against him revealed clearly how deeply he believed in his own impartiality. This associate noted that Hammarskjold felt that the Communist states did not really question his impartiality and his sole loyalty to the United Nations and that their criticism resulted solely from the fact that he and the United Nations were hampering them in furthering their goals in Africa.[62]

Hammarskjold's support for a unitary executive in the United Nations Secretariat was closely tied to his thinking about the impartiality of that body since suggestions for the reconstruction of the Secretariat's executive came in response to claims that it was not acting in an impartial manner. At the time of its initial attacks against Hammarskjold in September 1960, the Soviet Union proposed that the Secretariat should be directed by three men (a "troika") who would be drawn from the Western, Communist, and nonaligned groupings and whose unanimous consent would be required for any executive decision.[63] The Soviet Union had charged that this was necessary since no individual could be neutral and impartial under present world conditions. Some quarters in the

West were also mentioning at this time that the Secretariat was working in directions which were contrary to their interests and that it should therefore be organized on an intergovernmental basis.[64]

In his critique of the Soviet proposal Hammarskjold argued both that it was in conflict with the original conception of the Organization and that it would be extremely detrimental to the future ability of the Organization to promote international peace. On the first point he noted that the decisions in San Francisco in 1945—to have the appointment of Secretariat members subject solely to the approval of the Secretary-General, not to require fixed-term appointments for Secretariat members, and not to have Deputy Secretariats-General elected by the representative organs and directly responsible to them—were due to the desire of the framers of the Charter to secure the political independence of the Secretariat by freeing it from national influences. In his estimation the Soviet plan would fall back into exactly what the San Francisco Conference was trying to avoid. In his discussion of the future impact of different forms of organization for the Secretariat, he noted that "the choice between conflicting views on the United Nations Secretariat is basically a choice between conflicting views on the Organization, its functions and its future." [65] His attitude was that an international civil service, which was loyal solely to the United Nations and which had a unitary executive, was one of the most important and crucial bases of power which the Organization had at its disposal in promoting the resolution of conflicts and building higher forms of international cooperation. He opposed the Soviet and other proposals for the Secretariat's reorganization because their acceptance would to a large extent prevent the representative organs from delegating diplomatic and operational powers. They would be prevented from making such delegations of power because an intergovernmental Secretariat would be paralyzed by divisions within it and would thus be ineffective as an executive agent. Hammarskjold expressed his thought on what it would mean to accept a three-man executive for the Secretariat and to sacrifice the principle of an impartial Secretariat when he said at Oxford University in May 1961:

Such a passive acceptance of nationalism rendering it necessary to abandon present efforts in the direction of internationalism symbolized by the international civil service—somewhat surprisingly regarded as a cause of tension—might, if accepted by the Member nations, well prove to be the Munich of international cooperation as conceived after the first World War and further developed under the impression of the tragedy of the second World War.[66]

Hammarskjold appears to have felt that the existence of a unitary executive in the Secretariat and a respect by the Members for its impartiality represented both the possibility for greater international cooperation among states and the attainment of a significant degree of loyalty to the idea of an international community on the part of both the international civil servants and the nations themselves.

In evaluating the skills of the members of the Secretariat as a basis of power of the Organization, Hammarskjold viewed the skills of one group as particularly important. This was the small group of men who occupied high positions in the political sections of the Secretariat. There were a number of reasons for this judgment. First, he believed that the United Nations could exert its greatest influence in international crises and that in such circumstances it was only possible to involve a small number of men. He favored the involvement of only a small group both because it lessened the risk of public knowledge of United Nations activities and because international crises demanded quick decisions. He had a saying which he often used on the 38th floor of the Secretariat building to illustrate his ideas on this matter: "It is not wise to have too many men on deck during a storm." [67] Second, the great majority of the people in the Secretariat, 89 per cent,[68] are involved in the Organization's economic and social activities. Although he had great respect for this aspect of the United Nations' operations, he thought that it could not have a very great impact on international politics at this stage of history. At the same time it should be noted that he thought very highly of men like Philippe de Seynes, David Owen, and Paul Hoffman who were in charge of the United Nations' economic and social operations. Third, while Hammarskjold had great respect for the professional quality of many staff members throughout the Secretariat, this view did not apply to the entire staff. In fact, he once asked one colleague whether he thought that it would be possible for the Secretariat to do the same amount of work in certain professional areas with half the number of people if it were free to recruit only on the basis of skill and without regard to geographical distribution.[69] Another member of the Secretariat pointed out that although Hammarskjold accepted the political necessity of recruiting personnel on the basis of geographical distribution, and although in his last years he brought a number of Africans and Asians into high positions, he felt very uncomfortable at certain times about having to recruit on any other basis than that of skill. This Secretariat member attributed this attitude to his background in the Swedish civil service where there was little or no political patronage and where all jobs were acquired on the basis of competitive exams.[70]

While Hammarskjold had certain reservations about the professional capabilities of some members of the Secretariat, this did not hold true for his evaluation of his own abilities nor for that of the other Secretariat officials who shared "the top deck of the ship during storms." One theme which emerged clearly from *Markings* was his struggle to maintain humility while dealing with people whom he considered of a lesser ability. One entry in *Markings* reflects on this problem of some talented men: "Praise nauseates you—but woe betide him who does not recognize your worth." [71] More than one man who worked with him in some capacity made a remark similar to the following one: "Hammarskjold thought that he could perform a diplomatic task better than anyone else, and he was right." [72] While the above attitudes attributed to Hammarskjold should be noted, it should also be pointed out, first of all, that they are common to many statesmen, and second, that he was often obliged to undertake extensive diplomatic activities because of delegations of authority to him by the representative organs and because of the reputation of his office. One of the most articulate and comprehensive statements of Hammarskjold's diplomatic abilities has been made by his Executive Assistant, Andrew W. Cordier. He remarked:

During my 17 years in United Nations work and activity, I worked intimately and observed the methods of hundreds of high-level diplomats from all parts of the world. For some of them I have the highest regard for their skill and effectiveness in negotiation, but none of them quite compared with the incredible resourcefulness and effectiveness of Dag Hammarskjold. He combined sound, hard realism with an extraordinary imagination. When others saw no further possibility for progress, he devised a means and a pattern of further negotiation, for eventual breakthroughs in tough and baffling problems. His convincing and brilliant analysis of issues and his unique and effective techniques in carrying them to further stages of solution were combined with an energy which astounded collaborators and observers alike.[73]

Adlai Stevenson has also commented on this matter: "Of all his talents, this, perhaps was his greatest—a conciliatory spirit matched with a brilliant gift for evoking unanimity." [74] While Hammarskjold would not have indulged in an evaluation of his own talents as glowing as Cordier's and Stevenson's, he nevertheless was realistically aware of his own strengths and of their relevance to the political activities of the United Nations.

Added to Hammarskjold's own innate skills as a basis of power was the sense of religious mission which he had about his position. This led him to drive himself in making the United Nations succeed. He had this sense of mission from the time that he came to the United Nations. One of his first entries in *Markings* for the year 1953 reads: "Your prayer has been answered, as you know, God has a use for you. . . ." [75] He clearly recognized his religious obligation, and this probably led him to extend himself beyond what might ordinarily be expected of a man in his position. Per Lind, who knew Hammarskjold very well before and after he became Secretary-General, remarked that his sense of mission about the United Nations and his desire that it become a more influential force in world politics was due more to the influence of other dedicated Secretariat members on him than to his religious orientation.[76] Whether this is so is difficult to say, but it can be stated that he had a strong sense of mission about the Organization and his job.

Hammarskjold had considerable respect for the higher echelons of the Secretariat upon whom he relied a great deal. During his tenure as Secretary-General he tried to improve the caliber of men at all levels of the Secretariat, but he paid particular attention to the higher echelon positions. In following such a political course he resisted the pressure of Members to "dump" certain individuals on the Secretariat, and he demanded men of high caliber. During his first several years as Secretary-General he obtained Philippe de Seynes of France as Under-Secretary for Economic and Social Affairs and Ilya Tchernychev of the Soviet Union as Under-Secretary for Political and Security Council Affairs only after considerable negotiations with their governments. Hammarskjold rejected a number of nominations by the Soviet Union before he accepted Tchernychev, whom he had known as the Soviet ambassador to Sweden.[77] He also attempted to recruit a number of skilled diplomats whom he could use for specific United Nations missions. Two of these were Sir Humphrey Travelyn of Britain and Geoffrey Murray of Canada. Both men, who were accustomed to busy diplomatic lives, left the United Nations because of lack of work.

Instead of retaining a large number of high-ranking political officers in the United Nations Secretariat who could be used for specific diplomatic missions, Hammarskjold tended to call on national diplomats who were seconded to the United Nations. Examples of such men are: Rajeshwar Dayal of India and Galo Plaza of Ecuador in the Lebanon crisis of 1958; Baron Beck-Friis of Sweden in the Thailand-Cambodia dispute of 1959; and Herbert de Ribbing of Sweden in the Buraimi Oasis dispute (Britain vs. Saudi Arabia) of 1960–1961. Hammarskjold could usually find diplomats whom he respected to perform missions for the United Nations on a term basis, and this freed the Organization from keeping a sizeable group of unemployed diplomats on its staff. There was one crisis in which his store of diplomatic acquaintances was not sufficient to fill the United Nations posts in the field. This was the Congo crisis. There were so many men required in the United Nations Operation in the Congo that he was forced to call upon some men with whom he had little or no personal acquaintance.

THE DIPLOMATIC FACILITIES
OF THE UNITED NATIONS

Hammarskjold felt that the total diplomatic framework of the United Nations had an independent influence on international politics apart from the formal legal authority which the Organization's organs possessed. This influence was often reflected in authoritative statements of the United Nations organs, but at the same time it grew more out of the presence of the United Nations' diplomatic context than it did from the legal posture of the resolutions. Hammarskjold voiced his evaluation of this permanent multilateral framework in 1959 when he wrote:

The permanent representation at Headquarters of all Member nations, and the growing diplomatic contribution of the permanent delegations outside the public meetings—often in close contact with the Secretariat—may well come to be regarded as the most important "common law" development which has taken place so far within the constitutional framework of the Charter.[78]

By their constituting an important "common law" development he meant that the constant multilateral negotiations and the continual formulation of opinions regarding disputes within this context were asserting an influence on international decisionmaking which was not present in the past. He felt that increasingly states were influenced by having to accept mediation attempts by parties in this context and were having to take the opinions which emerged from this context into their decisions. He remarked that on many international matters there emerged

an opinion independent of partisan interests and dominated by the objectives indicated in the United Nations Charter. This opinion may be more or less articulated and more or less clear-cut, but the fact that it exists forms the basis for the evolution of a stand by the Organization itself, which is relatively independent of that of the parties.[79]

At other times he commented regarding this influence that "the tendency in the United Nations is to wear away, or break down, differences" [80] and that while "States are far less inclined than individuals and groups to be affected by the fact that negotiations are taking place and by the way they are going; still they are affected." [81] At the heart of this development there lay a phenomenon which Hammarskjold had observed prior to his having come to the United Nations—namely, that there is "an interdependent effect between outer criticism and inner insecurity which grows in strength with the intensity of international collaboration and with the degree of uniformity in fundamental ideological reactions between nations." [82]

It was also Hammarskjold's view that the constant process of multilateral interaction and the periodic formulation of consensuses on different problems among large groups of Members actually added strength and influence to the formal organs of the United Nations. He wrote that

While in one sense reducing the practical importance of the public sessions of the various organs, this development has basically tended to give these organs greater real weight in present day diplomacy. The public debate, and the decisions reached, gain added significance when the attitudes presented in public result from practically uninterrupted informal contacts and negotiations.[83]

This judgment of Hammarskjold's was closely tied to his opinion that private diplomacy is more conducive to agreement than public debate, and therefore any established system for private negotiations within the United Nations framework is likely to make the Organization a stronger force for peace.

Hammarskjold also viewed the diplomatic facilities as a basis for power for the Organization in that it gave the Secretariat, and more specifically the Secretary-General, the opportunity to influence negotiations concerning major international problems which were being held by the Members. He once remarked that the Secretariat "has creative capacity. It can introduce new ideas. It can in proper forms take initiatives. It can put before the Member governments new findings which will influence their actions." [84] Hammarskjold always felt that, while there were pressures for the peaceful settlement of disputes and for the creation of broad consensuses within the body of permanent delegations, the Secretary-General as a result of his impartial stature could be an important factor in assisting these tendencies. His years at the United Nations are replete with examples where he assisted in the settlement of conflicts and more particularly in proposing the use of United Nations means of action in their settlement. In some cases he was largely responsible for proposing a certain course of action which the multilateral organs adopted, and in other cases he significantly influenced the formulation of new mandates for existing United Nations operations through such initiatives. It was partly as a result of such activities that Andrew W. Cordier once described Hammarskjold as the "chief legislator" in the Organization.[85] Without the continued presence of national delegations in New York he could never have exerted the kind of influence on the creation and direction of United Nations enterprises which he did.

The Nature of the United Nations' Membership

Throughout his tenure Hammarskjold thought that one of the Organization's major sources of strength in international politics was its broad membership which included most of the states in the world. It was his view that, as a result of the growing interdependence in the world, consultation and joint decisionmaking among all states was a practical necessity to achieve peace and promote other values, and that the United Nations was the logical and intended vehicle for such activities. In his 1959 Introduction he wrote:

It still seems sometimes to be forgotten that—whatever views may be held about the United Nations as an institution—the principle of organized international cooperation on a basis of universality which is at present reflected in this Organization is one which has emerged from bitter experiences and should be now considered as firmly established. No international policy for the future can be envisaged which does not recognize this principle and is not willing to give it adequate representation in practice.[86]

While Hammarskjold thought that the Organization's membership would automatically make it an important framework for conflict settlement and cooperation in the world, he felt that insofar as it fell short of realizing the principle of universality, its role in international politics would be undermined. In fact, he even stated that if it were perceived that the Organization did not realize sufficiently the principle of universality in practice, there could be a movement which would seek to create a new international organization which would do so.[87] On one occasion he noted that one of the reasons for the collapse of the League of Nations was its failure to achieve universality.[88]

While he did not state so explicitly in any of his statements on the question of universality, the concrete question to which he was primarily addressing himself was the absence of Communist China from the United Nations.[89] He stated privately to colleagues that Communist China must be brought into the Organization in the near future and that its absence was impeding the Organization's playing a fruitful role in respect to many problems in Asia.[90] He evidently did not make his views public because of the likely reaction by the United States Government. While his opinions on this matter were never set forth explicitly in any public statements, they were readily understood by the Members. In fact, one of his major statements during his very first year as Secretary-General specifically rebutted all of the major arguments which are generally brought up by the United States against the representation of Communist China. He first hit at the argument that it should not be admitted because it was not a "peace-loving" state when he stated: ". . . the idea of the United Nations as a club to which only the like-minded will be admitted, in which membership is a privilege and expulsion is the retribution for wrong-doing, is totally unrealistic and self-defeating." [91] He noted that the realistic "working hypothesis" of the Organization must be trying to find a way "of somehow living together," and that the only road to this was seeking "peacefully negotiated agreements" between the very heterogeneous states of the world.[92] From this point he went on to rebut the charge that the Organization would be immobilized by a state which frequently employed the veto by pointing to the possibility of working through the General Assembly.[93] He finished his discourse by remarking that in reality it was not the veto power of any state which hindered a settlement of a conflict "but the hard fact that such settlements require agreement and acceptance by the parties to it." [94]

Chapter Three

Hammarskjold's Strategies and Tactics for Promoting the Peaceful Settlement of Disputes

As has already been noted in the previous chapter, the United Nations does not possess very substantial permanent bases of power, and therefore it relies to a large extent on the voluntary contribution of bases of power by its Members in its attempts to influence situations. Because of this condition any suggestion that the United Nations apply certain means of action to a situation in order to try to influence its outcome must be based on a judgment that a sufficient number of states with sufficient bases of power think that it is in their interest to concert some of their power through the United Nations or in cooperation with the United Nations. These calculations are not always easy to make, and as has been suggested in the previous chapter, the willingness of the Members to contribute their power may rest *inter alia* on their evaluation of the permanent bases of power of the United Nations. This is especially the case where the means of action to be used is directed by the Secretary-General and the Secretariat. Hammarskjold was very conscious of this fact, and he was therefore careful in following certain tactical principles which would gain the respect and confidence of the Members.

While successful strategies do require sufficient bases of power to influence the outcome of a situation, many strategies—if not most —are designed without any kind of sure knowledge that they will be able to draw on the necessary bases of power or that the power upon which they can draw will be sufficient to influence the situation in the manner desired. Politics seldom lends itself to that kind of predictability. At the same time certain probabilities can be estimated, and plans for maximizing the power of the United Nations in particular operations can be designed. During his tenure Hammarskjold thought that the probabilities of the United Nations influencing the outcomes of conflicts depended upon the kinds of conflicts that it was trying to affect and whether the Secretariat and the Members used United Nations means of action in accordance with certain tactical principles.

The following analysis of Hammarskjold's strategic and tactical principles for the peaceful settlement of disputes will include his views on the ways in which the United Nations Members, the representative organs, and the Secretary-General should employ four different means of action. They are: (1) negotiations among the Members at the United Nations; (2) mediatory missions (usually by the Secretary-General); (3) fact-finding missions; and (4) recommendations by the representative organs. One instrument of peaceful settlement, namely, the International Court of Justice, will not be discussed here since Hammarskjold never suggested during his tenure that any specific conflicts be referred to the Court.[1]

Apart from the distinction among different means of action another distinction which will appear often in Hammarskjold's strategies for both the peaceful settlement of disputes and controlling the use of force is that between disputes over interests inside the Western and Communist blocs and disputes over interests outside the blocs. As will be explained more fully later, Hammarskjold thought that the United Nations' ability to constructively influence a conflict depended upon the locus of interests in dispute. If they lay within the blocs (for example, the status of Berlin), he felt that the Organization could seldom play a constructive role; but if they lay outside (such as the status of the Suez Canal), then it might play an influential and positive role. This distinction does not concern whether members of the Western and Communist alliances were influential parties in the conflict but whether the conflict concerned their actual territorial and political status. Indeed, Hammarskjold assumed that the Great Powers (especially the United States and the Soviet Union) would almost always be influential parties in any international conflict, but he felt that their policies differed toward conflicts within and outside the territorial sphere of their alliances in such a way as to allow an active United Nations role in one set of conflicts and not in another.

Strategies

1. In conflicts over interests within the blocs, the United Nations representative organs and the Secretary-General should generally abstain from any attempts at mediation and the passage of resolutions, since the opposition of one or both blocs is likely to make such actions ineffective and is likely to alienate one or both blocs from cooperation with the United Nations and the Secretary-General on other matters more amenable to the Organization's influence. At the same time, if such conflicts pose very serious threats to international peace, the United Nations organs should initiate mediatory missions and/or pass resolutions which suggest substantive bases of settlement.

In setting forth this strategy it is necessary to state initially that while Hammarskjold accepted it for the greater part of his tenure (1956–1961), he did not prescribe it for the Organization during his first several years as Secretary-General. In fact, from mid-1953 to mid-1955 he actually viewed the peaceful settlement of conflicts between the Western and Communist alliance systems in Europe and the Far East as the most important task of the United Nations. In the discussion of this strategy Hammarskjold's reasons for initially trying to involve the United Nations in the settlement of conflicts over interests within the blocs will first be presented, and then his reasons for recommending that the Organization generally refrain from such involvements and turn its attention elsewhere will be examined. The discussion will end with a presentation of the only major involvement which the United Nations and Hammarskjold had in a dispute over interests within the blocs—namely, the dispute between the United States and Communist China in 1954 and 1955 over China's imprisonment of some American fliers captured during the Korean War.

In Hammarskjold's first general report to the United Nations Members in July 1953 he wrote: "The efforts of governments to control and moderate those conflicts that constitute an immediate danger to world peace—and above all the 'East-West' conflict—must command first attention in day-to-day decisions." [2] He added that the movements for political, economic, and social equality within and between nations also posed serious threats to international stability, but there was no doubt that he thought that the United Nations should turn its primary attention to Cold War conflicts in Europe and the Far East. In fact, in late 1954, just prior to his trip to Peking to mediate the dispute over the imprisonment of American airmen, he remarked to a diplomat that he expected the most serious threats to international peace in the near future to arise in the Far East.[3] The reasons why Hammarskjold thought that the major future crises were likely to arise in such areas and why the United Nations should attempt to settle them are not too difficult to discern. Despite the conclusion of the Korean War in the summer of 1953, the intense antagonisms between the Communist and Western states and their construction of powerful military machines did not subside. In fact, during this time both sides, especially the United States and China, engaged in active saber-rattling or "brinkmanship" in an attempt to force the other side to accept its demands. Apart from the constant threats which were posed by the immediate confrontations of these antagonistic politico-military coalitions, Hammarskjold also probably felt that the United Nations should concern itself with conflicts over interests within the blocs because there were no other serious threats to international peace at that time. The threats which were to soon appear in the Middle East and in the Afro-Asian world in general as a result of rapid decolonization and a shift of the Cold War to those areas did not seem very serious during the years 1953–1955. Hammarskjold must have no doubt been a bit skeptical about the ability of the United Nations to influence threats to the peace arising from the military confrontation of the blocs, given both their overwhelming military might and their veto power in the Security Council, but he evidently did not see an alternative role for the Organization.

In mid-1955, about the time of his successful mediation of a direct East-West conflict (the American-Communist Chinese dispute over the Chinese imprisonment of American fliers), Hammarskjold's perception of international politics and of how the United Nations might be able to influence it appears to have changed. He no longer saw conflicts between the Cold War blocs over their immediate territorial spheres as the main object of the United Nations' strategies for peaceful settlement. Rather, he looked to conflicts over interests outside their geographical boundaries as the most profitable area in which the Organization could employ its means of peaceful settlement. Such conflicts did not involve primary interests of the two blocs although some of them were viewed as very important to their security and other foreign policy goals.

There were several reasons why he adopted this new strategy. First, he observed in 1955 and 1956 a lessening of tensions between the blocs which outwardly had manifested itself in an Austrian peace treaty [4] and the resumption of diplomatic relations between the Soviet Union and West Germany. These actions of the bloc states, together with their mutual realization of what a direct nuclear clash might bring, seemed to indicate to Hammarskjold that there was less likelihood that they would attempt any direct military actions against each other's territories. Second, he perceived that the birth of a number of new states, mainly from Africa, would add an element of instability to world politics. In his Introductions of 1955 [5] and 1956 [6] Hammarskjold stated that the Organization should concern itself primarily with the conflicts between the countries of Africa and Asia and the historic West rather than with the threat of a military clash between the Western and Communist states in Europe or the Far East. Third, although he did not mention it in any public utterances, he was undoubtedly aware of the change in Soviet strategy which took place in 1955 and 1956 and which had its clearest expression at the Twentieth Party Congress in February 1956. This new strategy was based on a policy of "peaceful coexistence" which recognized the impossibility of "victory" in a nuclear war and which viewed the underdeveloped countries as the main battlefield in which the competition between Soviet communism and Western capitalism would be waged.[7] With this change in Soviet strategy it was natural for Hammarskjold to decide that the United Nations' focus for peaceful settlement should change.

Another reason that Hammarskjold directed the United Nations' means of peaceful settlement at conflicts not involving primary interests of the blocs was that he thought that the United Nations could seldom influence conflicts over their primary interests. In his estimation the Organization was unable to affect their primary interests (for example, their political and military control over their respective European spheres) both because the Security Council could not act as a result of the veto provision and because the General Assembly could seldom concert the political power which would be necessary to influence one of the super-powers and its allies. He most articulately set forth this position in his 1960 Introduction when he wrote:

With its constitution and structure, it is extremely difficult for the United Nations to exercise an influence on problems which are clearly and definitely within the orbit of present day conflicts between power blocs. If a specific conflict is within that orbit, it can be assumed that the Security Council is rendered inactive, and it may be feared that even positions taken by the General Assembly would follow lines strongly influenced by considerations only indirectly related to the concrete difficulty under consideration. Whatever the attitude of the General Assembly and the Security Council, it is in such cases also practically impossible for the Secretary-General to operate effectively with the means put at his disposal, short of risking seriously to impair the usefulness of his office for the Organization in all the other cases for which the services of the United Nations are needed.[8]

Hammarskjold knew how important the support of the Great Powers was to the Secretary-General in almost any task that he might undertake, and he did not want to risk his utility by alienating one or more of the Great Powers by taking a position which opposed what it or they considered vital interests. He believed that in conflicts outside of the blocs the security of the Great Powers was not so vitally at stake and that it was not in their self-interest to become militarily embroiled with each other in a competition for these interests.

While Hammarskjold believed in "a kind of division of responsibility" in international politics in which the Great Powers dealt with disputes within the geographical boundaries of the blocs, he thought that the General Assembly should formulate its views on such conflicts if they seriously endangered international peace. As has been previously mentioned, he feared that many Members of the General Assembly might vote in accordance with the wishes of the Great Powers which could exert considerable pressure on them, but in extreme crises he probably hoped that they would put the international community's interest in peace first. In respect to the Berlin situation, which was quite tense during the summer of 1961, he wrote in his 1961 Introduction:

The community of nations, represented in the United Nations, has a vital interest in a peaceful solution, based on justice, of any question which—like this one—unless brought to a satisfactory solution, might come to represent a threat to peace and security.[9]

As it turned out, there was no call for the General Assembly to influence a peaceful settlement of this question or any other direct interbloc conflict apart from the disarmament problem after the Sino-American dispute of 1954–1955, but Hammarskjold never dismissed it as a possibility.

As has been mentioned, the Sino-American dispute of 1954–1955 was the only direct conflict between a Communist and a Western state in which both the United Nations General Assembly and Hammarskjold tried to achieve a peaceful settlement. While the conflict itself is atypical of most of the conflicts between the two blocs at that time, it is an interesting dispute to study from the point of view of both the United Nations' involvement in it and the impact which this role had on the future political activities of the Organization. It was in this conflict that Hammarskjold demonstrated to the United Nations Members that the Secretary-General could be a very valuable agent of peaceful settlement for the representative organs, and in doing this he significantly altered their own policies toward the use of the Organization.

The dispute arose in mid-November 1954 when the United States learned that Communist China had imprisoned a number of its fliers, who had been shot down during the Korean War, because it claimed they were spies. The United States retorted that they were not spies and that their imprisonment was contrary to the repatriation of prisoners provisions of the Korean Armistice Agreement. In order to try to put pressure on Communist China to release them, the United States submitted the dispute to the United Nations Gen-

eral Assembly on December 5, 1954, and called for a resolution condemning the Chinese action and demanding the prisoners' release.[10]
This particular issue took on much more ominous overtones for
international peace than might have been expected because of the
nature of the relations between the United States and Communist
China and the state of American internal politics at that time. The
antagonisms between the two countries were especially acute near
the end of 1954 as a result of the Chinese Communist bombardments
of the island of Quemoy, the recent anti-communist Manila Pact
Conference, and the negotiations which were taking place between
the United Slates and Nationalist China concerning the signing of a
Mutual Security Pact.[11] They were heightened too by Secretary of
State Dulles's strategy of "brinkmanship," which constantly seemed
to put the Far East on the verge of a serious war. As a result of these
especially hostile relations the honor and political resolve of the two
countries became stakes in the struggle over the fliers. The internal
political situation in the United States which augmented the threat
to the peace which Communist China's imprisonment of American
fliers posed was the existence of the "China lobby" and its allies in
Congress, who included, among others, Senators Knowland, Mc-
Carthy, Jenner, and Bridges. This group was constantly urging
stronger measures upon the Eisenhower administration against the
Chinese Communist government. For reprisals in this particular
case, Senator Knowland was urging a blockade of China,[12] and Senator McCarthy favored cutting off all trade with Western countries
that traded with Communist China, "unleashing Chiang to attack
the soft underbelly of the China mainland", and waging "war if
necessary to secure the release of the United States prisoners." [13]

Under these rather ominous circumstances the United States
brought the problem to the United Nations, and the General Assembly held five meetings on it from December 8 to 10. On December 10 the General Assembly passed a resolution which was spon-
sored by sixteen nations, including the United States. It declared
that the imprisonment of the fliers violated the Korean Armistice
Agreement, and condemned their trial and imprisonment by the
People's Republic of China. It also requested that the Secretary-
General "make continuing and unremitting efforts" to seek their re-

lease.[14] Although Hammarskjold, as will be described later, had serious reservations about the political sagacity of the condemnation of China's action, he viewed the resolution, and more particularly the request that he as Secretary-General try to secure the release of the airmen, as his first real opportunity to make the Organization an effective instrument of peaceful settlement in the Cold War. On the same day that the resolution was passed, he decided to ask the Prime Minister of the State Council and the Minister of Foreign Affairs of the People's Republic of China, Chou En-lai, if he could come to Peking to discuss the problem with him.[15] In this dispute he felt apparently that his personal diplomatic activity was required to bridge the gap in communications between the United States and China. One purpose of his mission was mediatory in that he was going to try to get the Chinese to accept a certain position, but another was to act as a channel of communication through which the conflicting parties could understand the views and motives of the other. According to Hans Engen, the Norwegian Ambassador to the United Nations, his decision to go to Peking was motivated also by his estimation that the Far East was likely to pose the greatest threats to international peace in the near future.[16] Therefore, he wanted to know and to understand at first hand the leaders of one of the major parties in the area so that he and the United Nations could play an active peaceful settlement role in any future conflicts in the region.

Chou En-lai accepted Hammarskjold's request to come to Peking, and between January 6 and 10, 1955 they and their advisers held four talks. One part of their conversation involved a very detailed presentation by Hammarskjold of his position that the airmen were under the United Nations command in Korea and therefore should be released and an equally detailed statement by Chou En-lai of why he thought the airmen were spies.[17] Another part concerned a discussion of complaints which Chou En-lai brought up against the United States and its allies in Asia. Regarding Chou's complaint that the United States had aggressive designs against the People's Republic of China, Hammarskjold noted that he had heard similar claims about the motives of the People's Republic in the West. He then remarked that he hoped that his mission might be able to break through the mutual distrust and hostility between

China and the United States and set their future relations on a better course. Hammarskjold sympathized with two of Chou's charges. These were that Communist China had wrongfully been denied admission to the United Nations and that some Chinese students in the United States were not being allowed to return to the People's Republic of China. On the latter point he said that he would talk to United States Government officials about the possibility of granting these students visas. Although Chou did not accept Hammarskjold's reasoning regarding the prisoners, he agreed at the end of the talks to comply with two of the Secretary-General's requests. He agreed, first, that the People's Republic of China would be guided by the policy regarding prison terms for foreigners which it announced at Geneva, namely, that the terms would be lenient and, second, that it would supply information to the prisoners' families regarding their health. Chou also went beyond Hammarskjold's requests in respect to the prisoners and mentioned that their families could come to China to visit them.

Although Hammarskjold returned to New York without any explicit promise of the prisoners' release, he interpreted Chou's last offers as intimating that with time and patience the prisoners would be released. They were released on August 1, 1955. Between the time of his negotiations in Peking and the release Hammarskjold kept in touch with the Chinese leaders through the embassy of the People's Republic of China in Stockholm. During these months he cautioned against rash actions and suggested gestures of good will to the officials of the United States. His advice was not always accepted, as when the United States rejected his suggestion that it allow the fliers' families to go to China. On the other hand, his proposal that the United States grant exit visas for the Chinese students who wanted to return to the People's Republic was accepted.

Although it is impossible to make an authoritative judgment regarding the influence of Hammarskjold's mission, the history of the crisis does indicate that it had considerable influence not only in securing their release but also perhaps in preventing an armed conflict in the Far East. The mission established a channel of communication between the conflicting parties and gained important time when an armed conflict might have broken out had there not been some hope of a peaceful settlement. Hammarskjold's talks with officials of both governments also added a voice of reason and objectivity to the policymaking dialogues within each government. Several people have mentioned that Hammarskjold looked upon this mission as one of the most important which he had performed—from the perspectives of both international peace and the development of the United Nations.[18]

In terms of the development of the Organization and of its means of peaceful settlement the importance of this Peking mission cannot be underestimated. The General Assembly initiated a completely new means of peaceful settlement when it asked the Secretary-General to do whatever he could to have the fliers freed. Prior to this time the Secretary-General had been asked to perform numerous technical jobs by the representative organs, but he had never been requested to undertake any missions to solve important interstate conflicts. Trygve Lie during his tenure had tried on his own initiative to solve or influence the resolution of some disputes,[19] but he had never been asked by the representative organs to perform such roles. The General Assembly turned to Hammarskjold in December 1954 because some of the Members had come to know of his diplomatic skill and tact and because there was no other course open on which they could agree. This combination of a General Assembly or Security Council recommendation to states which were involved in a conflict combined with a request to the Secretary-General to help the parties come to an agreement soon became one of the major approaches of the United Nations in trying to further the peaceful settlement of conflicts. From this point on in the history of the Organization, recommendations by the General Assembly and Security Council continued to play key and essential roles in the work of the Organization, but the use of the Secretary-General as a diplomatic agent by the representative organs was the element that gave their resolutions an operative dimension. Hammarskjold had not deliberately sought such a role for himself as a part of his policy to return the United Nations to the work of serious peaceful settlement, but when the opportunity arose, he seized it.

   2. *In conflicts between Western and Communist states, the United Nations Members and the Secretary-General should try*

to persuade the parties to hold negotiations within United Nations structures where the mediatory influence of the Secretary-General and the nonaligned Members and the norms of the Organization might be able to further a peaceful settlement.

During Hammarskjold's tenure he tried on several occasions to persuade the Great Powers to hold their negotiations within United Nations structures or at least to allow the Organization to provide the conference services for the meetings. While these Great Power conferences usually concerned European security problems or the issue of disarmament, they sometimes concerned crises outside the blocs. Hammarskjold presented the advantages to be derived from holding Great Power negotiations at the United Nations after the plans for a summit meeting of the four Great Powers, India, and the Secretary-General at the United Nations in August 1958 fell through. Although this meeting was supposed to deal with the Lebanon crisis, which did not involve the primary interests of the blocs, his ideas concerning the value of a meeting in the United Nations can be applied to any Great Power negotiations. Concerning the advantages he wrote:

Not only would the Security Council have provided a firm procedural foundation for the planned discussions between the heads of government; more important, it would have provided them with a clearly defined legal framework and would have eliminated elements of uncertainty concerning purposes and principles which easily might complicate deliberations in other forms, unless far more extensive preparations had been made than are required for a meeting of the Security Council.[20]

Other reasons why Hammarskjold favored Great Power negotiations within the United Nations were that they would tend to eliminate the high expectations which accompany such meetings when specially staged and that they would be able to take advantage of the various kinds of mediatory and third-party assistance which the United Nations had developed.[21] He had often been impressed by the conciliatory influence which he and the majority of Members had had on the Great Powers in different crises which had been brought to the United Nations, and he hoped that gradually this influence might be brought to bear on more of their encounters.

There were two specific occasions on which Hammarskjold encouraged the Great Powers to hold summit conferences at the United Nations. During the first part of 1960 he tried to have the Big Four summit conference, which was finally held in Paris and which broke up over the U-2 incident, held at the headquarters of the Organization. While three of the Great Powers were moderately receptive to the idea, President de Gaulle's vehement opposition to the proposal prevented it.[22] The other occasion when Hammarskjold supported the convening of a summit conference at the United Nations was the Middle East crisis in the summer of 1958, but the proposal of such a meeting was finally turned down by the Soviet Union. While this conflict concerned interests outside the blocs, the diplomacy surrounding it reveals a great deal of Hammarskjold's thinking concerning the relation of the organization to high-level Great Power talks. The first event which led to the proposal of a Great Power summit conference at the United Nations was the suggestion of Premier Khruschchev of the Soviet Union on July 19 that the leaders of the four Big Powers, India, and the Secretary-General meet at the summit to discuss the Middle East problem.[23] On July 22 President Eisenhower responded by agreeing to such a summit meeting, but he proposed that it be held within the framework of the Security Council.[24] Khruschchev accepted this proposal, but the parties soon turned to arguing about procedures and other matters. At the beginning of August, Khruschchev made a sudden trip to Peking, and upon his return he rejected the idea of a summit conference. In its place he proposed the convening of a special session of the General Assembly.[25] Most observers thought that Peking had pressured Moscow into rejecting the idea of the meeting within the Security Council because Nationalist China would be represented.[26]

Before Khruschchev rejected the proposal for the summit conference at the United Nations in which the Secretary-General would take part, Hammarskjold had given strong support to it. He saw it as a recognition of the increasing importance of the Organization in international politics and of the need for an impartial representative who could facilitate agreement among the national delegates. He had long been trying to persuade the Great Powers that the Organization provided an excellent framework for negotiations, and the proposal for a summit conference at the United Nations seemed to prove that his efforts were bearing fruit.

While Hammarskjold preferred to have Great Power negotiations at the United Nations, he felt that a second-best method for promoting the peaceful settlement of East-West conflicts was for the Organization to provide the conference services for such meetings. This meant that the Organization would provide the physical facilities and perhaps translation services for the meeting. While such an arrangement did not provide the immediate mediatory services of the United Nations diplomatic facilities in New York, it did give the Secretary-General and the Members some opportunity and justification for making their views heard. One Great Power meeting where the Organization did provide such services was the Big Four Foreign Ministers meeting in Geneva in May 1959. In a speech in Copenhagen just prior to that conference he remarked on the favorable effects of such arrangements:

This is more than a purely formal relationship. It reflects the fact that, should the parties find themselves in need of the kind of assistance the Organization can render in any other respects, they can ask for such assistance and will get it. To begin with, this means only various practical arrangements, but the assistance can go further without changing the basic situation, which is that the foreign ministers' conference as such is independent of the Organization, and that the United Nations at the present stage neither has nor can have any policy position as a party to the conference.[27]

In the Geneva meeting of May 1959, the fact that the United Nations was providing the conference services at the Palais des Nations gave Hammarskjold an opportunity to discuss a number of problems with the foreign ministers assembled there. It is possible to surmise that he viewed such arrangements solely as "a foot in the door" for the United Nations and that he hoped to see such conferences formally within the United Nations framework in the future where the Organization could employ a broader range of its means of peaceful settlement. Although he generally placed European security problems out of the United Nations' purview during his tenure, he probably hoped in the long run to have negotiations concerning them and the determination of their final solution well integrated into the United Nations system of peaceful settlement procedures.

> *3. In conflicts over interests outside the blocs, the United Nations representative organs and the Secretary-General should undertake actions whose purposes are to promote peaceful relations among and political independence for the disputing states and to exclude the Cold War powers from any direct involvement which could lead to a serious international military conflict and to a perpetuation of the local conflict.*

This strategy represents the central policy which Hammarskjold prescribed for the United Nations in its attempts to settle conflicts over interests outside the Western and Communist blocs, and it underlies most of his other strategies toward such conflicts which are articulated in this chapter. It should also be mentioned that all of the calculations which are present in this strategy for the peaceful settlement of disputes are also valid for his strategy for controlling the use of force in such conflicts.

As has been previously pointed out, Hammarskjold's ideas regarding the United Nations' role in international politics began to change in 1955. Beginning with that year he felt that the United Nations should concentrate on resolving conflicts whose locus lay outside of the territorial spheres of the Cold War protagonists. This change in his thinking was due to his perceptions of a relative stabilization of relations between the blocs in Europe and to a lesser extent in the Far East, a change of focus of the Cold War from Europe to the less-developed countries, the likely emergence of many new African states, and increased friction and tension in the Middle East. This change was reflected very clearly in his Introductions from 1953 to 1956. Whereas in 1953 he viewed the conflicts between the Cold War blocs as the prime objectives for the United Nations' means of peaceful settlement,[28] in 1955 the focus of his strategies for the United Nations was quite different. In his 1955 Introduction he wrote:

The peoples of Asia today, of Africa tomorrow, are moving towards a new relationship with what history calls the West. The world organization is the place where this emerging relationship in world affairs can most creatively be forged.[29]

He also noted in that same document that

in the next ten years the peace and stability of the world will be strongly affected by the evolution in Africa, by the national awakening of its people, by the course of race relations and by the manner in which the economic and social advancement of the African people is assisted by the rest of the world.[30]

From these statements one can detect that Hammarskjold's paramount concern had become the new political and economic relationships which are being forged between Africa and Asia and the West—and the role of the United Nations in influencing the nature of these relationships.

By 1956 his thinking appears to have moved even further toward a recognition that the problems arising from Africa and Asia should be the primary focus of the Organization. In his Introduction of that year he listed what he believed were the three great challenges of our time, and he placed "the relationship of the peoples of Asia and Africa with the peoples of Western traditions" and "the economic development for that majority of mankind which has so far shared so little in the fruits of the industrial age" before "the unresolved conflict between the ideologies that divide the world." [31] The only means that he then suggested that the United Nations utilize in relating itself to these problems were economic and technical assistance and a greater use of the United Nations organs. He did not articulate the strategies which the representative organs and the Secretary-General should follow in order to alleviate the problems posed by the emergence of the new African and Asian states until after the Organization had been involved in several crises in the Middle East and Africa.

Hammarskjold's strategy for handling these conflicts outside the blocs did not emerge in practice until the series of crises in the Middle East in 1956, and it was not clearly articulated until his 1960 Introduction. Andrew W. Cordier summarized Hammarskjold's strategy very well when he said that in a crisis the Secretary-General sought "to elbow the cold war out of the situation, lower the tension, isolate the cold war element in it—then to the solving of the problem." [32] The ways in which he sought to "elbow the cold war out of the situation" and hence to alleviate the threat of a larger international war were to introduce United Nations means of peaceful settlement or its means for controlling the use of force and to exclude the Great Powers from any direct role in these operations. The major purpose of such a policy was to remove any excuse of unilateral Great Power intervention to "solve" the situation which might exacerbate the conflict and provoke a counter intervention by the opposing Cold War alliance. These original conflicts might be between two states in the area or between a "Western" country and an African or Asian state, or they could involve both kinds of conflict. In his 1960 Introduction, which is largely concerned with this strategy, he spoke of the United Nations' ability to use means of settling disputes, deterring armed conflicts, and restoring the peace all under the rubric of "preventive action" or "preventive diplomacy." [33] He wrote:

Preventive action . . . must in the first place aim at filling the vacuum so that it will not provoke action from any of the major parties, the initiative for which might be taken for preventive purposes but might in truth lead to counter action from the other side. The ways in which a vacuum can be filled by the United Nations so as to forestall such initiatives differ from case to case, but they have this in common: temporarily, and pending the filling of a vacuum by normal means, the United Nations enters the picture on the basis of its non-commitment to any power bloc, so as to provide to the extent possible a guarantee in relation to all parties against initiatives from others.[34]

In the same Introduction he also described some of the non-permanent bases of power on which the Organization could rely in acting in conflicts outside the blocs. One was the support or at least the acquiescence which the Great Powers gave to United Nations operations as a result of their judgment that such support would be likely to avoid undesirable complications with the opposing bloc and the Afro-Asian grouping. Another was the support which the African and Asian states would give to the United Nations out of an interest in protecting and strengthening their own independence. Concerning the support of the Great Powers he wrote: "Agreement may be achieved because of a mutual interest among the big Powers to avoid having a regional or local conflict drawn into the sphere of bloc politics." [35] He apparently surmised that the Great Powers would accept United Nations operations because they would judge that their unilateral entry might lead to a serious East-West conflict, that United Nations actions at least prevented intervention by the other bloc, and that refusal to accept United Nations actions would alienate the Afro-Asian countries. In respect to the interest which the African and Asian states had in supporting United Nations operations in their regions, he said:

Whether the countries concerned call themselves non-committed, neutral, neutralist or something else, they have all found it not to be in harmony with their role and interests in world politics to tie their policies, in a general sense, to any one of the blocs or to any specific line of action supported by one of the sides in the major conflict.[36]

Hammarskjold's calculation, which by 1960 was based on experience, was that the new states would prefer to have the United Nations perform certain peace-oriented functions in their area rather than risk the chance of undercutting their independence by allowing or asking the Great Powers to assume such tasks. He perceived that whether a new state was having a conflict with a neighboring state or with a Great Power, it would generally consider the United Nations as a politically more acceptable and more effective source of aid. Such an arrangement with the United Nations rather than with certain Western and Communist states was more acceptable because it was less likely to undermine the independence of the new state, and was more effective because it was more apt to elicit the cooperation of all interested countries and to discourage the opposition of any states that might be in disagreement with it. As will be observed in the following description of the specific strategies which Hammarskjold prescribed for the United Nations, his policy of keeping the peace by isolating conflicts in Africa and Asia from the Cold War led him to promote a policy of nonalignment or neutralism for the non-Western states. This policy, needless to say, was not always appreciated by the Great Powers.

4. *In interstate conflicts over interests outside the blocs, the United Nations representative organs should make recommendations for the solution of the disputes and/or should delegate mediatory responsibilities to the Secretary-General in order to prevent an outbreak of fighting between those states and in*

order to prevent a continuing conflict from leading to Great
Power intervention on opposing sides.

During Hammarskjold's tenure there were only two conflicts
between states over interests outside the blocs in which either the
Security Council or the General Assembly recommended specific
settlement proposals and requested that the Secretary-General promote their implementation.[37] There were other occasions when
they recommended settlements and mediation where large-scale violence had broken out or where the immediate conflict was civil
rather than interstate in character, but these are dealt with in separate strategies in this study. The two occasions when there were
formal resolutions of the representative organs were the Arab-Israeli
dispute in the spring of 1956 and the Middle East crisis of 1958.

Hammarskjold's activities during the Arab-Israeli dispute of
early 1956 and his views on the United Nations' involvement in this
conflict clearly illustrate the policies which have been articulated in
this strategy and in the previous one. Despite the fact that this was
the first conflict over interests outside the blocs in which he became
actively involved, his overall strategy of "preventive diplomacy,"
which he elaborated five years later, is very easily identifiable in his
approach to this problem.

Hammarskjold had privately and unsuccessfully tried to assume
the role of a mediator in the Arab-Israeli conflict during 1954 and
1955, but it was not until early 1956, when the conflict became more
serious as a result of the parties' violations of the Armistice Agreements, that both he and the Organization assumed very active roles.
Apart from the growing seriousness of the dispute, another factor
which led to a more active role for Hammarskjold was the new
prestige which he had gained as a result of his successful mediation
of the Sino-American conflict of 1954–1955. Hammarskjold's role in
trying to settle the disputes between Israel and her Arab neighbors
began in January 1956, when on his own initiative he visited Prime
Minister Ben-Gurion in Jerusalem and President Nasser in Cairo and
discussed with them the gradual decay of the Armistice Agreements
of 1949. Both men described their states' violations as reactions to
comparable actions of the other state.[38] When he returned to New

York, representatives of the Western powers consulted with him about possible ways to create greater stability in the area. At that time Britain wanted the United States and France to reiterate their Tripartite Declaration of 1950, which proclaimed that the three powers would act against any breach of the peace in the area, and to take preparatory measures to back up their pledge. The United States refused to go along with the British plan because the Tripartite Declaration was considered as a Western imperialist doctrine by the Arabs and because the administration did not want to ask for the Congressional approval.[39] When the Western states approached Hammarskjold about the possibility of taking the problem to the Security Council, he was rather critical of it since he feared that the debate would lead to stronger Western and Soviet commitments respectively to Israel and Egypt and hence to an exacerbation of the conflict. He preferred that the Great Powers privately back his own diplomatic efforts with the parties. When the Western states announced that they had decided to take it to the Security Council, he suggested that any proposal should not reflect a "tripartite" orientation since that would most likely bring forth a Soviet veto and intensify the Cold War aspects of the problem.[40] Hammarskjold's motive throughout these preliminary talks was to persuade the Western and Communist states to forego attempts to achieve influence in the area at the expense of their Cold War rivals and to support stability in the region.

When the Security Council did meet, the Western proposal was submitted only by the United States in order to avoid giving it a "tripartite" aura. This proposal, which was passed, requested the Secretary-General to survey the situation along the armistice lines between Israel and her four Arab neighbors, and

request[ed] the Secretary-General to arrange with the parties for the adoption of any measures which after discussion with the parties and with the Chief of Staff he considers would reduce existing tensions along the Armistice Demarcation Lines.[41]

The resolution also recalled three previous resolutions which had proposed measures for a reduction of tensions along the armistice lines, and it suggested that possible measures which the Secretary-General might negotiate with the parties were the withdrawal of forces from the armistice lines, full freedom of movement of United Nations observers, and the establishment of local arrangements for preventing violations of the Armistice Agreements. In Hammarskjold's estimation the introduction of the resolution solely by the United States and the mandate for quiet diplomacy by the Secretary-General were conducive to the peaceful settlement of the problem. He appears to have thought that his own negotiations with the parties and whatever behind-the-scenes support the Great Powers might give him would be most effective if all of the negotiations with the parties were private.

From April 6 to May 6 he traveled back and forth between the capitals of Israel and its four Arab neighbors. On May 9, 1956, in a report on the results of his trip, he announced that the five parties had all agreed not to violate the cease-fire provisions of the General Armistice Agreements and that the only permissible recourse to armed force was in a case of armed attack as set forth in Article 51 of the Charter. He noted that this exception did not allow any acts of retaliation in response to minor forays from the other side of the border.[42] Although Hammarskjold was supported in his efforts by the Western Great Powers, the basis of power which made the difference in achieving the accord was his own skill as negotiator. General E. L. M. Burns, who was then the head of the United Nations Truce Supervisory Organization, has written regarding Hammarskjold's personal influence:

the great burden of this negotiation was undertaken by Mr. Hammarskjold himself. Throughout this grueling programme his stamina was astonishing; he never seemed weary, nor did his perceptions flag. His name had become synonymous with diplomatic skill, and he deployed his great resources throughout the four weeks of his mission. . . .
Eventually, by dint of great persuasiveness, moral force, and persistence, Mr. Hammarskjold got the agreement of all parties to the principle that the provisions of the cease-fire article must always be observed, unless the opposing party broke them first.[43]

At the end of his trip Hammarskjold reflected on the nature of the influence which the Secretary-General backed by a Security Council resolution could bring to bear on such a problem. In a statement upon his return to New York he said:

the assignment has shown that the United Nations can be directly helpful to member governments in their wish to reestablish order and maintain peace; helpful, not by imposing its will, but by bringing out what is common ground for agreement to the parties in a conflict and crystallizing it in a way which gives the governments a firm point from which they can move forward.[44]

It is very difficult to classify the kind of role which he played here and which he was often to play in the future in traditional terms such as good offices, conciliation, mediation, and arbitration. It had characteristics of conciliation and mediation in that he strove to "bring . . . out what is common ground for agreement" and to persuade the parties to accept the cease-fire clause, but at the same time he was a channel of communication and an interpreter of a situation to the governments involved. He was a very pragmatic man in addition to having idealistic goals, and he always allowed the situation to dictate what kind of personal role could be most advantageous for peace. Hammarskjold's pragmatism also carried over to his ideas regarding the kinds of solutions which he and the United Nations should strive to achieve in different situations. His realistic acceptance of a partial solution to the Arab-Israeli problem in 1956 was set forth in his May 9 report:

The final settlement is probably still far off, but even partial solutions to the harassing problems of the region would be a contribution to the people of the region and to the peace of the world.[45]

Although Hammarskjold had received the cease-fire assurances from the parties, he returned to New York in May with a fear that war might be imminent in the area. In the light of this fear he talked to representatives of the Great Powers and asked them to restrain the parties from any belligerent actions and to persuade both sides to abide by the Armistice Agreements. He realized that the parties' assurances to him would be effective only if they were supported by the Great Powers that had backed his mission to the Middle East. He hoped that when the Security Council met to review his trip to the Middle East, they would take a joint approach to the problem which would put some substantial power behind his and the United Nations' activities in the area. When the Security Council met in early June, the Western states refused to adopt a four-power approach and to sponsor jointly with the Soviet Union a resolution, as Hammarskjold had hoped they would do, although they did decide that only Britain should introduce the Western resolution in order to rule out any "tripartite" flavor.[46] In the preambular clause of this resolution Britain called for efforts to try to solve the Arab-Israeli problems on a "mutually acceptable basis," but the Arab states strongly opposed this clause.[47] Mr. Ahmed Shukeiry of Syria saw in it an attempt to force the Arab states into peace negotiations, with the condition that Israel must find the terms acceptable. He thought that it would mean that Israel could veto the terms of the General Assembly resolution on the partition of Palestine and the various resolutions which urged Israel to offer repatriation and financial compensation to the Arab refugees.[48] Despite Bulganin's and Khruschchev's agreement with the British in April on the need for a peace settlement in the Middle East on a "mutually acceptable basis," the Soviet Union backed the Arab states and refused to go along with the British injection of this clause in the Security Council resolution. Joseph Lash has suggested that perhaps the Soviet Union would not have supported the Arab complaint on this point if the West had sanctioned a four-power resolution.[49] This was surely Hammarskjold's hope, but it is difficult to say whether it would have been the case. As it turned out, the Security Council resolution supported only the Secretary-General's past efforts and asked him to proceed along the same course of action in the future.[50]

Following the resolution Hammarskjold continued to press the parties through private diplomatic channels to respect the cease-fire accord and the Armistice Agreements; but he realized that he did not have the necessary bases of power to apply against the parties since there was a split between the "Superpowers" on the issue. With the Suez Canal nationalization of July 26, 1956, any hope which Hammarskjold had of encouraging a Great Power consensus on the problems of the Middle East disappeared.[51] At that time Secretary of State Dulles took the attitude that Arab-Israeli friction should be left to the United Nations,[52] but Hammarskjold was not very confident about his ability to use the Organization's means of peaceful settlement in an effective manner without a consensus among and concerted pressure by the Great Powers. Although he did not explicitly say so, he probably regarded the situation as a case of "over-reliance" on the Secretary-General. By September 1956 the situation along the Arab-Israeli frontiers had reverted to a situation of constant forays across the borders,[53] and Hammarskjold's progress of the previous spring had been completely undermined.

While the United Nations' representative organs were not very successful in achieving a peaceful settlement of the previously discussed dispute, they were more fortunate in the Middle East crisis of 1958. The recommendation of a settlement by the General Assembly and its use of the Secretary-General as a mediator did not occur until the end of August 1958, but in order to understand these activities some explanation of the crisis is necessary. It is also desirable at this point to present a detailed background of this crisis, since Hammarskjold employed other strategies in this crisis and since the specific applications of these strategies, which will be discussed in this and the following chapter, will be better understood by a background knowledge of this complex conflict.

At the root of the Middle East crisis of 1958 were two major conflicts. One was the conflict in the Arab world between the forces of radical nationalism, which were led by the United Arab Republic (a union of Egypt and Syria), and the forces of political conservatism, which were led by the Arab Federation (a loose confederation of Jordan and Iraq). In this particular dispute the government of Lebanon had a tacit alliance with the forces of political conservatism. The other conflict was a civil dispute between the conservative government of Lebanon, which was led by a Christian president (President Chamoun), and a large segment of the Moslem population, which tended to be radical in its political views. Both of these conflicts were complicated at that time by the fact that the conservative forces in each conflict were formally aligned with Western states and the radical forces were tacitly aligned with the Soviet Union. The tacit alignment of the United Arab Republic with the Soviet Union was strengthened just at the time of this conflict when in May 1958 President Nasser visited Moscow.

Promoting Settlement of Disputes

The intra-Arab and Cold War conflicts of the Middle East were initially activated in the spring of 1958 by the outbreak of the civil war in Lebanon. In order to understand why this civil conflict arose, some explanation of Lebanese internal politics is necessary. The country itself is about evenly divided between Christians and Moslems, and as a result of this distribution an agreement was made between the two groups at the time of independence in 1946 that the Christian community should not seek outside protection from the West and that the Moslem community should not seek a union with Syria or a broader union with all Arab states. This accord had been adhered to up until 1957 and had been the basis of the country's political stability. In 1957 President Chamoun violated the agreement when he accepted the Eisenhower Doctrine, which clearly placed Lebanon within the Western defense system. The Moslem community in Lebanon was disturbed by this political tack by the Chamoun government, and they became even more antagonistic to the government when rumors began to circulate at the beginning of 1958 that Chamoun was going to try to have the constitution amended so that he could run for another term when his term expired in September 1958.[54] Some Moslem groups sought and obtained military assistance from the United Arab Republic in order to try to overthrow the government, although the amount of aid was not as extensive as the Chamoun government claimed.[55]

The question of the Lebanese civil conflict was initially brought to the United Nations on May 22, 1958, when the Lebanese government complained that the United Arab Republic was seeking to overthrow it by sending arms and men into its territory.[56] Between June 5 and 11 the Security Council debated the issue, and after several meetings which were dominated by charges and counter-charges by the disputing states and their Great Power allies, it finally agreed to dispatch an observer force to Lebanon to determine whether infiltration of arms and men was taking place. On July 13, just several weeks after the force was established, the internal Lebanese situation suddenly improved when the disputing factions were able to agree privately on an individual to assume the presidency following Chamoun's departure in September; he was the head of the army, General Guad Chehab.[57] Then, almost as quickly as the situation seemed to improve, it became much worse as a result of the overthrow of the pro-Western government in Iraq. This led the United States and Britain to send troops to Lebanon and Jordan respectively in order to protect the pro-Western governments there. Despite the fears of some observers, the Soviet Union and the United Arab Republic did not attempt any armed action against these two governments or the Western troops on their soil; but they did try to obtain a condemnation of the American and British actions and implicitly of the Lebanese and Jordanian governments by the United Nations Security Council.

After the Soviet Union failed to obtain a condemnation and a call for the withdrawal of Western troops in the Security Council, it decided to call for a meeting of the General Assembly in order to seek a similar resolution. It was at this session of the Assembly, which lasted from August 9 to 21, that the Members of that body both elucidated the principles for the settlement of the conflict between the Middle Eastern states and delegated responsibility for seeking the implementation of these principles to the Secretary-General. The particular resolution which was passed became known as "the Arab Good Neighbor Resolution," [58] and its contents mirrored the suggestions which Hammarskjold had made at the beginning of the session.[59] The resolution reaffirmed the Arab League's noninterference pledge, proposed that the Secretary-General create "practical arrangements" for upholding the purposes and principles of the Charter in Lebanon and Jordan which would allow the early withdrawal of foreign troops, and suggested that the Secretary-General continue to study plans for Middle East economic development. Hammarskjold strongly approved of the substance of this resolution because it was primarily a local settlement among the disputing Arab states and represented a decision by those states not to allow themselves to become embroiled in the Cold War. Apart from approving of the substance of the settlement, Hammarskjold was also pleased that the United Nations diplomatic context had been influential in the emergence of the settlement and that the Secretary-General was empowered to assist the Middle Eastern states in its implementation. Regarding the role which the multilateral diplomatic machinery of the United Nations played in finding a settlement, he remarked on the day following the passage of the resolution that

> to my mind yesterday was one of those days in the life of this Organiza-
> tion when it showed its valuable contribution to present politics in the
> international field and to present diplomacy.
>
> I should like, for once to "sell" this Organization a little bit by say-
> ing that I can assure you that I have enough experience of international
> affairs and diplomacy to say that the picture which we have today would
> not have come about without the services which this Organization can
> render.[60]

Four days after the resolution was passed Hammarskjold embarked on a three-week tour of the Middle East, during which he
explored with the governments of the region how the General Assembly's request for practical arrangements to promote peace in the
region could be fulfilled. When he returned to the United Nations,
he set forth in a report to the General Assembly his ideas regarding
the nature of the "practical arrangements" which should be set up
and the functions which they should perform.[61] He suggested a
United Nations presence in Jordan which would be composed of a
Special Representative of the Secretary-General with a small staff
and liaison offices under his authority in Beirut and Damascus.[62]
He explained the functions of this presence when he wrote:

> In the period of transition, when it is justified to hope that the Arab na-
> tions will succeed in their efforts to establish a good neighbor policy but
> while frictions and departures from the main line may still be feared, the
> practical arrangements must in the first instance aim at keeping under re-
> view the degree of implementation of the general policy line and provide
> for means to set straight what may seem to be going wrong.[63]

He thus saw the practical arrangements as a means of providing him
and the Organization with objective information whereby they
could judge the compliance of the states with the Good Neighbor
Resolution and as a means of providing the local governments with
United Nations advisers and mediators.[64] With direct information
from the region he hoped that if a serious dispute began to appear,
the Secretary-General and, if necessary, the representative organs
could try to solve it before it developed into a serious conflict. The

liaison offices under the Special Representative in Beirut and Damascus were charged with providing channels of communication until normal communications were established between the different Middle Eastern states involved. Because normal communications were restored soon after the personal representative of the Secretary-General, Ambassador Pier Spinelli, arrived in Amman, it was never necessary to establish the liaison offices in the other two cities; nor was it necessary to appoint a roving representative to visit Cairo and Baghdad periodically.

One of the functions which the United Nations presence in Jordan performed was the monitoring of radio broadcasts from Cairo and Damascus. Hammarskjold saw the radio attacks as an important cause of the tension in the area and their frequency and intensity as an indicator of the degree of implementation of the Good Neighbor Resolution. Although the radio attacks against the Jordanian government were not halted during the Special Representative's activity there, there was some abatement in their intensity.[65] The office of the United Nations also served repeatedly as a calming and mediatory agent at times when it appeared that there might be armed violence between Jordan and the United Arab Republic forces in Syria. An incident in November 1958 which nearly led to an armed conflict was the pursuit by U.A.R. jet aircraft of a Jordanian plane in which King Hussein was riding. The Special Representative's office counseled moderation to the parties. Ambassador Spinelli also reported the facts of the incident to the Secretary-General, who in turn counseled the U.A.R. against a repetition of such incidents.[66]

During his trip to the Middle East in September 1958, Hammarskjold decided that there was no present need for an additional United Nations presence in Lebanon besides the observer force already there.[67] He thought that the change in government, which took place in September, would remove the primary cause of tension and would remove the threat to international peace which the nation's internal politics posed during the summer months. In his report he noted that following the withdrawal of UNOGIL new stabilizing measures would be considered, but by December he saw no need for such measures.

> *5. In conflicts between states over interests outside the blocs, the Secretary-General should independently engage in mediation in order to prevent armed conflict between the states involved and intervention by the Cold War powers.*

During Hammarskjold's tenure most of his mediatory activities were undertaken on his own initiative rather than at the behest of the Security Council and the General Assembly. However, it should be pointed out that in independent mediations he kept key delegations, including members of the Security Council, informed of the progress of his negotiations. In undertaking such mediations Hammarskjold followed his overall approach to such conflicts of trying to persuade the disputing parties to eschew alignments with the Cold War blocs and of seeking Western and Communist support for stability and peace in the area in conflict. His approach to independent mediation was always very flexible regarding the ways in which he sought to bring the disputing parties to a settlement, but there were a series of tactical principles which tended always to guide his activities. These will be presented in the second part of this chapter. It should be mentioned that Hammarskjold never embarked upon independent mediations with any certainty of success. He acted when he perceived a need for mediation and when he thought that the particular attributes of his office might prove to be helpful in attaining an agreement.

The majority of Hammarskjold's independent acts of mediation and his first independent mediation centered on the Middle East. During 1955 and early 1956 Hammarskjold made some attempts to bring Israel and Egypt together in order to gain acceptance of the Armistice Agreements, but his major activities in this matter were carried out at the behest of the Security Council in the spring of 1956. His first major independent mediation in a Middle East dispute did not occur until after the dispute over Egyptian nationalization of the Suez Canal arose in the summer of 1956. His attempt to find a peaceful settlement of this dispute did not occur until October, when Britain and France brought the issue to the Security Council after two Western-sponsored conferences in London had failed to obtain Egyptian consent to their proposals. The first meeting of the

Security Council convened on October 5, and the five major representatives at the meeting were Dulles, Lloyd, Pineau, Shepilov, and Fawzi. Hammarskjold feared that if the talks progressed within the Council under the light of public scrutiny, little would be accomplished except drawing the dispute further into the Cold War and inflaming the emotions of the conflicting parties, and hence making compromise more difficult. He therefore proposed a plan whereby the talks would be held within the confines of his office following initial statements in the Council.[68] From October 9 to 12 negotiations were held in Hammarskjold's office between Lloyd, Pineau, and Fawzi, with the Secretary-General acting as a kind of chairman. Ambassador Engen of Norway, who was quite close to Hammarskjold during this period, said that his approach in these discussions was similar to his approach in almost all other negotiating circumstances. First, he tried to facilitate communication between the parties to a dispute. In this case, getting the Foreign Ministers into his own office took care of this. Second, he intervened in the dialogue between the parties to encourage agreement in any manner which he thought was politically proper. Pineau has remarked that Hammarskjold did not intervene to propose solutions but rather noted the points on which he thought there was a possibility of agreement.[69] In this role of suggesting possible areas of agreement he both summarized what he felt was a consensus among the parties and subtly suggested his own ideas concerning an agreement.[70] Near the end of the talks, Hammarskjold on his own initiative undertook to draw up six principles upon which he thought that the three countries could agree.[71] The parties accepted his principles, and they were incorporated into a Security Council resolution on October 13, 1956.[72] At the same meeting an operative section in the resolution, which was put forward by Britain and France and which proposed the creation of a governing board for the canal similar to the one which had been approved by the Second London Conference, was vetoed by the Soviet Union in accordance with the express wishes of Egypt.[73] While the problem had not been completely solved, Hammarskjold was confident that it was on the way to solution. He was especially confident since Lloyd, Pineau, and Fawzi all agreed to meet with him within several weeks—probably in Geneva.⁷⁴ Apart from his pleasure with the apparent progress toward a settlement, Hammarskjold was also pleased because the negotiations had demonstrated again the utility of United Nations diplomatic facilities.

Following the Security Council meeting on October 13, Hammarskjold continued to explore possibilities for the implementation of the six principles with the parties. One letter which he wrote to Fawzi is very interesting from the point of view of assaying the extent to which he felt that he could adopt an independent mediatory role in such negotiations. He began this letter of October 24 saying:

> what I do is not to put out any proposals of my own, nor to try to formulate proposals made by you or any of the others. Just as I did at the end of the private talks in New York, I just wish, in my own words, to try and spell out what are my conclusions from the—entirely non-committal—observations made in the course of the private talks, interpolating on some points in the light of my interpretation of the sense of the talks where they did not fully cover then the ground.⁷⁵

What his "interpolating on some points" turned out to be in the letter was a proposal which the Egyptians had been rejecting in numerous forms ever since they had nationalized the Canal. This proposal was that a joint organ or a delegated organ should be set up for fact-finding, reconciliation, and arbitration and that it should settle any disputes which arose between Egypt and an organization of the users.⁷⁶ In making this suggestion Hammarskjold surely was going against his commitment in the letter to withhold any proposals of his own. His statement that he did not intend to pursue this independent course indicated a certain reluctance on his part to commit himself as Secretary-General to an independent point of view, but he was not deterred from doing so. The substance of his proposal showed that despite his interest in peacefully facilitating the colonial withdrawal of the Western states from Africa and Asia, he was ready to help them retain some interests in the area and to help them save their "amour-propre."

Following the United Nations' efforts to restore peace and to obtain the withdrawal of foreign troops from Egypt after the Suez invasion, the United Nations and Hammarskjold returned to the problem of trying to settle various conflicts between Israel and her Arab neighbors and between Egypt and the former owners of the Suez Canal. One of the first conflicts in which the United Nations became involved was the conflict between Egypt and the former stockholders of the Suez Canal Company regarding compensation for the Egyptian nationalization of the canal. The negotiations concerning this problem lasted from the spring of 1957 until the announcement of agreement on February 26, 1959. The first problem which arose was: who were to be the parties to negotiate with the Egyptian government?; and it was not solved until February 1958. During the negotiations over this procedural problem Hammarskjold was a sounding board for the proposals of different states, and through such talks and through different suggestions he helped the parties come to an eventual agreement.[77] With the commencement of negotiations on the substantive problem in February, Hammarskjold was joined in his mediatory activities by Mr. Eugene Black, the president of the International Bank for Reconstruction and Development. According to Hammarskjold, Black's activities centered on the economic problems while his own centered on the political-legal ones.[78] According to one participant in these talks, Hammarskjold would either pave the way for the submission of proposals by Black by talking to the parties, or he would put pressure on the parties to agree to Black's suggestions after the bank president had made them. In these talks he described his task as that of finding a "common denominator" rather than as that of being a "mediator." [79] From reports of his activities in these negotiations, his denial of acting in any mediatory capacity is inaccurate in that he did at times suggest certain courses of action and solutions. However, his description of his task as that of finding a "common denominator" does describe another aspect of his role. This was his position as an impartial interpreter of ways in which the policies of the different parties might be reconciled. In assessing the reasons for the final agreement, Hammarskjold interpreted the United Nations' role as having been highly influential and, in fact, indispensable.[80]

During the years 1957 to 1959 Hammarskjold became involved several times with the relations between Israel and her Arab neighbors. On one occasion when a conflict seemed possible between Israel and Jordon over the status of Mt. Scopus, he was successful in helping the parties to settle their differences; but on two other occasions when he attempted to mediate the larger differences between Israel and her neighbors, he was not so successful. These unsuccessful attempts both occurred in 1959, when he tried to promote a settlement of the Israeli-Egyptian dispute over the former's right to use the Suez Canal and a general peace treaty between Israel and the Arab states.

Hammarskjold's mediation of the Mt. Scopus dispute occurred in late 1957 and the first half of 1958. The issue in this conflict was an Israeli-Jordanian controversy over the nature of the convoys that Israel was allowed to send to Mt. Scopus. Mt. Scopus is an enclave in Jordanian territory northeast of Jerusalem which according to the General Armistice Agreement was to be a demilitarized possession of Israel.[81] In November, 1957 the Jordanian authorities complained that Israel was abusing these rights by bringing in too many supplies, especially gasoline. The conflict became very heated. Jordan declared that it no longer had any confidence in Colonel Leary, an American who was the acting head of the United Nations Truce Supervisory Organization since the transfer of General E. L. M. Burns to UNEF.[82] Hammarskjold was deeply concerned that the situation might lead to an armed conflict, so he decided in early December to visit Israel and Jordan to try to persuade the two states to arrive at an agreement. As he remarked following his trip: ". . . it is much better to keep the car on the road than to try to get it out of the ditch." [83] During his visit he talked to both governments and persuaded them to let Lieutenant-Colonel Flint, a Canadian who was the head of Mixed Armistice Commission, arbitrate the dispute as to what the Israeli convoys would be allowed to bring into the Mt. Scopus area. He said that a military man like Colonel Flint could calculate such a question in an impartial and technical manner.[84] On December 5 the Secretary-General announced that Jordan and Israel had come to an agreement and that they would permit United Nations personnel to check on its implementation.[85] Since Hammarskjold thought that there was a need for a stronger United Nations presence in the area until the new agreement had been in successful operation for a period of time, he announced that he was appointing a personal representative to oversee the new agreement. On

December 16 he appointed Ambassador Francisco Urrutia of Columbia to the post.

During early 1958 the conflict erupted again. In April Hammarskjold sent Under-Secretary Ralph Bunche to work with Ambassador Urrutia, and in June he delegated his Executive Assistant, Andrew W. Cordier, to inspect Mt. Scopus and to negotiate with the two governments. Then, during the latter part of June he made another trip himself to Amman and Jerusalem to discuss not only the Mt. Scopus problem but also other points of conflict between Israel and Jordan. His mediation was evidently quite successful since the friction between the two parties soon abated. John C. Campbell has written about this and other similar efforts at peaceful settlement by the Secretary-General:

On a number of occasions the Secretary-General has acted as a conciliator and pacifier, reducing temperatures when they were dangerously high, a task which no governmental representatives could have accomplished so successfully. But his powers are necessarily limited.[86]

Hammarskjold recognized both the power which his position of international impartiality lent to his activities and the limited resources which his office possessed. For this reason, prior to the Mt. Scopus negotiations and most other negotiations he spoke with the representatives of the Great Powers and other interested states in order to obtain their support. In minor disputes, such as that over Mt. Scopus, the Soviet Union was generally willing to support the Secretary-General's efforts, but this was not the case when it came to any attempted mediations of the larger issues in dispute between Israel and the Arab states.

One of these larger issues was the conflict between Israel and Egypt over Egypt's refusal to allow ships going to and from Israel to pass through the Suez Canal. This prohibition was contrary to the General Armistice Agreement between the two countries[87] and against a Security Council resolution of September 1, 1951.[88] Egypt claimed that since it was still in a legal state of war with Israel, it had a right to bar Israeli ships from using the Suez Canal.[89] Before any talks between Egypt and other states could be reconvened on the status of the canal after the Suez invasion, Egypt made a unilateral declaration on April 24, 1957, concerning the future international status of the canal.[90] While the Egyptian declaration reaffirmed the Constantinople Convention of 1888, which states that all nations could use the canal in time of peace, and provided some arbitration procedures for the settlement of future disputes between Egypt and the users, Hammarskjold did not think that the declaration lived up completely to the six principles in the October 13, 1956 Security Council resolution and to the proposals in his letter of October 24, 1956 to the Egyptian government.[91] The declaration provided Egypt with a legal loophole for excluding Israeli ships under the rationale of exercising belligerent rights. In a press conference on April 25, 1957, Hammarskjold stated that the Securtiy Council resolution of September 1, 1951 was "the law, at least for the Secretary-General," but he noted that he was not "a policeman with a gun" and that all that he could do was to try to persuade Egypt to abide by the law through diplomatic persuasion.[92] At the same time, while implicitly criticizing the position of Egypt, he did note that Egypt's exclusion of Israeli ships was not the only violation of the General Armistice Agreements, and that in fact "non-compliance is widespread." [93] In making this statement, Hammarskjold was trying to show his impartiality in respect to the total problem, and thus was attempting not to alienate the Egyptian government with which he had to work on this and other problems in the future.

During the following several years Hammarskjold continually approached Israel, the Arab states, and other interested parties about settling peacefully the problem of Israeli passage through the Suez Canal and other Arab-Israeli problems in accordance with the law of the Armistice Agreements. His attempts at peaceful settlement became especially intense from early spring until September 1959. He remarked that during this period a day did not pass without his taking part in negotiations on the question of passage through the Suez Canal.[94] By summer he thought that relations were beginning to improve between Egypt and Israel and that the Great Powers were becoming more interested in stability in the area. He therefore counseled Israel that without fanfare it might try to send a ship through. Israel sent its cargo ship *Inge Toft,* but it was stopped.[95] The Secretary-General spoke out strongly against the action at a press conference soon after the incident and remarked that he found a definite contradiction between the United Arab Republic's policies and the resolutions of the Security Council.[96] Hammarskjold seldom made such outspoken criticisms of a state's policies. He did so only when he thought that his own voice might add that extra element of pressure which would swing the policies of a state in a new direction.

This public intervention did not cause an immediate change, but it was followed by new negotiations which opened up a new possibility for progress on the issue. In talks with the parties he suggested an arrangement by which Nasser could retain his public opposition to the passage of Israeli cargoes but at the same time allow them through the canal. The United Arab Republic would allow Israeli goods to pass through the canal provided they were under the legal title of another state. Israeli exports would be required to bear the title of the importing state, and Israeli imports would be required to bear the title of the exporting state. In the negotiations Foreign Minister Fawzi agreed to this, but when the plan was actually tried in December, 1959, the United Arab Republic stopped the ship *Astaypalea* and would not allow it to proceed. When Hammarskjold heard that the plan had been thwarted, he angrily called Cairo and sent messages to Nasser and Fawzi, but to no avail. In January 1960 he visited Cairo and tried to persuade Nasser to reverse his position. Nasser told him that the plan was off because Israel was campaigning against a World Bank loan to the United Arab Republic to improve the canal. He called Israel's action a "provocation" and characterized it as being against the spirit of the agreement. He remarked too that the papers of the *Astaypalea* were not in order.[97] This was the last attempt which Hammarskjold made to solve the problem. He thought that he had exhausted for the time being any power which he might exert on the parties. Until some stronger support would be given by the Great Powers to his efforts, he did not see any possibility of success for the Secretary-General. Since the Soviet Union would not put pressure on the United Arab Republic because of the political gains it reaped in the Middle East by supporting the Arab cause, and since the Western states did not want to push Nasser further into the arms of the Soviet Union by putting pressure on him to make concessions to Israel, any new effort by Hammarskjold had to wait until the international politics of the Middle East changed.

Soon after the attempt to secure Israeli passage through the canal had been thwarted, it appeared that a basic change in the international politics of the Middle East might be taking place. The hints of the possible change were revealed following a series of Israeli-Syrian clashes in January and February 1960. Following these incidents Mrs. Meir, the Foreign Minister of Israel, Mr. Lloyd, the Foreign Minister of Britain, and President Eisenhower all declared that the solving of the Arab-Israeli problem was up to the United Nations.[98] Hammarskjold considered these statements as a case of over-reliance on the Secretary-General at a time when national, and particularly Great Power, initiatives were required. In a press conference on February 18, 1960, he clearly but diplomatically set forth this view:

I think the reactions are natural as regards the role of the United Nations, and I firmly hope that this expression of views—that is to say, that the United Nations carries a responsibility—will be followed, on the part of those who have made the statements, by appropriate reactions and actions in the United Nations and in support of the United Nations.[99]

Shortly after this suggestion of "appropriate reactions and actions in the United Nations and in support of the United Nations," the Soviet paper *Izvestia* suddenly called for a relaxation of tensions and a calming of passions on both the Arab and Israeli sides. It accused both Israel and the United Arab Republic of violating the 1949 Armistice Agreements.[100] This unexpected support by the Soviet Union was greatly appreciated by Hammarskjold, and it gave rise to speculation that the Soviet Union was embarking on a new policy in the Middle East. Joseph Lash has written that Hammarksjold always believed that the best hope for a stabilization for the area lay in a Soviet-American agreement to work along common lines through the United Nations, with the Secretary-General as their executive agent, and that he always objected to the attempt of the three Western Great Powers to exclude the Soviet Union from a voice in the region.[101] As it turned out later, the Congo crisis proved that the Soviet Union was not ready to renounce its unilateral ambitions in Africa and the Middle East, nor to come to an understanding with the United States on the basis of their mutual interest in preventing a direct clash and in creating a broad international stability. Hammarskjold looked forward in his last years to the creation of such a consensus, but his hopes were, at best, a bit premature.

During 1959 Hammarskjold also tried to persuade Israel and the Arab states to conclude a general peace treaty or at least to take some steps on the road to such an accord. The reasons why he attempted mediation at this time were similar to those for his attempted mediation of the Suez Canal question, and his failure to succeed can also be attributed to conditions similar to those which led to the failure of that mission. His attempt to achieve a general settlement of the Arab-Israeli problem took the form of an addendum to a report on the work of the United Nations Relief and Works Administration (UNRRWA) in the Middle East, which he submitted on June 15, 1959.[102] In the report he took the liberty of recommending some steps which would lead to the long-run relaxation of tensions in the Middle East. Before presenting this proposal publicly he carried on extensive diplomatic negotiations with Israel and the Arab states in order to try to obtain support for it. In this endeavor he thought he had been quite successful, but when it was announced, the Arab states rejected it. One Arab diplomat in an interview mentioned that although Hammarskjold had received some favorable responses to his proposal, it had not received official approval from the Arab governments. What had happened was that a number of the Arab representatives personally had agreed with Hammarskjold's thinking; but some Arab governments thought that the political situation in their countries would not permit its acceptance, and others still held out some hope of obtaining a more favorable situation for themselves. Whatever the outcome, it showed Hammarskjold's concern with mobilizing political support for a proposal privately before it was put forth publicly and his desire to introduce new and more positive thinking into the debate. John C. Campbell has attributed both an increased impatience by non-Middle Eastern states with Arab and Israeli inflexibility, and more moderate statements by Israel and the Arab states on this question, to the influence of Hammarskjold's report.[103]

The essence of Hammarskjold's report was that the Palestinian

Arab refugees, who numbered about one million, should be absorbed into the economic life of the Middle East through a vastly increased program of capital expenditures which he thought could be raised through future oil revenues and from outside assistance. The Arab states renounced the plan because they thought that it proposed resettling the refugees in an area other than Palestine, and Israel was not completely happy with it because Hammarskjold upheld the right of all the refugees to return to Palestine if they wanted to in accordance with a General Assembly resolution of 1948.[104] The Secretary-General believed that Israel should abide by the resolution just as the Arabs had to abide by those aspects of the General Armistice Agreements which they did not like. He privately voiced the view that very few refugees would choose to return to Palestine, but the Israelis still were not enthusiastic about the plan.[105] Although his plan for resettling the refugees and for investing $1.5 to $2 billion in the region by 1970[106] was not adopted by the Assembly, Hammarskjold thought that the Assembly would have to return to a plan similar to it in the future.[107] He always believed that an acceptance of the Armistice Agreements coupled with massive aid and refugee resettlement programs were the only bases on which a lasting peace in the region could be established. In Hammarskjold's thinking, as revealed in this plan, the United Nations was not to be the instrument for financing the development and thereby reconstructing the region, but was solely to be the instrument through which the parties could come to a long-range settlement of their differences. In setting forth his own proposal he was trying to spur the parties to make such a settlement through the representative organs by appealing to their reason and self-interest, by exerting whatever power his own office might have on them, and by mobilizing whatever support he could from the other Members for his plan.

Some of Hammarskjold's most interesting mediations, which were independently initiated, took place during the Middle East crisis of 1958. His mediatory efforts can basically be divided into two periods—June and July 1958 and August 1958. During the first period he dealt primarily just with Lebanon and the United Arab Republic, whereas in the second period, which followed the landing of American and British troops in Lebanon and Jordan, he engaged in mediatory activities among most the Arab states and the Cold War powers.

Hammarskjold's activities as a mediator between Lebanon and the United Arab Republic took place in late June and early July while he was in the Middle East setting up the United Nations Observer Force in Lebanon. He also tried at that time to mediate between disputing Lebanese factions, but this will be dealt with in another strategy. In his talks with both the Lebanese and the U.A.R. governments he sought to persuade them to cease all hostile propaganda and actions against the other so as to bring about peaceful relations between them and to prevent the possibility of any clash's drawing in the Cold War blocs. First, he went to Cairo to talk to President Nasser. He pointed out to Nasser the dangers to the peace and independence of the Middle East which any infiltration could cause and specifically asked him to modify the U.A.R.'s radio attacks against the Lebanese government.[108] Although he did not receive any promises that the U.A.R. would comply with this request, the broadcasts became slightly more subdued. He also asked Nasser to use his "good offices" with the Moslem political leaders in Lebanon. Nasser agreed, as long as the U.A.R. was not considered as a party to the dispute.[109] Hammarskjold then went to Beirut, where he talked to Lebanese officials. In his talks he tried to persuade them to take a less hostile stance toward the United Arab Republic, but most of his discussions concerned the internal Lebanese situation. He had less success in carrying on a constructive dialogue with some of the Lebanese officials, and particularly President Chamoun, since they felt that he and the United Nations observer force were unfriendly to their point of view.[110]

The crisis in the Middle East and Hammarskjold's independent efforts to solve it took a new turn when on July 15 the United States and Britain sent troops respectively to Lebanon and Jordan. Their dispatch of troops was in response to the overthrow of the pro-Western government in Iraq, which they feared might precipitate an uprising of anti-Western elements in those countries combined with possible external intervention by the United Arab Republic and the Soviet Union. In the immediate aftermath of these events Hammarskjold was unable to undertake an active mediatory role since most of the parties involved were more interested in condemning their adversaries than in seeking a settlement. His active mediation role did not commence until the beginning of the special session of the General Assembly on the Middle East crisis on August 8. Because he feared that this session might degenerate into mutual accusations among the Cold War powers and the disputing Middle East states, he elected to make the first speech at the session.[111] In this speech he set forth a series of constructive proposals for creating peace in the region. His hope was that these proposals would set the tone and the framework for the discussion at the session and would prevent the Members from falling into counter-productive condemnations. One of his suggestions was that "some form of United Nations representation in the country might be a desirable expression of the continued concern of the Organization for the independence and integrity of Lebanon." [112] He thought that this representation might serve the rest of the region also. Another proposal was that the Arab states in the region reaffirm their Arab League commitments to nonaggression and noninterference.[113] His third proposal, which was not in the field of peaceful settlement, concerned a program of economic aid to the region.[114] Of these three suggestions, perhaps the key one was the Arab noninterference pledge in that it aimed at a settlement which was basically local in character and which would exclude any direct involvement of the Great Powers in the area. Following his speech Hammarskjold worked hard through diplomatic channels to persuade the Members to accept a peaceful settlement along the lines which he had proposed. He remarked to a Swedish journalist, Sven Ahman, that this was the first time he had found himself "lobbying for a plan." His success in influencing the nature of the discussion and the final settlement can be recognized readily in the speeches by the national delegates during the emergency session and in the final resolution. For example, President Eisenhower's proposals to the Assembly reiterated the suggestions of the Secretary-General, although he also asked for a strong police force to protect Lebanon and Jordan.[115] James Reston of *The New York Times* attested to Hammarskjold's influence on the President's address when he wrote that it was "very largely the product of . . . Mr. Hammarskjold's fertile mind." [116] His influence on the character of the final resolution can be seen in that it mirrored his proposals except for the fact that there was solely a commitment to further study of an economic development plan rather than a decision to establish such a program.[117]

One individual with whom Hammarskjold worked very closely in the diplomatic efforts to solve the Middle East crisis was Ambassador Hans Engen of Norway. Whereas Hammarskjold as Secretary General could not actively pressure the Members to omit condemnations of America and Britain for fear of alienating the Soviet Union and some other states, Engen could. During the session Engen spent numerous hours with Fawzi trying to persuade him not to give in to Gromyko's insistence that the resolution condemn the Western states. Hammarskjold concluded that there was little likelihood that he could change Gromyko's position, but he thought that he had a good chance of persuading the United States and Britain to accept his proposals and to give up their insistence on a strong police force to protect Lebanon and Jordan.[118] Both these states had come to the session determined that a United Nations force would have to be established in Lebanon and Jordan before they would leave. Together with Fawzi, Hammarskjold persuaded Dulles and Lloyd that Nasser did not aim to overthrow the governments of Jordan and Lebanon and that they should rely on mutual commitments among the Arab states. He suggested also that the United Nations should remain in the area to help the local states solve their disputes and maintain their independence. He pointed out that another function of the United Nations presences would be to provide America and Britain with excuses for withdrawing their troops in that they could point to the creation of substitute security arrangements.[119] His argument carried weight with the Western states. On the day that the resolution was passed, both Dulles and Lloyd stated that the American and British troops would be withdrawn as soon as substitute United Nations arrangements could be established.[120]

In 1958 Hammarskjold also assumed a mediatory role in a dispute between Tunisia and France. While there was never any fear of a serious Cold War conflict growing out of this dispute, there was a real fear that armed conflict might arise between the two states concerned. The conflict arose in February 1958 when French planes operating in Algeria against the Algerian rebels bombed the Tunisian town of Sakiet Sidi-Youssef. In retaliation Tunisia cut off the flow of supplies to French troops which were on its territory under treaty arrangements signed at the time of Tunisian independence in 1955. The issue came to the United Nations on February 13, when Tunisia asked for a meeting on the situation and when France on the following day called for a meeting to consider the question of Tunisian assistance to the Algerian rebels.[121] Because an armed conflict between the troops of the two countries seemed quite possible, Hammarskjold engaged in vigorous diplomatic activity to persuade the two sides to settle their problem in a peaceful manner. First, he appealed publicly to the Tunisian government to allow the provisioning of the troops.[122] He feared that an outside French force might try to reach the French encampment and in so doing come into conflict with Tunisian troops. In negotiations with the Tunisian representative Hammarskjold was told that Tunisia would allow the provisioning if the French did not abuse the right. This meant that the French should not supply additional military goods to their forces and that they should not impede activities of the Tunisian government within its own borders. The Secretary-General then talked to the representative of the French government and received promises from him that France would honor the Tunisian request.[123] In performing this function Hammarskjold acted both in a mediatory capacity and as a channel of communication at a time when communication between the two governments had all but disappeared. On February 17 he announced that the two parties had agreed that France could resume the supplying of its troops under the stipulations laid down by Tunisia.[124] This ended Hammarskjold's activity in the crisis, since at a Security Council meeting on February 18 the parties agreed to accept the offers of the United States and Britain to mediate the substantive issues in their conflict.

In two disputes Hammarskjold appointed personal representatives to perform mediatory missions instead of undertaking them himself. One was between Thailand and Cambodia, and the other was between Saudi Arabia and Britain. The mediation of the Thailand-Cambodia dispute is very interesting both from the point of view of the procedures by which Hammarskjold initiated it and from the point of view of the way in which he sought to prevent it from becoming embroiled in the Cold War. The dispute attracted his attention twice—once during the period 1958–1959 and again in 1960. The substance of the dispute in 1958 concerned the political activities of refugees, press and radio attacks against each other, troop activities along their border, and the ownership of the Temple of Preah Vihear.[125] During the fall of 1958 negotiations on these points broke down, and on November 24 Cambodia announced that it was temporarily suspending diplomatic relations with Thailand. The Thai government soon retaliated with a similar action.[126] On December 1 and 8 the Cambodian and Thai governments respectively complained to the Secretary-General about the provocative behavior of the other.[127] Hammarskjold talked privately to the representatives of the two parties and found that they were interested in restoring relations. He then decided that the assistance of a third party, representing the United Nations, might facilitate agreement. However, he thought it better not to request the Security Council to consider his proposal and the conflict itself at a public meeting. He reasoned that if the Western and Communist states had an opportunity to make public pronouncements on the conflict, they were likely to differ on the merits of the positions of the Thai and Cambodian governments. He feared that this might embroil the conflict in the Cold War and aggravate the conflict itself.[128] Instead, he solicited privately the approval of the members of the Security Council for his plan to send Ambassador Baron Beck-Friis of Sweden to the two Southeast Asian states as a mediator. Since none of the Great Powers saw the conflict as very vital to their interests, they raised no formal opposition to his plan. After approximately a month of diplomatic activity in Thailand and Cambodia the work of Ambassador Beck-Friis bore fruit, and on February 6, 1959 both Southeast Asian nations announced jointly that they were renewing diplomatic relations.

Hammarskjold was satisfied with the result of this mission because it did not embroil the conflict in Cold War politics and did not result in a rigidifying of the positions of the two states. In a press conference on the day before the resumption of relations was announced, he noted:

> Without in any way making this a precedent, I responded to the invitations and a representative was sent there, with the acquiescence of the members of the Security Council. You can see how much more effective and smooth-working such a technique is than the regular one, which involves all the meetings and debates, and so on. That is a good case in point to demonstrate how, pragmatically, we can find better ways to do the job without at all departing from the Charter . . . .[129]

Besides revealing the flexibility of the Charter, this operation also pointed out to Hammarskjold the new independence which the Secretary-General had achieved in the peaceful settlement field. In a speech in Copenhagen in May 1959 he said about the significance of the Beck-Friis mission:

> This action which may lead to the development of a new pattern—other governments have made two or three proposals of a similar nature—is an example of what I should like to call active preventive diplomacy, which may be conducted by the United Nations, through the Secretary-General or in other forms in many situations where no government or group of governments and no regional organization would be able to act in the same way.
>
> That such interventions are possible for the United Nations is explained by the fact that in the manner I have indicated, the Organization has begun to gain a certain independent position, and that this tendency has led to the acceptance of an independent political and diplomatic activity on the part of the Secretary-General as the "neutral" representative of the Organization.[130]

He recognized that not only were Members now bestowing powers upon him under Security Council and General Assembly resolutions, but that they were also coming to him privately for advice and asking him to undertake certain diplomatic activities on his own. Less than five years before, the Secretary-General had been given his first major diplomatic mandate by the General Assembly. Now he was being requested by Member States outside of the multilateral organs to undertake independent attempts at peaceful settlement on behalf of the Organization.

Hammarskjold also used his office as a means of peaceful settlement when the Thai-Cambodian dispute broke out anew in 1960.[131] In the summer of that year both states wrote privately to Hammarskjold and complained about the radio and press attacks against each other. Cambodia complained too that Thailand was harboring two Cambodians who had tried to kill Prince Sihanouk and that it was refusing to extradite them. Hammarskjold in negotiations with the two states suggested that they send representatives to New York for negotiations and that he would assign a personal representative to help them come to agreements. Hammarskjold probably would have undertaken the task personally if the Congo crisis had not demanded so much of his time. In September he asked Ambassador Hans Engen of Norway to be his personal representative, and from September to December Engen met repeatedly with Cambodian and Thai diplomats in New York and assisted them in coming to a series of agreements. Hammarskjold kept in contact with the negotiations through Engen. In December the representatives of Cambodia and Thailand signed ten letters of agreement covering numerous aspects of their relations in the Secretary-General's office in the presence of Hammarskjold and Engen.

Probably the least well-known conflict which Hammarskjold tried to settle was that between Britain and Saudi Arabia over possession of the Buraimi Oasis in the southern part of the Arabian Peninsula. In the dispute Britain was acting on behalf of two of the small political units on the southern and eastern edges of the Arabian Peninsula, the Trucial Shaikhdom of Abu Dhabi and the Sultanate of Muscat and Oman, whose foreign policies it administered with their legal consent. The area in dispute, the Buraimi Oasis, had long been a source of conflict between the Saudis and its smaller neighbors. In very recent history the oasis had changed hands several times. In 1952 the Saudis captured it from the Shaikh of Abu Dhabi and the Sultan of Muscat and Oman, and then in 1955 the Shaikh and the Sultan, with the help of Great Britain, recaptured it. During this last encounter large numbers of tribesmen who lived around the oasis and who were loyal to the Saudis were forced to flee to Saudi Arabia.[132]

The United Nations and Hammarskjold first became involved

in the conflict when Hammarskjold visited Saudi Arabia at the invitation of King Saud in January 1959. The king and his brother, Prince Feisal, reported to Hammarskjold that they were planning to take the conflict to the Security Council since they had been unable to receive satisfaction from diplomatic overtures made to Great Britain. Hammarskjold counseled them that they might succeed in focusing public attention on the issue by this method but that they were also likely to freeze the positions of the respective sides. They then asked Hammarskjold whether as Secretary-General he would try to promote a settlement of the conflict. He replied that he would if he could secure approval of the British. The British approved.[133]

Hammarskjold arranged that representatives of the two sides meet with him in his office. Meetings began in September 1959 with King Saud's personal representative, Abdur Rahmann Azzam, and the deputy head of the British Mission to the United Nations, Harold Beeley.[134] In August 1960 the parties agreed that the Secretary-General should appoint a special representative who would make an impartial report on the problem and would mediate the boundary dispute and the problem of the refugees in Saudi Arabia. They agreed also to discuss the resumption of diplomatic relations. Hammarskjold then appointed the Swedish Ambassador to Spain, Herbert de Ribbing, as his personal representative.[135] During Hammarskjold's remaining tenure as Secretary-General Ambassador de Ribbing was able to carry out only the fact-finding phase of his assignment, but his mission was continued after the Secretary-General's untimely death.[136]

> *6. In conflicts over interests outside the blocs, the United Nations representative organs and the Secretary-General should create observer and fact-finding groups as instruments of peaceful settlement when they will provide information which will assist the settlement of a dispute, when their employment may assist in gaining time for the conflicting parties to settle the dispute, and/or when their presence might provide an excuse for the withdrawal of a national military presence which is exacerbating the dispute.*

The observer group which best illustrates this strategy is the United Nations Observer Force in Lebanon (UNOGIL). This body was set up on June 11, 1958 [137] in order to report on the extent of the infiltration of arms and men into Lebanon from the United Arab Republic, which Lebanon had charged was very extensive. While the creation of this group was proposed by Sweden, it was Hammarskjold who had actually suggested the idea to Sweden.[138] He viewed it as both an instrument of peaceful settlement and an instrument for controlling the use of force. He appears to have thought that UNOGIL would act in support of peaceful settlement in several ways. First of all, he thought that it would provide information which would assist in the settlement of the internal Lebanese and the general Middle East conflict. Most important, he felt that it was likely to show that the amount of infiltration was not substantial and that this would take away the Chamoun government's excuse for staying in power, namely, that a serious external aggression was taking place. Hammarskjold was of the opinion that once the possibility that Chamoun would remain in power was removed, then the Moslem and Christian factions would begin serious negotiations to choose a successor who was acceptable to both groups. This, in turn, would end the opportunity for external assistance to the Moslem faction and hence the international crisis in the area. He also expected that any new government would adopt a less pro-Western and more neutralist foreign policy and that this would lessen the hostility of Lebanon's neighbors toward it and the likelihood of a war which pitted the radical nationalist and Communist states against the more conservative Arab countries and the Western states. Another way in which Hammarskjold hoped that UNOGIL might further a peaceful settlement was by giving the diplomats and the Lebanese factions time to settle their differences. He felt that as long as some kind of United Nations enterprise was involved in examining the substance of the conflict, the various parties would not engage in any military actions to try to resolve it.[139]

Hammarskjold's strategy may have had the influence which he desired, because on July 13, following a UNOGIL report that there was not extensive infiltration,[140] the internal Lebanese factions agreed on the head of the army, General Guad Chehab, as the next president.[141] But before this agreement was announced, the crisis took a new turn as a result of the landing of American and British troops in Lebanon and Jordon following the overthrow of the pro-Western government in Iraq. While Hammarskjold thought that these actions were unwise and unnecessary, and that they had undermined much of the progress which had been promoted by the United Nations and other parties, he perceived that in the new circumstances UNOGIL might assume a new role in the settlement of the crisis. He thought that an increase in its numbers and its continued presence might give the United States an excuse to withdraw its troops in that they could say that UNOGIL was performing the tasks which their troops had previously undertaken. This was one of the reasons that he announced on July 22 that he intended to increase the observer force's numbers despite the fact that the Soviet Union had vetoed a Japanese resolution to expand the force in the Security Council.[142]

While the United States did not choose to withdraw its troops soon after their landing, Hammarskjold hoped during the emergency session of the General Assembly in August that both it and Britain might be persuaded to do so. He felt that the retention of UNOGIL in Lebanon and the establishment of a United Nations presence in Jordan might facilitate their decisions to withdraw.[143]

Although Secretary of State Dulles and Foreign Minister Lloyd came to the General Assembly session with the hope that the United Nations would create a strong police force to protect the territorial integrity of Lebanon and Jordan, Hammarskjold and other diplomats persuaded them that some more modest United Nations presences coupled with a pledge of nonintervention by the Arab states would be sufficient. On August 21 the General Assembly passed "the Arab Good Neighbor Resolution," which requested the Secretary-General to create "such practical arrangements as would adequately help in upholding the purposes and principles of the Charter in relation to Lebanon and Jordan in the present circumstances, and thereby facilitate the early withdrawal of the foreign troops from the two countries." [144] Prior to its passage both Dulles [145] and Lloyd [146] agreed that their troops would be withdrawn as soon as the Secretary-General had created suitable substitute arrangements. Under the General Assembly resolution he stationed Pier Spinelli, the Director of the European Office of the United Nations, in Jordan, and he kept UNOGIL and its political officers in Lebanon and increased the number of men in the force. According to men who were acquainted with his thinking at this time, he viewed one of their primary functions as providing excuses for the withdrawal of the foreign troops in those countries.

7. *In a conflict over interests outside the blocs where the primary conflict is a civil war and where there is a threat of or an actual intervention on behalf of the civil factions, the United Nations representative organs and the Secretary-General should attempt to mediate the conflict in order to bring about an accord on the nature of the future internal order and hence in order to prevent an international war from resulting from external intervention on behalf of the internal parties. The Members and the Secretary-General should also urge the internal parties to support a neutralist foreign policy so as to discourage intervention by Cold War powers and local states.*

Since a number of the important international crises which the United Nations considered during the years 1953–1961 concerned civil strife in which external parties had an interest in the outcome, this strategy was a very important one from Hammarskjold's viewpoint. While it was applied most notably to the Congo crisis, it also guided Hammarskjold's activities in the Lebanese, Laotian, and South African crises.

The first occasion when this strategy came into play was the Lebanon crisis of 1958. As has been mentioned previously, Hammarskjold thought that once the Christian and Moslem communities could agree on a replacement for President Chamoun, the crisis would subside. Without the civil strife there would be no opportunity for intervention by either Middle Eastern or Cold War powers. In discussions with the leaders of the Lebanese factions at the end of June and the beginning of July 1958, Hammarskjold urged them to choose a new leader and to support a more non-aligned foreign policy stance for their country, although at all times he had to be very careful that his mediation did not appear as an attempt to dictate solutions to them. Andrew W. Cordier has remarked that Hammarskjold was limited to seeking to influence the internal political situation through "the power of suggestion" rather than "the power of direction." [147] Hammarskjold's ability to be an effective mediator was greatly hampered by President Chamoun's and his associates' distrust of him. These men thought that UNOGIL personnel had closed their eyes to a great deal of infiltration from the United Arab Republic, and Chamoun even voiced the opinion privately that Hammarskjold was a tool of Nasser.[148] The Chamoun government was also resentful of Hammarskjold's intimations that a less pro-Western and more neutralist foreign policy would tend to alleviate the tensions in both Lebanon and the Middle East. While the Secretary-General was not accepted as a mediator by the internal Lebanese factions, it is possible that his voice might have had some influence in leading the Christian and Moslem factions to agree on the generally respected and more neutralist General Chehab as the next president. Chehab's selection occurred on July 13, just a little over a week after Hammarskjold had left Lebanon.

During the Laotian crisis of 1959–1960 Hammarskjold was quite active in trying to bring the various internal factions together and to influence the nature of the governmental regime. Hammarskjold's conception of the most important prerequisite for peace in the crisis was the same as that in Lebanon, namely, a neutralist government which was supported by the major internal groups. In the Laotian crisis Hammarskjold was able to support this policy position with the 1954 Geneva Agreements on Indochina. The Agreements stated that Laos should have a government which included all internal political groupings, and they also limited the nature and amount of outside aid.[149]

In March 1959 Hammarskjold made a trip throughout Southeast Asia, including Vientiane, the capital of Laos. While there, he discussed the crisis with the king and several Laotian political leaders. He recommended to the pro-Western government of Prime

Minister Phoui Sananikone, which had been in power since 1957, that it pursue a policy of internal reconciliation and international nonalignment, and that it should reactivate the International Control Commission which had been set up by the Geneva Agreements to supervise the maintenance of the nation's neutrality. The Commission had been abandoned by Laos in 1958. The Laotian government rejected this advice and was backed by the United States.[150]

Hammarskjold and the United Nations became formally involved in the Laotian crisis following an outbreak of violence between government and Communist forces in August 1959. On September 4, while Hammarskjold was in Latin America, the Laotian government sent him a cable announcing that the North Vietnamese government was increasing its aggressive actions and requested "the prompt dispatch of an emergency force to halt aggression and to prevent its spreading." [151] It also asked the Secretary-General "to apply to this request the appropriate procedure." [152] Hammarskjold flew back to the United Nations headquarters immediately and brought the communication to the attention of the Security Council. He was not sure of the basis of the Laotian claims and foresaw little hope that an emergency force would be assigned. The Security Council decided to send a fact-finding subcommittee composed of representatives of Argentina, Italy, Japan, and Tunisia. Hammarskjold did not agree with the Soviet claim that the subcommittee was illegally constituted,[153] but he did not like the Western policy either of trying to impose a solution on the Soviet Union.[154]

While the fact-finding subcommittee was still in Laos, he learned that its findings did not substantiate the extensive claims of the Laotian government. He knew that neither these findings nor anything that the Security Council might do was likely to improve the situation, so he began to explore with the Secretariat and some of the delegations what kind of a United Nations presence might be established to promote peace and stability in the country and the area. When the Soviet Union was informed of Hammarskjold's intention to create a United Nations presence there, it released a press communique which strongly opposed his plan as unlawful and which stated that any future international action in Laos should be within the framework of the Geneva Agreements.[155] Hammarskjold conjectured that this adverse reaction might be solely for the benefit of the Chinese and the North Vietnamese, who were opposed to any kind of United Nations involvement which might impede the Communist Pathet Lao. He talked with Anatole Dobrynin, a United Nations Under-Secretary who often acted as an interpreter of Soviet policy for him, but Dobrynin did not inform him of such a Soviet motive.[156] Despite the absence of Soviet approval he decided to go to Laos for consultations and to arrange for the creation of a United Nations presence. He believed that the particular steps envisaged were within his legal prerogatives,[157] and he was quite sure that he understood the true motives behind the Soviet disapproval. Hammarskjold may have been correct in his judgment of the Soviet position in the light of the absence of any Soviet opposition after he had left for Laos and in the light of our present knowledge of the Sino-Soviet conflict.[158]

Hammarskjold arrived in Vientiane on November 12, and for four days talked with Laotian authorities. He again stressed the desirability of internal reconciliation and a neutralist foreign policy in line with the Geneva Agreements. He also talked with them about the possibility of establishing a United Nations presence which might help them achieve these goals. The outward nature of this presence was announced on November 15 when the Secretary-General appointed Mr. Sakari Tuomioja, the Executive Secretary of the United Nations Economic Commission for Europe, to review the economic situation of the country and to propose some development projects in which the United Nations might play a role.[159] While he hoped that Mr. Tuomioja's report would contain some practical proposals for integrating the country economically and hence politically, he did not envision the United Nations presence as primarily economic. The main functions of Mr. Tuomioja and his successor, Mr. Zellweger of Switzerland, were to act as advisers to the government on how Laos could maintain its independence and neutrality, to discuss how the United Nations might contribute to this policy, and to act as mediators among the internal Laotian factions. Other functions were to provide the Secretary-General with an independent source of information regarding the Laotian situation and to provide a ready channel of communication between the

Secretary-General and the Laotian government.[160] Since the government had agreed with Hammarskjold that policies of neutrality and internal reconciliation were the best means of maintaining the independence and security of the nation, the special representative also may have been stationed in Vientiane to remind the government periodically of the conclusions it had reached with the Secretary-General.

In early January 1960 a group in the Laotian armed forces staged a coup which was aimed at getting the government to adopt more anti-Communist and pro-Western positions. At the time Hammarskjold was traveling in Africa. He immediately sent a cable to King Savang Vathana of Laos urging a policy of "independent neutrality and democratic progress" and expressing the hope that "no changes will take place which could raise doubt with regard to the basic foundations of the policies of the country and the confidence they have created." [161] Obviously, he was urging the king not to allow the country to diverge from the neutralist course which it had been pursuing recently. Such an initiative directed at influencing the internal as well as the international policies of a country was surely an unprecedented step for him. It showed the extent to which he felt able at this point in his career to take policy stands in attempting to promote the peaceful settlement of conflicts.

Although Hammarskjold replaced his personal representative, Sakari Tuomioja, in March 1960 with the Swiss lawyer and politician, Dr. Edouard Zellweger, the latter had little opportunity to use his political and legal skills to any advantage on behalf of the United Nations. In April elections took place which gave a heavy victory to right-wing forces. Following this occurrence the problem took on a more and more East-West complexion, with an increasing outside involvement by the United States and by North Vietnam and its Communist allies. Throughout this crisis of 1960–1961 Hammarskjold saw little hope for any meaningful United Nations involvement as long as there was such an internal polarization of Laotian politics and substantial intervention by the Cold War powers. At one point during the 1960–1961 crisis the United States approached Hammarskjold about the possibility of a Security Council meeting on the problem and a consequent greater United Nations involvement, but he discouraged such a meeting or such an involvement until there was a greater community of interest between the Western and Communist blocs. He believed that a meeting would result in mutual accusations and that it would be impossible to reconstruct his own role in such a polarized situation.[162] While he did not see a great deal of hope of the United Nations' influencing the situation under these circumstances, he kept a United Nations representative in Laos in case the situation so changed that the representative might be able to play a mediatory role. As he remarked in a news conference in May 1961:

For the moment, and pending a solution of the purely political problem, the operation is therefore kept, so to say, in abeyance, in a kind of icebox, with its potentialities maintained but without any real activity.[163]

The issue of South Africa, which came before the Security Council in April 1960, is quite different from the other cases being discussed in this section. While in the other three situations (Lebanon, Laos, and the Congo) there were large and distinct factions in serious conflict with each other, in South Africa the situation was one of very effective control and subjugation of the majority of the population by a minority group. While the issue of the white minority's subjugation of the black majority had often been before the General Assembly since the founding of the United Nations, the reasons that it came to the Security Council in April 1960 were that a large number of Negroes were killed during a protest in Sharpeville and that the Western nations were becoming more sensitive to Afro-Asian pressure on the issue. On April 1, 1960 the Council passed a resolution condemning the South African policy of "apartheid" and requesting

the Secretary-General, in consultation with the Government of the Union of South Africa, to make such arrangements as would adequately help in upholding the purposes and principles of the Charter and to report to the Security-Council whenever necessary and appropriate.[164]

Hammarskjold initially planned to go to South Africa to speak to officials there in the summer of 1960, but the Congo crisis forced him to postpone his trip until January 1961. At that time he held talks with Prime Minister Voerwoerd and his associates over a period of several days, and during these meetings he pointed out the dangerous implications of the policy of "apartheid" for South Africa's internal stability and its peaceful relations with other states. Although no United Nations arrangements were set up in accordance with the Security Council resolution, several South African diplomats mentioned after Hammarskjold's death that no talks had created such doubt in Prime Minister Voerwoerd's mind about the racial policy of "apartheid" as had those with Secretary-General Hammarskjold.[165]

Probably the best known crisis in which the United Nations sought to bring about a reconciliation of warring factions in a single country was the Congo cirsis of 1960–1964. Because Hammarskjold was in office for only a little over fourteen months of this period, only that period will be discussed here. It was initially his hope that with the stationing of a United Nations force in the Congo to maintain civil order, the quarreling parties would resolve their differences; but this did not occur. By the fall of 1960, just three months after the United Nations force entered the Congo, there were four major centers of power: the Mobutu-Kasavubu government in Leopoldville, the Gizenga government in Stanleyville, the Tshombe government in Katanga, and the Kalongi government in South Kasai. The first two both claimed national jurisdiction, whereas the latter two sought control solely of their local areas. It should also be mentioned that the Gizenga government was allied with former Prime Minister Lumumba, who was confined to his official residence in Leopoldville until November, when he tried to escape and fell into the hands of the Mobutu-Kasavubu government.

During the summer Hammarskjold confined his activities to privately urging the parties to settle their differences through negotiations,[166] but after the overthrow of Prime Minister Lumumba by President Kasavubu in September and the emergence of rival claimants for the leadership of the Central Government, he began to think that a more active peaceful settlement role by an outside party would be necessary. In November he supported the creation of the Congo Conciliation Commission by the Congo Advisory Committee, since he thought that the recommendations voiced by this group of fifteen national representatives might form a policy around which internal and external parties could rally. Then, in December he suggested to the Members that they pass a resolution requesting United Nations officials in the Congo to promote the convening of the parliament.[167] He suggested this course because by this time he felt that only such a national meeting and an acceptance of the national parliament as the final authority in the Congo could lead the country from the political morass that it was in. The representative organs did not accept his position then, because many Members feared that Lumumba might re-emerge as the leader of the government. Following Lumumba's death in Elizabethville in February, the fear of his re-emergence gone, the Security Council soon supported Hammarskjold's suggestion that the United Ntaions undertake to persuade the internal parties to reconvene their parliament in order to choose a new national government.[168] In March the Congo Conciliation Commission, which was composed of all states with troops in the United Nations force, supported the call of the Security Council for a new and more active role for the Organization in trying to mediate the internal disputes.[169]

In order to persuade the quarreling parties to convene the parliament, Hammarskjold sent a representative, Robert Gardiner, to the Congo for the specific purpose of mediating among the parties on this matter. He first arranged to have three representatives of President Kasavubu and three representatives of Antoine Gizenga's government in Stanleyville meet in ONUC Headquarters for the purpose of arranging a new session of parliament. With Gardiner's mediatory assistance they agreed that the parliament would be convened at Lovanium University outside Leopoldville under protection of ONUC forces.[170] When the parliament finally met on July 15, United Nations personnel continued their mediatory activities in helping the conflicting factions to agree upon a government. In this work Gardiner and Mohammed Khiari of Tunisia were quite active.[171] On August 2 a new national government was formally chosen with a former labor union leader, Cyrille Adoula, as Prime Minister. Only one area in the Congo, the Province of Katanga, refused to recognize its authority. With the formation of the Adoula government, Hammarskjold thought that the worst of the crisis had passed since most internal parties and external states supported it.

While some states would have preferred a different group in power, their ability to intervene and to turn the Congo into an international battlefield was hampered by the lack of dissident factions to assist.

Hammarskjold's last mission for the United Nations was a trip to the Congo for the purpose of trying to mediate a settlement between the head of the Katanga government, Moise Tshombe, and Premier Adoula of the Central Government. Hammarskjold was of the opinion that the United Nations force was succeeding in removing the mercenaries fighting for the Katangese government and that with their disappearance Tshombe would have to make his peace with the Central Government. He therefore left for the Congo on September 12 with the hope that his mediatory services could expedite a final settlement.[172] As it turned out, Tshombe's mercenaries had the upper hand in their battle with the United Nations forces in Katanga when Hammarskjold arrived, and the Secretary-General therefore decided that he had to negotiate a cease-fire with Tshombe. On September 17, the plane in which he was flying to meet Tshombe crashed in Ndola, Northern Rhodesia, and he was killed.

Tactics

During Hammarskjold's tenure one of the most important factors in the growth of the United Nations' influence was his formulation of tactical principles for its means of action. He realized that sufficient political support for United Nations operations could be maximized by the sensitivity of the Secretariat and the Members to the present nature of international politics. His tactical principles reflected his own sensitivities to the international system and the psychology of its members. These principles were not set forth by Hammarskjold in the form that they are presented here, but were formulated by the author after a study of the late Secretary-General's actions and statements.

NEGOTIATIONS

1. The Members should generally use private, rather than public, negotiations when they are trying to resolve conflicts, since

> *such negotiations encourage frankness and a willingness to compromise.*
>
> 2. *The Members should use the General Assembly and the Security Council for public negotiations when their pronouncements are likely to perform an enlightening function, to put pressure on states to accept mediation or compromises or to follow peaceful policies, or to strengthen United Nations principles. But the Members should avoid public negotiations when they are likely to freeze the positions of states.*

Hammarskjold's two tactical principles spelled out above center on a single problem—whether the Members of the United Nations should carry on their negotiations for peacefully settling disputes in private or within the public forums of the Organization. Regarding the introduction of organs of public diplomacy into international politics, which first took place with the creation of the League of Nations in 1919, he wrote:

The form of international organization, beginning with the League and continuing in the United Nations, has been aptly described by Professor Philip Jessup as parliamentary diplomacy. This parliamentary diplomacy, with its public debates, is in part the reflection of a desire to introduce democratic procedures in the field of international politics. Back of the introduction of parliamentary diplomacy is also the belief prevalent at the end of the First World War that the catastrophe might have been avoided had the peoples been fully informed by the governments about their international agreements and policies.[173]

While Hammarskjold was a democrat in his outlook on international society, he found that his predilection to democratize international politics by inviting public participation in the negotiating process often came in conflict with his desire to see disputes settled peacefully. His primary reservation about public negotiations was that they tended to freeze the positions of states rather than to encourage compromise. Since he viewed the Organization as primarily an organ of reconciliation, anything which inhibited the willingness of states to compromise their positions in the interest of international peace was detrimental to its work. On this question he has remarked:

Publicity is right and necessary in multilateral diplomacy. However, it also represents a danger. Open diplomacy may, as a prominent delegate to the United Nations recently pointed out, easily become frozen diplomacy. This comes about when open diplomacy is turned into diplomacy by public statements made merely to satisfy segments of domestic public opinion or to gain some propaganda advantage elsewhere.[174]

There is the temptation to play to the gallery at the expense of solid construction. And there is the risk that positions once taken publicly become frozen, making compromise more difficult.[175]

As a rule Hammarskjold thought that disputes were more likely to be settled peacefully in private conversations between national representatives and the Secretary-General where calm reason and the mediatory influence of outside parties were likely to make themselves felt. Usually, he preferred to leave the working out of compromises to private talks and the announcement of their results to the public organs. Concerning this approach, Andrew W. Cordier once remarked that Hammarskjold's "method modified the Wilsonian slogan of open covenants openly arrived at to open covenants quietly arrived at." [176]

While Hammarskjold did tend to oppose public diplomacy, he believed that at times it could perform a valuable function in encouraging agreement. In favor of "conference diplomacy" he noted that it

can subject national policies and proposals to the sharp tests of worldwide appraisal, thus revealing the strength, or weakness, of a cause that might otherwise have remained hidden . . . . It can activate the sound instincts of the common man in favor of righteous causes.[177]

While he saw limited value for public diplomacy at this stage of history, he looked forward to the day when such methods could be used in international politics without fear of their freezing national positions and impeding compromises. In fact, he thought that successful public diplomacy was a sign of progress toward a more organized and stable world order. He once expressed his ideas on this question when he wrote:

Legislators and members of parliaments in our democracies have long been used to . . . the compromises that are fashioned every day in the legislative process, to accepting defeat as well as victory in voting as part of the normal course of politics. Neither the diplomats who practice multilateral diplomacy on the public stage nor the governments they represent are yet fully acclimated to this new aspect of international relations.[178]

Hammarskjold hoped that the international community would soon accept public bargaining as many national communities do now, but he was under no illusion as to its acceptance during his years as Secretary-General.

RESOLUTIONS OF THE SECURITY COUNCIL AND GENERAL ASSEMBLY

1. The General Assembly and the Security Council should not condemn the policies of states while simultaneously offering means of settlement or a solution for a conflict in which they are involved. Such condemnations only encourage intransigence.

Throughout Hammarskjold's writings and actions as Secretary-General one very clear theme is that it is extremely unwise to level condemnations at states if one is trying to settle a conflict with them in a peaceful manner. In respect to the representative organs of the Organization, this conviction came out very clearly in Hammarskjold's attitude toward the General Assembly resolution of December 11, 1954, which both requested the Secretary-General to try to secure the release of the United Nations fliers in China and "condemn[ed]" the trial and imprisonment of the fliers as contrary to the Korean Armistice Agreement.[179] At the time that this was passed, he privately expressed regret about the condemnation since he knew that the Chinese Communist government would never consent to negotiate with him if his mission was carried out under the General Assembly mandate. To have done so would have been tantamount to admitting its guilt before the negotiations had even begun, and Hammarskjold knew that the pride of any government would have forbidden such an admission. In order to increase the possibility that the Chinese government would talk to him about the problem, he disassociated his request to negotiate with it from the General Assembly resolution and asked to speak to the Chinese Foreign Minister under his independent powers as Secretary-General.[180] This succeeded, and the arrangement later became known as the "Peking Formula." In reminiscing about the above mandate in 1961, Hammarskjold said:

I have always considered that one of the classic examples of bad handling of a matter was the handling by the General Assembly of the China prisoner issue in the fall of 1954, when, in one and the same resolution, the General Assembly condemned Communist China and asked for negotiations with that country.[181]

He noted at the same time that it was always necessary to keep a negotiator "in a position to negotiate with those with whom he had to deal" [182] and that such condemnations are almost sure to undermine such a position.

REQUESTS FOR MEDIATION
BY THE SECRETARY-GENERAL

1. The United Nations Members should not ask the Secretary-General to undertake mediatory missions unless he has a good chance of success and unless they, and particularly the Great Powers, are willing to support his activities by exerting independent pressure on the parties concerned. Unsuccessful efforts at mediation are likely only to bring discredit on the Secretary-General and the Organization and are likely to open the Secretary-General to hostile criticisms.

According to people who were associated with Hammarskjold during his years as Secretary-General, he was periodically frustrated by the tendency of states and especially the Western Great Powers to call upon him to try to solve a particular dispute when they were not willing to give his diplomatic efforts the necessary behind-the-scenes support to achieve the task. He thought that any attempts on his part to persuade states to solve their conflicts peacefully without adequate support by the Members might undermine the effectiveness of his own office as a consequence of possible attacks on him and as a consequence of the public failures in which they were likely to result. He also seems to have concluded that such unsuccessful operations by the Secretary-General on behalf of the

United Nations were likely to discredit states' respect for the Organization and thus lessen their willingness to comply with future requests of the Security Council and the General Assembly. By this attitude Hammarskjold did not mean that all requests for his services had to be assured of success beforehand. On the contrary, he believed that an element of uncertainty and a risk to his office were present in almost all operations which he undertook. He did expect, however, that the states requesting him to do something would honestly try to apply their power behind his efforts.

A reference to this problem of over-reliance on the Secretary-General is contained in a letter to Mr. Max Ascoli, editor of *The Reporter*. In this letter Hammarskjold was commenting on an editorial which Ascoli had written castigating the Eisenhower administration for placing too much responsibility in the Suez crisis in the hands of the Secretary-General.[183] According to Andrew W. Cordier, Hammarskjold was not supporting Ascoli's criticism of United States policy in this letter. Hammarskjold was in fact very satisfied with United States policies throughout the Suez crisis. In his letter to Ascoli he was only supporting the thesis that a policy by the Members of placing too much independent responsibility on the shoulders of the Secretary-General could be very damaging to his office in the long run.[184] He wrote:

It is one thing that, in the vacuum which suddenly developed in the Suez crisis, I had, for what it was worth, to throw in everything I had to tide us over; it was one of those irrational and extremely dangerous situations in which only something as irrational on a different level could break the spell. But it is an entirely different thing, every time the great powers run into a deadlock, to place the problem in the Secretary-General's hands with the somewhat naive expectation that he can continue to turn up with something. It is a matter of course that a continued use of the office of the Secretary-General in that way sooner or later leads to a point where he must break his neck politically. If as in the Suez situation, the very facts, as established by the policy of the various big powers, force the Secretary-General into a key role, I am perfectly willing to risk being a political casualty if there is an outside chance of achieving positive results. But if the Secretary-General is forced into a similar role through sheer escapism from those who should carry the responsibility, there is place for a solid warning. Politically, the Secretary-General should be, and is, most expendable, but he should not be expended just because somebody does not want to produce his own money.[185]

In early 1960 he made another statement concerning over-reliance on the Secretary-General to solve and stabilize conflicts. This occurred when increasing friction along the Israeli-Syrian armistice lines prompted political leaders of the United States, Britain, and Israel to say that the resolution of the disputes between Israel and Syria was up to the United Nations—meaning the Secretary-General—to solve.[186] Hammarskjold was a bit exasperated at this buck-passing, and in a press conference he remarked:

I can do some things—which I have tried—that are easier for the Secretary-General to do in the ways available to him than for the other organs. There are things which the other organs can do and the Secretary-General cannot do. It is a question for everybody who has responsibility in this case to judge when we pass from a situation which should be handled by the means available to the Secretary-General to a situation which requires action by one of the other organs.

My own feeling is that there is a certain tendency at present in some quarters to forget this difference of responsibilities and to expect from the Secretary-General action which rightly belongs to the Security Council.[187]

Hammarskjold did not have any grand illusions regarding his ability to solve single-handedly serious international conflicts. At times he concluded that his position and his own diplomatic abilities allowed him to play a key role in persuading states to solve their disputes, but he always felt the need for substantial constellations of national power behind his negotiating efforts.

MEDIATION BY THE SECRETARY-GENERAL

1. In assuming any mediatory role, the Secretary-General should have the consent of one of the representative organs or the parties directly concerned, and he should generally strive to gain the approval of the Great Powers. Such support increases his acceptability to the conflicting parties and generally assures a significant constellation of power behind his efforts; and it also avoids alienating the United Nations Members.

Because Hammarskjold was very cognizant of the precarious political position which the Secretary-General occupied in a world dominated by nation-states, he always wanted to have the necessary legal and political support from the Members for any attempt to promote the peaceful settlement of a dispute. As a rule he preferred to have a mandate from the Security Council or the General Assembly for such ventures, although at times he found the informal consent of the relevant parties to a dispute to be satisfactory. Oscar Schachter, the director of the General Legal Division of the United Nations, has explained Hammarskjold's desire for clear legal backing for any negotiating roles when he wrote:

frequently, there are objections to any conciliation efforts, and influential groups within the states concerned (or perhaps external forces) may make it difficult for the governments to agree to a third-party "volunteer." However, when the third party is buttressed by firm legal authority —that is, when his "locus standi" rests on the rules and procedures to which that state has formally committed itself, that in itself becomes a cogent factor in overcoming resistance.[188]

While Hammarskjold usually preferred to base his activities on formal mandates,[189] he also found it possible and sometimes even desirable to obtain the consent of the parties concerned. While he felt that the Secretary-General had the legal prerogative to undertake such activities on his own initiative,[190] and while he felt that the consent of the parties concerned generally gave him sufficient political backing, he often solicited the approval of the Great Powers since their policies so often affected the willingness of the parties to settle their differences. Apart from that, he was concerned that he not give an impression of excessive independence which might alienate these states. On occasions he solicited approval of his activities at the monthly informal luncheons of Security Council members,[191] and at other times he contacted the permanent members of the Security Council separately. In the case of his dispatch of a personal representative to Thailand and Cambodia in December 1958 to help those parties settle their differences, he solicited the approval of each member of the Security Council by letter. In October 1959 Hammarskjold let it be known that he was contemplating sending a personal representative to Laos who could be a mediatory agent between any internal or local Southeast Asian parties that might request his services. The Soviet Union strongly objected to his plan, but Hammarskjold continued with it anyway since he felt that it was within his legal powers and that the Soviets really did not object to his policies. He felt that they had announced their opposition to appease the Chinese and North Vietnamese, who were opposed to any United Nations role in the area, and that they were really in sympathy with his efforts to uphold the Geneva Agreements.[192] Whether he was or was not correct in his calculations, his approach to the problem does show his concern with the views of the Great Powers to such independent mediations.

2. *The Secretary-General should seek private approval for his mediatory missions from the parties concerned and possibly from the Great Powers, rather than a mandate from the representative organs, when public debates would only exacerbate the conflict by forcing the parties to take public positions and by encouraging Great Power alignments.*

During Hammarskjold's discussions with states prior to his mediations of the Arab-Israeli conflict in the spring of 1956 and the Thailand-Cambodia dispute in 1958–1959, he sought private backing for his activities for both of the reasons set forth in this tactic. In 1956 he was especially concerned with the possibility that a public debate would lead the Western states and the Soviet Union to become more committed respectively to Israel and the Arab states. He feared that such a development would drag the dispute further into the Cold War and would make it more difficult to settle. While in the end he was unable to prevent a public Security Council meeting and to secure the private backing of the Great Powers for his mediation, he was able to persuade the three Western powers to abjure submitting a tripartite resolution and to allow just the United States to submit it in order to avoid giving it a "Western" aura.[193]

In the Thailand-Cambodia dispute he initially secured from the two states concerned a request for mediatory assistance, and then he privately wrote to the members of the Security Council and asked them whether they would approve his dispatch of a mediator. In this case he particularly feared that a public debate would lead the two parties to take public positions and to make public accusations which would make compromise very difficult, but he was also concerned that a debate might encourage an East-West alignment which would probably have seen the United States siding with Thailand and the Soviet Union backing Cambodia. This would probably have encouraged intransigence on both sides and would have brought Southeast Asian problems further into the Cold War context, with the result of threatening peace in the area and in the world.[194]

The other case in which Hammarskjold encouraged disputing parties not to seek a public United Nations meeting but to agree to his private mediation was the dispute between Saudi Arabia and Britain over possession of the Buraimi Oasis in the southern part of the Arabian peninsula. On a visit to Saudi Arabia in January 1959, he was told by King Saud and Prince Feisal that they intended to bring the issue before the Security Council. Hammarskjold advised them that this would probably just freeze the positions of the parties in the dispute by forcing the states to commit themselves to public positions and by leading them to take very antagonistic attitudes toward each other. He therefore suggested that Saudi Arabia consent to private mediation by himself and that he would seek the consent of Britain to such a mediation. In September 1959 a mediation agreement was arrived at, and Hammarskjold assigned a Swedish diplomat as mediator.[195]

> 3. *In private negotiations the Secretary-General should only take positions as to how a conflict should be resolved when he is quite sure that he will not alienate parties from cooperating with him in that conflict and perhaps in future ones.*

As Secretary-General, Hammarskjold did not enter negotiations between disputing parties with a preconceived idea of what kind of substantive position he could take. While he did suggest possible settlements to disputing parties, he was very careful at the same time not to alienate one of the parties by his position so that he undermined his chances of working with that party in that conflict and perhaps in future ones. This problem of course did not arise if Hammarskjold's participation in a negotiation were based upon a mandate by the Security Council or the General Assembly to seek a particular solution. However, such precise mandates were not the

bases for the majority of his attempts to further peaceful settlements. One of Hammarskjold's best statements on the role of the
Secretary-General in situations where he did not have a clear legal
position to uphold was made when he arrived in New York to assume the position of Secretary-General. He said:

The public servant is there in order to assist, so to say from the inside,
those who take the decisions which frame history. He should—as I see
it—listen, analyze and learn to understand fully the forces at work and the
interests at stake, so that he will be able to give the right advice when the
situation calls for it. Don't think that he—in following this line of personal policy—takes but a passive part in the development. It is a most active one. But he is active as an instrument, a catalyst, perhaps as an
inspirer. . . .[196]

Although in later years Hammarskjold felt a bit freer to take substantive positions than this statement might connote, the image
which it implies of a very cautious adviser and analyst for the disputing parties is a very accurate description of his activities throughout his tenure as Secretary-General. One of the most authoritative
evaluations of this approach of Hammarskjold's was set forth by his
Executive Assistant, Andrew W. Cordier, in 1961:

He must and does play the role of counsellor judiciously. On some issues
the Secretary-General may not, and sometimes should not express his
views. Or again he may take an intermediate stance and express his views
in a somewhat marginal manner. As he once said in a press conference,
"A car can often be driven by only a light touch of the wheel." [197]

Hammarskjold had to judge for himself on each occasion whether
and to what extent he could reveal his own ideas as to how a dispute
might be settled.

One Arab diplomat who was present at a number of negotiations on Middle Eastern problems in which the Secretary-General
took part remarked that Hammarskjold "was very sensitive to the
sensibilities of nations' sovereignty" and "never tried to assume the
role of a powerful arbiter." [198] At the same time this diplomat admitted that the parties often sought and respected his advice. Hammarskjold near the end of his tenure once expressed his reservations
about any attempts at arbitration by the Secretary-General when he
said:

Promoting Settlement of Disputes

If I were to be rash enough to . . . try to establish myself as a kind of arbiter passing judgments on what is being done and how it is being done, I think I would definitely take a step which would . . . eliminate the role of the Secretary-General for diplomatic purposes and in negotiation contexts.[199]

He knew that any effort to force himself as an arbiter on parties or any public declarations that he might make which would put one or several of the parties in a bad light would be likely to lead to a refusal on the part of those parties and perhaps others to seek and to trust the Secretary-General's services in the future. When he once referred to the position of the Secretary-General as a "suicide job," [200] he meant that his efforts to influence conflicts always held out the possibility that he could so alienate Member States that his future effectiveness would be seriously damaged. Mr. Sven Ahman, a Swedish journalist, who reported this statement, noted that this concern did not come from a desire "to save his job" but from the desire "to save the possibilities of the office." [201]

The one occasion on which Hammarskjold did speak strongly in favor of the Secretary-General's taking substantive positions in negotiations with conflicting parties was a speech which he gave in Copenhagen in May 1959. At that time he noted that his positions should be "based on the Charter and its principles and thus express what may be called the independent judgment of the Organization." [202] In his discussion of "the independent judgment of the Organization" he implied that this judgment was not only his but also the judgment or opinion of the majority of the Members as well. He noted:

This opinion may be more or less articulate and more or less clear-cut but the fact that it exists forms the basis for the evolution of a stand by the Organization itself, which is relatively independent of that of the parties.[203]

In other words, he saw his role largely as giving voice and operational meaning to a consensus which had grown up among the Members regarding the manner in which a particular dispute should be settled. His own role was not that of an independent oracle but that of a spokesman for the Members and the Principles and Purposes of their Organization. While Hammarskjold preferred to speak on behalf of a consensus among the Members, this was not always possible since there were sometimes significant differences among the Members regarding how a dispute should be resolved. One example of his participation in talks on a conflict where there was little international consensus was his participation in negotiations over the status of the Suez Canal in October 1956. In such circumstances any of his substantive opinions had to be guarded and oblique and often had to be included in his summaries of areas of common agreement.[204]

> *4. The Secretary-General should seldom publicly take a position as to how a conflict should be resolved since such action is very likely to alienate one or more of the conflicting parties and is likely to cast doubt upon his impartiality and his diplomatic discretion. Only when a public judgment is likely to be regarded as impartial by almost everyone should he make it.*

Shortly after he became Secretary-General in 1953, Dag Hammarskjold had an interview with *The New York Times* correspondent A. M. Rosenthal in which he speculated on the extent to which the Secretary-General should take it upon himself to make public judgments of the Members' actions. He said that he had given some thought to the possibility that the Secretary-General should be a man of such drama and personal impact that he could create public loyalties to the United Nations. He noted that this approach had the advantage of not allowing the Members to ignore the Organization whenever they chose, but he then went on to say:

But the price is too high. The nations would lose confidence in a Secretary-General who seemed bent on the spotlight even if he did it for the good of the United Nations. Loss of confidence: too high a price.[205]

Although Hammarskjold did make several public judgments of states' action during his tenure, the basic choice which he made in 1953 regarding this aspect of the activities of the Secretary-General never changed. In 1960 he voiced this same idea again in a news conference when he said:

I shall not go out to the public in general and condemn any member nation. If I did that, I would harm the operations of the United Nations more by reducing the value of the Secretary-General than I would help the Organization by upholding the principles in these concrete cases.[206]

His preference to try to assert his influence in private negotiations was a product of both his civil service and diplomatic background and his considered judgment that his position would soon lose all utility in negotiations if states resented his past actions or feared a public reproval by him.

While Hammarskjold feared the consequence of any public judgments of states' actions, he did not preclude them as a function of his office. In his Copenhagen speech of May 1959 he remarked that in about one out of every ten situations in which he had an opportunity to express an opinion on an international conflict, "the situation require[d]" that he make a public judgment. At the same time he noted that in making such judgments the Secretary-General had to "be prepared to see his future value as a negotiator endangered or even lost. In the latter case, he ought naturally, to resign from his post." [207] In this statement he mentioned his remarks following the uses of force in the Hungarian and Suez crises as examples of such public judgments.[208] While these statements in 1956 were aimed at trying to influence the states involved to restore the peace rather than at promoting the peaceful settlement of a conflict, his statements at the time of the Suez and Hungarian crises do provide an indication of when he thought that public judgments were permissible to influence the settlement of disputes. In Hammarskjold's statement to the Security Council on October 31, 1956, following the Israeli attack against Egypt and the Anglo-French ultimatum to Egypt, he first noted that "as a servant of the Organization, the Secretary-General has the duty to maintain his usefulness by avoiding public stands on conflicts between Member Nations." [209] He then implied that there were two kinds of circumstances in which he should risk the future usefulness of his office and take public stands. One was where states committed major violations of the Principles and Purposes of the Organization, as he thought occurred in the Suez and Hungarian crises, and the other was where "such an action might help to resolve the conflict." [210]

Regarding the circumstance where there is a major violation of the Charter, he said:

the discretion and impartiality . . . imposed on the Secretary by the character of his immediate task may not degenerate into a policy of expediency. He must also be a servant of the Charter, and its aims must ultimately determine what for him is right and wrong.[211]

Two occasions other than the Suez and Hungarian crises on which he did make public criticisms of the policies of Member States for violations of the Charter were the refusal of the United Arab Republic to permit Israeli ships through the Suez Canal in 1959 [212] and the presentation of a disarmament plan by the Western states in 1960 which proposed the creation of an International Disarmament Organization outside the framework of the United Nations.[213] While Hammarskjold thought that such public statements risked the future effectiveness of his office, he believed that the risk could be diminished greatly if they could be made to appear very impartial. As he once noted about such statements: ". . . the Secretary-General must have the full confidence of the Member States, at least as to his independence and his freedom from personal motives." [214] At the time of his criticisms of the Israeli, British, French, and Soviet actions in 1956, he maintained a position of impartiality in the eyes of the Members as a result of the consensuses among the Members on the actions of the four states. In the case of his criticism of the United Arab Republic in 1959, his impartiality was not openly questioned because he based his position on a resolution of the Security Council. His criticism of the Western proposal for an International Disarmamant Organization in 1960 did not have explicit support from the Members, but his impartiality was not questioned for several reasons. First of all, the problem was not very controversial since there was little likelihood that an IDO would be created in the near future. Second, he was able to speak out on the issue with little repercussion from the Great Powers because they recognized his right to speak on matters which concerned the future development and effectiveness of the Organization. By accepting his initiative they accepted his right to represent what might be called "a UN interest" in this very limited sphere of international politics.

Promoting Settlement of Disputes

During Hammarskjold's tenure he also made several statements when he thought that "such an action might help to resolve the conflict." Although such statements differed from the positions of some Members, they were not meant as criticisms but rather as attempts to get parties to accept a settlement which was proposed by a neutral agent. Examples of such statements were Hammarskjold's support for disarmament proposals of the Soviet Union and the United States in the Security Council on April 29, 1958,[215] his proposals of August 9, 1958 for a settlement of the Middle East problem,[216] and his report to the General Assembly of June 15, 1959 on a long-term solution for the Arab-Israeli conflict.[217] As was the case with his public criticisms of Members' policies, he tried very hard in these public attempts at mediation to maintain his impartiality in the eyes of the Members. He attempted to maintain his impartiality in his intervention in the Security Council disarmament debate by supporting one proposal of each bloc, but this attempt failed when Ambassador Sobolev reprimanded his intervention. Hammarskjold was more successful in having the impartiality of his proposals accepted when he suggested a number of bases of agreement for the Middle East crisis on August 9, 1958. In the first place, since he was the first person to speak at the emergency session of the General Assembly, he was not opposing the proposals which any Members had previously put forth. Second, the proposals themselves for a noninterference pledge by the Arab states, an economic development program for the area, and a United Nations presence in the region were by their nature very difficult for any Member to oppose publicly. The Soviet Union did try to seek another solution to the problem, but it never openly criticized Hammarskjold for his proposals. In Hammarskjold's report to the General Assembly of June 15, 1959, in which he suggested programs of economic development and resettlement of the Arab Palestinian refugees as bases of an Arab-Israeli peace settlement, he attempted to maintain his impartiality by faithfully following the terms of the General Armistice Agreements and Security Council resolutions and by not criticizing any of the parties involved. His ideas were rejected by the Arab states and Israel, but there were no attacks on the Secretary-General himself.

5. The Secretary-General should try to find legal bases for any substantive positions that he takes publicly or privately since the parties are more likely to accept solutions to which they have previously committed themselves and since they are less likely to question his impartiality if he supports established substantive accords.

As has been pointed out, Hammarskjold came to the United Nations well imbued with the importance of law in maintaining order and in promoting social values in both national and international societies. During his tenure as Secretary-General the importance of law in international decisionmaking continued to play a key role in his thinking and in his actions. Throughout his attempts to have Members settle their disputes peacefully he always sought to base his positions on legal norms. These legal norms can be classified into four categories: resolutions of the United Nations' representative political organs, specific legal agreements between the parties involved, the Principles and Purposes of the Organization, and accepted principles of international law. One reason why he tried to base his suggestions on such legal norms was that the parties usually felt some sense of legal obligation to accept his proposals. Another motive for following such a policy was that the parties were less likely to criticize his views or impartiality if the parties and/or the community of states had previously committed themselves to the specific or general outlines of his proposals.

The legal bases upon which Hammarskjold preferred to rest his positions were resolutions by the Security Council or the General Assembly since they were explicitly binding on him as Secretary-General. Throughout his efforts to persuade Israel and the Arab states to solve their differences peacefully, he relied on specific resolutions supporting the General Armistice Agreements. In an informal conversation with Sven Ahman, Hammarskjold remarked that he preferred to have very precise mandates from the Security Council and the General Assembly regarding solutions to particular problems that he was to seek rather than vague mandates or no mandates at all. He noted that in this preference he was manifesting the habits and preferences which he had acquired in the Swedish civil service. He also remarked that the reason that he had a different conception of the office of the Secretary-General from his predecessor, Trygve Lie, and from Paul Henri Spaak, who was nearly chosen for the position in 1946, was that by profession they were politicians and he was a civil servant.[218]

There were a number of instances where Hammarskjold based his positions on specific legal agreements between states. One example was his reliance on the Korean Armistice Agreements in his talks with Chou En-lai in 1955 about the imprisonment of United Nations fliers in China. Another was his support for the Geneva Agreements of 1954 on Indochina in his discussions about the Laotian crisis of 1959–1960 with both the Laotian government and other interested states. In his continual involvement in the Arab-Israeli conflict he always supported the General Armistice Agreements, but these agreements also had the explicit support of the Security Council.

While Hammarskjold preferred to base his substantive positions on the General Assembly and Security Council resolutions and specific legal agreements between states, he also found the Purposes and Principles of the Charter to be of value when the former legal sources were not available. He viewed those principles as "some basic rules of international ethics by which all Member States have committed themselves to be guided," [219] and although he recognized their general character, he thought that they were "specific enough to have practical significance in concrete cases." [220] Oscar Schachter has explained both the utility of the Purposes and Principles for Hammarskjold in taking stands on individual problems and the overall importance of the principles to him when he wrote:

Faced with conflicting national demands and expectations, he relied on these principles and on other generally accepted legal concepts as a manifestation of the long-range major policies to which all governments had committed themselves. He did this not merely in deference to formal authority, but on the premise that the fundamental principles of the Charter and international law embodied the deeply-held values of the great majority of mankind and therefore constituted the moral, as well as the legal, imperatives of international life.[221]

While these principles provided Hammarskjold with important normative bases for some very difficult decisions, they also were sufficiently flexible so that he could adapt his position to the particular needs of the very complex crises with which the United Nations had to deal.[222]

Most of the situations in which Hammarskjold publicly invoked the principles of the Organization were either armed clashes between states or his establishment or direction of U.N. peacekeeping forces, but there was one occasion on which he did invoke several purposes and principles of the Organization in order to influence the outcome of a public debate. This occurred in April 1960 when he tried to influence the discussion among the Great Powers regarding the organization of an international disarmament body. In a speech before the Ten-Nation Committee in Geneva he argued that the plan which the Western states had proposed for an International Disarmament Organization would undermine the purposes of the Organization to promote the peaceful settlement of disputes and the maintenance of peace.[223]

> 6. *The Secretary-General should generally announce any agreements which he concludes with national governments since governments will be less likely to violate a public accord than a private one.*

This tactical principle became an established policy of Hammarskjold's during his trip to the Middle East in April 1956, which was undertaken to persuade Israel and her Arab neighbors to respect the Armistice Agreements. After he had obtained commitments from these states to uphold the cease-fire provision of the Agreements, a press communique from Cairo intimated that the Egyptian government did not intend to adhere to such a policy. He immediately sought a meeting with President Nasser, at which he obtained a commitment that Egypt would be guided by the previous agreement. He then issued a public communique in which he stated that all of the states had committed themselves to uphold the cease-fire clause. He did this in order to make it more difficult for these states to go back on their commitments.[224] Emery Kelen, a member of the United Nations' Office of Public Information, has written: "From that time on, he used to send to the headquarters detailed communiques to be released to the press, which then served to nail down the conferees to agreements reached." [225]

> 7. *The Secretary-General should do nothing to embarrass or humiliate a nation which he hopes will enter negotiations on a dispute and/or compromise its previous position, and he should in fact try to find means of preventing it. States are unlikely to modify their policies if this involves a public humiliation.*

In trying to persuade states to settle their differences peacefully, Hammarskjold always seemed to be very conscious that governments were not likely to compromise their positions if they were humiliated or forced to "lose face" internationally and with their own peoples. He also appeared to believe that if the United Nations were influential in embarrassing states in such a manner, they would not be likely to cooperate with the Organization in the future.

The best example of Hammarskjold's many attempts to promote a compromise by a state in a conflict by seeking to avoid any humiliation for that state was his handling of the negotiations with Communist China in 1954 and 1955 in order to secure the release of the United Nations fliers imprisoned there. The first instance in this mission where he tried to save the face of Communist China was his adoption of what came to be called the "Peking Formula." The essence of this formula was that when a state does not recognize the authority of a resolution of the Security Council or the General Assembly which the Secretary-General has been asked to try to implement, he can request and undertake negotiations under his independent diplomatic powers flowing from the Charter rather than under the authority of the resolution. By adopting this legal justification for his negotiations, the Secretary-General is able to discuss the problem with the state without the state's having to recognize the authority of the Security Council or General Assembly resolution. Hammarskjold's action of divorcing his mission from the General Assembly resolution in this case was especially important since he knew that the Chinese Communist government would not negotiate with him if he associated himself with the General Assembly's condemnation of its policies. In the telegram which he sent to the Chinese Premier Chou En-lai, he did not enclose the resolution, and he asked the Chinese Premier if he could talk to him since he felt "a special responsibility" in this case.[226]

In an interview in 1960 Hammarskjold described his understanding of the "Peking Formula" when he said:

The Peking Formula meant that if an organ of the United Nations asks the Secretary-General to do something and does so without delegating its authority, he has only the authority vested in him under the Charter, although he is, of course, guided by the resolution.[227]

He went on to note that this legal position allowed the Chinese to say: ". . . we don't care a damn about your instructions, but we recognise your authority. You are an independent organ of the United Nations. What your relationship is to the Security Council or the General Assembly is your business." [228] That this particular legal and diplomatic device was crucial in his ability to persuade the Communist Chinese government to accept his request to come to Peking for negotiations can be seen in a news release of the official Communist Chinese news agency on January 4, 1955. It quoted the Indian paper *Indian Express* as saying that Hammarskjold "would have very little chance of success if he acted on the unilateral resolution of the United States." [229] Another indication of his having gauged the reactions of the Chinese correctly was Chou En-lai's answer to the Secretary-General, which came in two cablegrams. The first one stated that "in the interest of peace and relaxing of tension" he was willing that the Secretary-General come to Peking to discuss "pertinent questions," and the other was a sharp denunciation of the General Assembly's resolution which stated that the United Nations was not justified in interfering in an internal matter such as the conviction of spies by a Chinese court while failing to condemn the dispatching by the United States of spies to carry out subversive activities.[230]

The only other occasion on which Hammarskjold used the "Peking Formula" was in connection with his talks with officials of the South African government in New York and in South Africa in

1960 and 1961. These talks occurred as a result of a Security Council resolution on April 1, 1960, which was passed following the Sharpeville riots. That resolution

request[ed] the Secretary-General, in consultation with the Government of the Union of South Africa, to make such arrangements as would adequately help in upholding the purposes and principles of the Charter and to report to the Security Council whenever necessary and appropriate.[231]

The South African government, as it has always done, rejected the authority of the United Nations over the problem of its internal race relations, which it claimed to be within its domestic jurisdiction. Thus, in order to talk with the government authorities and in order to present his own views on the problem, Hammarskjold agreed to conduct the negotiations on the basis of the "Peking Formula." After consultations with the South African government he announced on April 19, 1960:

The consultations rendered necessary by the provisions of paragraph 5 of the Security Council's resolution of 1 April 1960 will be undertaken on the basis of the authority of the Secretary-General under the Charter. It is agreed between myself and the Union Government that the consent of the Union Government to discuss the Security Council's resolution with the Secretary-General would not require prior recognition from the Union Government of the United Nations authority.[232]

The Secretary-General went to South Africa in January 1961 for several days of talks with Prime Minister Verwoerd under this arrangement.

To return to the Peking mission, Hammarskjold took several other steps in connection with those negotiations which were aimed at saving the face of the Chinese government and thus at inducing it to become more conciliatory. The first was his statement at the beginning of the negotiations with Chou En-lai that his mission to Peking should not be construed as challenging the legal right of the Chinese courts to try and convict the men.[233] This statement of respect for the sovereignty of the Chinese state was very important since China was still smarting under the memory of the extraterritorial jurisdiction which had been imposed upon the Chinese state by the Western nations for almost a century prior to World War II.

Hammarskjold also took several steps in the negotiations which were aimed at providing the Communist Chinese government with face-saving devices for freeing the prisoners. He realized that the conflict would never be settled unless a way could be found for the Chinese to release the prisoners without appearing to give in to the pressure of the United Nations and the United States. He first recalled in the talks with Chou En-lai that the Chinese had mentioned at the Geneva Conference of the previous year that there was a traditional Chinese policy of commuting sentences for good behavior. Then, he mentioned that the Chinese might be willing to provide the families of the prisoners with pictures of them and information about their health. Hammarskjold's obvious intention here was to give the Chinese a humanitarian justification for releasing the prisoners. The Chinese actually went a step beyond Hammarskjold on this last proposal and told him that the prisoners' families could come to China to visit the prisoners if they so wished. When Hammarskjold completed the negotiations, he was very optimistic that some face-saving rationalizations for allowing the release of the prisoners had been found and would soon bear fruit. When Secretary of State Dulles decided not to permit the families to visit the prisoners, Hammarskjold was very disappointed,[234] but he continued to negotiate with the Chinese through the Communist Chinese embassy in Stockholm about the release of the prisoners. It is interesting to note that when the Communist Chinese government did decide to release the fliers at the end of July 1955, it informed the Secretary-General on his birthday that the motive for its actions was not because of the Assembly decision but because of its desire to maintain and strengthen its friendship with the Secretary-General.[235] As Joseph Lash has remarked, the face-saving device which they finally used to explain the release of the prisoners was "personal courtesy" to Hammarskjold.[236] The choice of this explanation could be interpreted as an expression of thanks to him for his sensitivities to the feelings and the diplomatic needs of the Communist Chinese government.

There were several other occasions on which Hammarskjold

tried to find face-saving devices for parties which would aid the peaceful settlement of conflicts. One such occasion was in 1958 when Hammarskjold proposed that a personal representative of the Secretary-General and a small United Nations staff be stationed in Jordan. This United Nations presence was supposed to concern itself with any disputes which Jordan might have with its neighbors, but it was also placed there as a face-saving device which would allow the British troops in Jordan to withdraw. The presence of these troops was exacerbating the tension between Jordan and some of its neighbors and between Britain and some Arab states, and the creation of the United Nations presence was supposed to enable the British to say that the United Nations had created a substitute security arrangement for its forces and that it could therefore withdraw. Hammarskjold's retention of UNOGIL in Lebanon and an increase in its personnel was supposed to serve a similar function for the United States in that country.[237]

Another aspect of Hammarskjold's strategy to prevent embarrassment to disputing governments who compromised their positions or whom he hoped would compromise their positions in negotiations was his refusal to condemn their policies or to triumph after their compromise. On this latter point Ambassador Hans Engen remarked that Hammarskjold had one of the most valuable traits which a diplomat can possess, and that was that "he did not triumph after victory." [238] He noted that after the Secretary-General had succeeded in getting a diplomat to back down from a position, he never assumed a superior or triumphant air nor did he ever mention publicly that he had persuaded a state to surrender a previous stand. Hammarskjold expressed his philosophy behind this strategy in *Markings* when he wrote: "The other's 'face' is more important than your own." [239]

Chapter Four

Hammarskjold's Strategies and Tactics for Controlling the Use of Force

During Dag Hammarskjold's tenure as Secretary-General the most publicly noticeable change which occurred in the practices of the United Nations was the development of means for controlling the use of force. This change was highlighted by the creation of the United Nations Emergency Force in the Middle East (UNEF) and the United Nations Force in the Congo (ONUC). To a significant extent the creation of these means of action and their successful deployment were the product of the political sagacity and skill of Secretary-General Hammarskjold. While he was by no means the only person responsible for their creation, his thoughts and actions left the most profound mark on their character.

Strategies

1. In a conflict over interests within the blocs, the United Nations should not undertake any order-maintenance or administrative responsibilities because it is constitutionally unprepared to exercise such responsibilities and because any dispute over United Nations activities might undermine many of the Organization's other activities. At the same time an observation mission whose purpose would be to deter certain national actions by providing impartial information on the activities of certain states would be acceptable if it were approved by the states of each bloc.

Hammarskjold's general reluctance to involve the United Nations in conflicts over interests within the blocs was even greater when it came to taking measures for the purpose of controlling the use of force than it was in initiating actions to achieve the peaceful settlement of disputes. The reason for this greater reluctance was that measures to control the use of force generally have a greater influence on the issue in dispute and therefore are more likely to illicit the opposition of the Western and Communist states.

The strategy which is set forth above and which illustrates Hammarskjold's opposition to the Organization's assuming administrative and military responsibilities in areas within the blocs is best illustrated by Hammarskjold's approach to the Berlin problem in the late 1950s. During 1958 and 1959 there was considerable friction between the two blocs over the future status of Berlin, and there were some suggestions, by Premier Khrushchev among others, that Berlin and the access routes to the city from West Germany be placed under the authority of the United Nations. The assumption of such proposals was that the United Nations administration and force would not be obstructed by the two blocs and that the Organization itself was constitutionally and politically equipped to handle such tasks. Hammarskjold was not so sanguine about the likelihood of the Communist and Western states' indefinitely accepting such a status for the city, and he also believed that there were very serious legal and political problems inherent in the assumptions of such authority by any of the organs of the United Nations. In a press conference on May 21 he remarked that such an administration and force

requires obviously, back of it, somebody who can give the proper kind of directives and instructions, and those directives and instructions, in a case like the present one—the Berlin one—would have to be of a very serious political nature. I would like you to tell me whether you believe that the United Nations at present is so organized, constitutionally, that there is any organ which would be entrusted with that kind of policy decision back of a potentially fighting force.[1]

Although he did not elaborate on the constitutional inability of the different organs to direct such an enterprise, it is fairly easy to surmise what he meant. The General Assembly did not have the legal powers to pass binding decisions and to take enforcement action.

The Security Council could not have performed the role of such an executive authority since it could be prevented from taking needed decisions as a result of the veto provision. As far as a possible delegation of authority to the Secretary-General was concerned, Hammarskjold most likely rejected that because he did not want to have to interject himself into such a politically sensitive position between the two blocs upon whose tolerance and good-will almost all of his functions depended. He probably surmised that both he and the United Nations as a whole would ultimately have been the object of extensive attacks by one or both blocs because of the decisions which they would have had to make, and such an alienation of one or both blocs would have undermined almost all other functions which the Secretary-General and the United Nations might be able to perform in the world. Hammarskjold did not rule out a more limited "presence" such as a United Nations observer group which would report on compliance with a Great Power agreement and which would thus act as a deterrent against any violations of the agreement, but that was as far as he was willing to involve the Organization.[2]

The general line of reasoning presented above tends to be born out by a statement which he made to Ambassador Hans Engen of Norway at about this time that he did not want the United Nations to be saddled with "another Danzig."[3] Although he did not elaborate on the Danzig analogy, a brief glance at the history of that semi-internationalized city and its connection with the League of Nations in the interwar period provides some insights into why he feared a United Nations involvement in Berlin. Following the war, Danzig, which had a predominantly German population, was placed within the Polish customs union, and its foreign affairs were placed under the control of the Polish government. At the same time it was given an independent democratic government which was to control the internal affairs of the city. In order to implement this rather strange arrangement, it was decided that the League should appoint a High Commissioner who should seek to mediate any disputes between Poland and the government of Danzig and who should act as a guardian of the constitution of the city.[4] Throughout the history of this arrangement the League and its High Commissioner were often the object of attack by the different parties, and after the accession to power of the Nazi Party in Germany and Danzig in 1933 the League's functions were gradually eroded away.[5] These attacks and this erosion of its role were due to the fact that the League was constitutionally not prepared to assume such functions and because the Members were unwilling to take action against a Great Power. From the League's experience with this venture Hammarskjold probably drew the conclusion that both the idea of an internationalized city which was coveted by one or more of the Great Powers and the bestowal of political functions in such a city on an international organization could undermine the reputation of the Organization and could exacerbate rather than lessen tensions in the long run.

> *2. In an interstate conflict over interests within a single bloc, the United Nations representative organs should abstain from any measures aimed at deterring or halting military action (for example, strongly-worded resolutions, observer or military forces) which would lead a superpower to think that other states were seeking to undermine its security interests and which might prompt that superpower to initiate military action outside its bloc. The Secretary-General should refrain from any condemning statements which would seriously alienate that superpower and hence undermine his ability to work with that state in the future.*

Hammarskjold's adherence to this strategy came out most clearly during the United Nations' consideration of the crisis in Hungary in November 1956—and more particularly during the several days just prior to the Soviet invasion of Hungary on November 4. The first question which arose for the United Nations on the Hungarian question was whether it should take action to deter a possible Soviet attack. The question faced the Organization for a period of fifty-eight hours from the time that it received a message from Premier Nagy at approximately 12:30 P.M. on November 1, which called on the United Nations and the Great Powers to protect Hungary's political independence,[6] until approximately 10:30 P.M. (New York time) on November 3, when the full-scale Soviet intervention in Hungary began. During the fifty-eight hours not only did the Secretary-General refrain from making a public statement regarding the problem, but he also seemed purposely to avoid making one. The Secretariat did not even announce the reception of the cablegram from the Hungarian premier calling for United Nations assistance until around 2:00 P.M. on November 1 when newsmen, who heard through other channels about its having been sent, questioned the Secretariat about it.[7] When the Security Council did have meetings on the problem on November 2 and 3, the Secretary-General did not attend, but delegated Under-Secretary Protitch to represent him at these meetings.

One of the reasons for the decided hesitancy on Hammarskjold's part to involve himself and the United Nations in the Hungarian crisis was his own and the United Nations' preoccupation with the Suez crisis in which there was already armed conflict; but it appears that there were other reasons too. Another reason might have been a belief that the Soviet Union would honor its pledges to negotiate the peaceful withdrawal of its forces with the government of Premier Nagy. Another might have been a fear that any action which threw the Organization and its Western members against the Soviet Union could have risked a world war. Hammarskjold probably shared this latter fear with the United States administration, which was blocking any kind of United Nations action during the days just before the attack.[8] One statement which supports this idea was made by Dr. Conor Cruise O'Brien, who at the time was a member of the Irish delegation at the United Nations. In his book *To Katanga and Back* Dr. O'Brien wrote: ". . . on Hungary, Hammarskjold worked with the United States, and the services of the Secretariat may not have been without importance in enabling the explosive Hungarian issue to be buried." [9] The remarks of two other participants in United Nations diplomacy at that time also tend to substantiate this shared common evaluation although they did not indicate any actual cooperation between Hammarskjold and the United States. Charles Cook, a member of the United States delegation to the United Nations, remarked that it was the opinion of his delegation that Hammarskjold was acting out of an excess of caution because of a fear that the Soviet Union might initiate a full-scale war if it saw a serious diplomatic challenge from the United

Nations and the West.[10] A member of the Secretariat on the other hand explained that there was a consensus in the high echelons of the Secretariat during the first few days of November that as long as the United States did not propose that the United Nations take some action, it could not and would not do so.[11] Whether there were any actual consultations and agreements between Hammarskjold and United States Government officials is not too important; but what is important is that Hammarskjold feared any attempts by the United Nations to deter a Soviet attack and that he could not see the necessary political support for any action among the Members.

Following the announcement of the Soviet invasion at the United Nations just before midnight on November 3, a Security Council meeting was called for the very early hours of the morning of November 4. Hammarskjold drew attention to the statement which he made in the Security Council on October 31 following the Israeli attack on Egypt and the Franco-British ultimatum and said that it also applied to this situation.[12] In essence the statement said that the actions of the states which were being considered were contrary to the principles of the Charter.[13] The very mild and oblique nature of this criticism showed his hesitancy to make any kind of statement which would so embarrass the Soviet Union as to complicate the Suez crisis and his future relations with the Soviet government. Although Hammarskjold's mild criticism and the General Assembly's resolution demanding that the Soviet Union withdraw its troops from Hungary immediately [14] could be viewed as sanctions aimed at terminating the attack against the territorial integrity of Hungary, Hammarskjold apparently did not view them in this light. According to an individual who was quite close to him at the time, he never thought that his or the General Assembly's positions would force the Soviet Union to reverse its course of action in Hungary and that any stronger actions against the Soviet Union would have risked a world war. He believed that the Organization had to defend its principles by taking the above stands, but he was quite sure that the violation of these principles would stand.[15]

> 3. *In military conflicts over interests within a single bloc, the United Nations representative organs and the Secretary-General should undertake studies and make critical judgments of*

aggressive behavior in order to show the extent of international opposition to such actions and thus deter similar future actions.

While Hammarskjold did not think that the previously discussed criticisms which were leveled at the Soviet Union for its actions in Hungary would modify its behavior in that crisis, he felt that such expressions of principle were very important. They might have the effect of deterring similar future actions by showing states the extent of the opposition to such policies within the international community and the censure that they would have to expect from the Organization for such activities.[16] Apart from Hammarskjold's own statement and his support for the resolutions of the General Assembly, he also suggested on January 5, 1957 that the General Assembly appoint a committee to make a detailed report on the crisis and that the committee obtain a great deal of its information by interviewing many of the refugees who had fled Hungary.[17] This proposal followed a number of unsuccessful attempts by the Assembly to send personnel to Hungary to report on the situation and to seek implementation of the Assembly's resolutions. The General Assembly accepted his proposal on January 10, 1957, and appointed five countries to the committee.[18] In the summer of 1957 the committee submitted its report, which charged the Soviet Union with violating the political independence of Hungary and the human rights of its people.[19] On September 14, 1957 the General Assembly formally approved the conclusions of the study.[20] Like the United Nations actions previously discussed, this study and its adoption by the Assembly were supposed to deter future aggressions by showing the Soviet Union and all other countries the widespread opposition of states to such actions and the particular forms in which these censures could be expressed by the United Nations. In pursuing such a strategy Hammarskjold was trying to make all Members of the Organization more responsive to general norms of international behavior which are shared by the majority of the membership.[21]

4. In armed conflicts over interests outside the blocs, the United Nations representative organs and the Secretary-General should take stands against any attempts to alter the status quo by the

*use of force and should seek through negotiations to bring a
halt to the fighting in order to both restore the status quo and
prevent intervention by Cold War powers and thus a serious
escalation of the conflict. The representative organs should also
create peacekeeping forces which will supervise the withdrawal
of forces, provide excuses for the withdrawal of forces, deter
further armed clashes between the parties, and deter Cold War
powers from becoming militarily involved in the conflict.*

This strategy, like many of the strategies discussed in this chapter concerning conflicts over interests outside the blocs, is a specific
application of Hammarskjold's general strategy of "preventive diplomacy" outlined in Chapter III.[22] This general strategy aims at
both a prevention of violence between disputing states outside the
blocs and a prevention of intervention of Communist and Western
states (especially the United States and the Soviet Union) in these
conflicts with the possibility of an ensuing larger war between these
great military alliances. Hammarskjold's general perceptions of why
different states and groups of states are likely to support United Nations operations, which are designed to promote the above objectives, are presented in the discussion of "preventive diplomacy."

The one United Nations involvement which best illustrates this
particular strategy of Hammarskjold's was its role in the Suez crisis
of 1956. Another crisis in which parts of this strategy were applied
was the Bizerte crisis of 1961, which included a military clash between French and Tunisian forces.

Although UNEF was the most original and important means of
action used by the United Nations to terminate the armed conflict
in the Suez crisis that resulted from the Israeli attack on Egypt and
the intervention of Britain and France "to protect" the Suez Canal,
the Organization used other means of action to halt the conflict before that force was created. The first attempt to restore the peace
occurred at a Security Council meeting on October 30 which was
called to consider the threat to the peace posed by the Israeli action
and the Anglo-French ultimatum. Although the meeting was formally requested by the United States, Hammarskjold told the Security Council the following day that he would have called for it him-

self under Article 99 if the United States had not done so.[23] At the meeting on October 30 he privately supported the resolution of the United States which was vetoed by Britain and France. This resolution called for the restoration of the status quo through the withdrawal of the Israeli troops, and requested Members not to introduce military forces into the area.[24] Then, on October 31 he made a statement in which he implicitly said that the actions of Israel and the planned actions of Britain and France were contrary to the Principles and Purposes of the Charter,[25] and he privately supported a Yugoslav resolution which transferred the question to the General Assembly.[26] Although Hammarskjold was, according to associates, initially discouraged about the possibility of stopping the actions of the three countries in Egypt, he thought that the United Nations had to try to halt their actions by showing them the extent of the opposition to their policies in the international community. When the General Assembly on November 2 passed the resolution by the United States which had been rejected by the Security Council, it asked the Secretary-General to report on the compliance of the various parties.[27] The Assembly then asked him on November 4 to negotiate a cease-fire with the parties.[28] These mandates led Hammarskjold to become a very active and important diplomatic agent in the efforts to end the armed conflict, and between November 4 and 6 he formally negotiated a cease-fire among the parties.

From its beginning, Hammarskjold probably feared that the crisis would touch off what he had recently come to view as one of the most likely threats to international peace. This was an armed conflict between the Great Powers over interests in Asia, the Middle East, or Africa. In this particular case there was a real possibility that if Britain and France continued their actions, the Soviet Union would send military assistance to Egypt, and that such a development might then force the United States to intervene on the side of its Western allies. When the Canadian Minister of External Affairs, Lester Pearson, came to the United Nations on November 1 and 2 with the idea of replacing the British and French with a United Nations force to police the area while a settlement was being negotiated, Hammarskjold was initially doubtful whether Pearson's suggestion was appropriate at that time. He did not regard the possibilities of establishing such a force and of working for a lasting peace settlement as very good while the parties still seemed to be quite committed to carrying out their original intentions.[29] At the same time he was convinced that some approach had to be devised which would give the British and the French an excuse for halting their actions. As he remarked to a friend, they had to be given "another road to run on." [30] He soon began to see that although the United Nations could not create a force to halt Britain, France, and Israel, it could create a force which they could claim was taking over for them. The pressure to get them to halt their activities would have to be applied by the Members apart from the opposition which they expressed in their General Assembly resolution, but the Organization could make their decision easier by providing them with a face-saving device. The British Prime Minister, Sir Anthony Eden, had remarked in the House of Commons on November 1, in an attempt to make the British and French action appear respectable, that the British and French would halt their operation if a United Nations force were created to maintain peace in the area.[31] This statement, along with the support for the idea of a United Nations force by Canada, the United States, and other Members, evidently convinced Hammarskjold by November 3 that a United Nations force might be just the action which would allow the three states to back down gracefully. He also appears to have felt that there was a real need for a force which could supervise the restoration of the status quo and thus prevent any unnecessary friction between Egypt and the three invading states. At that time he thought the force would be needed only for a period of several months while the troops were being withdrawn from Egypt.[32] He did not envision that it would remain indefinitely along the armistice lines as a deterrent to any future armed conflict between Israel and Egypt.

Before and after the General Assembly resolution of November 4 which requested the Secretary-General to submit a plan for a force,[33] Hammarskjold discussed the nature of the force with Secretariat and national officials. During these talks he put forth two reservations to Pearson's initial proposal, and the United States concurred with his ideas.[34] He first of all opposed Pearson's suggestion that the force should include the French and British forces which were already in the area.[35] Aside from the fact that he knew that Egypt would strongly oppose their inclusion, Hammarskjold was interested in isolating the conflict as much as possible from the Cold War, and one means of doing this was to exclude all Great Power forces from that area. He most likely surmised that if the Western Great Powers were included in the force, the Soviet bloc would demand that some of its troops be included, and that any future disagreement over the use of the force might bring the two opposing blocs into conflict on Egyptian soil. The other point in Pearson's proposal which Hammarskjold opposed was the suggestion that the force's entry into Egypt should not depend on Egyptian consent.[36] As a result of his own respect for the law of the Charter and international law, he believed that the Organization could not impose a force on Egypt on the basis of a General Assembly resolution, and as a result of his conversations with Egyptian and Afro-Asian representatives he thought that the force could not obtain the necessary backing with such a stipulation.[37]

When Britain and France did accept a general cease-fire on November 6, they utilized the face-saving device of accepting the substitution of the United Nations force which had initially been proposed by Lester Pearson; and they remarked that "they warmly welcome[d] the idea . . . that an international Force should be interpolated as a shield between Israel and Egypt, pending a Palestine settlement and a settlement of the Suez Canal." [38] Prior to their announcement the General Assembly had already taken significant steps toward creating the force. On November 5 it approved the first report of the Secretary-General on the nature of such a force, created a United Nations Command for the emergency force, and requested that troops be recruited from states other than permanent members of the Security Council.[39] On November 7, the day after the final cease-fire, the General Assembly approved the second report of the Secretary-General, which set out in greater detail the functions of the force.[40] In that report the Secretary-General summarized the functions of UNEF when he wrote:

the functions of the United Nations Force would be, when a cease-fire is being established, to enter Egyptian territory with the consent of the

Egyptian Government, in order to help maintain quiet during and after the withdrawal of non-Egyptian troops, and secure compliance with the other terms established in the resolution of 2 November 1956. The Force obviously should have no rights other than those necessary for the execution of its functions, in cooperation with local authorities.[41]

This interpretation was to receive numerous challenges before the restoration of the status quo was achieved, but it weathered the storm created by the opposition of Israel, France, and Britain.

Although all of the parties involved had accepted both the cease-fire and the creation of a United Nations force to supervise the withdrawal of non-Egyptian troops from Egypt, the threat to international peace arising out of the crisis still existed. The actual consent of Egypt for the entry of the force had still not been obtained; the British and French still desired to use the presence of their troops in Egypt to pressure Egypt into accepting a greater voice for themselves in the management of the canal; and the Chinese and the Russians were offering "volunteers" to fight for Egypt.[42] Hammarskjold concluded that under these conditions United Nations troops had to be introduced into Egypt as quickly as possible in order to deter the entry of the Soviet and Chinese "volunteers" and in order to deter a recrudescence of fighting between Egyptian troops and the troops of Israel, Britain, and France. His evaluation of the problem at that time was described by General Burns, the commander of UNEF, in his book *Between Arab and Israeli.*

[I]t was urgent at that time, Mr. Hammarskjold and his advisers believed, to get some troops into Egypt at once. It was felt that it would be a race between UNEF's getting established on the ground and "volunteers" from Russia and Communist China and other similarly oriented countries arriving in Egypt to assist the Egyptian forces to expel the invaders. It was thought quite possible that such volunteers might be sent, and that the Middle East might develop into another Korea, with the forces of the West, nominally under the aegis of the United Nations, ranged against the forces of the Communist countries and deployed in Egypt and possibly other Arab countries.[43]

The key to the problem was thus to get President Nasser to accept the entry of the force which would deter the armed conflicts which Hammarskjold so feared. The aspirations of Britain and France to use the presence of their forces to pressure Egypt into accepting some form of internationalization of the canal was also a problem, but the overwhelming feeling in the General Assembly against such a policy lessened the likelihood that this could become a serious problem.

The first move which the Secretary-General made to get UNEF into Egypt was to obtain Egypt's consent to the entry of a small group of officers from the United Nations Truce Supervisory Organization (UNTSO). He hoped that they could arrange for a separation of the troops and for the entry of the UNEF contingents. Egypt consented, and Hammarskjold immediately dispatched the commander of UNTSO, General Burns, and ten of his officers to the canal region. William Frye has written of the effect which these officers had on the situation immediately following the cease-fire.

> Tempers were at white heat, and a single incident of the wrong kind could have revived full-scale fighting. The physical presence of the ten observers, with United Nations insignia, flags, arm-bands, etc., had a re-markable psychological effect, according to eyewitnesses, calming the at-mosphere and giving promise of full United Nations intervention to come.[44]

The Secretary-General's next move was to order a build-up of the United Nations troops in Italy so that it would be very difficult for President Nasser to refuse the entry of the force.[45] The next and the major problem was to get Nasser to agree to the entry of these troops that were building up in Italy. Hammarskjold pointed out to him that Egypt had committed itself to accept the force by approving its creation, but Nasser wanted to make sure that they agreed on certain common interpretations of UNEF's mandate.[46] His main fear was that the force would be used to occupy the canal area and that it would then be used to put pressure on Egypt to accept the internationalization of the canal. Hammarskjold promised him that "except for a possible 'staging area' in the region of the Canal, UNEF would have 'no functions' there once the area ceased to be a battle zone." [47] Hammarskjold also promised him that the clearance of the canal would not begin until all French and British troops had left Egypt and that French and British ships would not be used in the clearance operation.[48]

Controlling the Use of Force

Another issue, which arose at about this same time and which nearly blocked the entry of UNEF into Egypt, was a dispute between Nasser and Hammarskjold over the procedures for terminating the force's stay in Egypt. Nasser said that it should be solely up to Egypt to say when it should leave,[49] and Hammarskjold stated that since Egypt had accepted the General Assembly resolution which created the force, the General Assembly was the proper organ to make such a decision.[50] His viewpoint on this issue was closely tied to his desire to prevent the conflict from ever evolving into a direct Western-Communist struggle. He particularly feared that Nasser at a later date might order the force out of the country and obtain foreign assistance (probably Soviet) when he was interested in using the canal for political purposes or in renewing the conflict with Israel. Such an action would very likely have brought Western troops into the area as a countermove to that of the Soviets, and this could have sparked an international war. While on November 14 Nasser felt compelled to allow UNEF to enter Egypt, he continued to reject Hammarskjold's views on this topic. Hammarskjold then decided to fly to Cairo to talk to the Egyptian president about this issue, and on November 17 he persuaded Nasser to accept his interpretation, partially by threatening to take the issue to the General Assembly. At the same time he was able to facilitate Nasser's retreat by drawing up a vague agreement which they understood but which did not give the appearance of a victory by either party.[51]

Following the settlement of the above issue, the main problem which Hammarskjold and UNEF faced lay in persuading Israel to withdraw from the Sinai peninsula. While the British and French withdrew their forces by December 22, Israel was still balking in January 1957 at leaving the Gaza Strip and the western coast of the Gulf of Aqaba without certain assurances. The assurance that it wanted in respect to the Gulf of Aqaba was that its ships would be permitted free passage through the Straits of Tiran which led to the Israeli port of Elath. In respect to the Gaza Strip it proposed further negotiations with the Secretary-General, but it implied that it wanted to stay there.[52] Hammarskjold gave some support to the Israeli's demand that its ships be assured free passage through the

Straits of Tiran, but he clearly rejected its desire to stay in Gaza, since that would have constituted a clear violation of both the *status juris* and the General Assembly's mandate that all troops should withdraw behind the armistice lines.[53]

On February 11 Israel compromised its original plan to remain indefinitely in Gaza, but it said that it would not withdraw unless the United Nations assumed administration of the territory. Although Hammarskjold did not publicly reject the Israeli demand that the United Nations should assume political control of Gaza, he privately told Lester Pearson that the United Nations did not have the legal right to assume such a responsibility against the wishes of Egypt.[54] Behind this position was probably a recognition that a decision by the United Nations to govern the Gaza Strip would be strongly rejected by the Afro-Asians and the Soviet bloc, with considerable opposition from the Latin Americans.[55] Hammarskjold agreed to Lester Pearson's suggestion that Pearson discuss the possibility of a United Nations administration with the Members, but he thought that it was legally and politically impossible to impose it on Egypt.[56] When Israeli authorities announced on March 1 that their troops would be withdrawn from Gaza, they hoped that the United Nations would assume permanent control, but Hammarskjold had never given them any assurances on this matter.

Following the Israeli withdrawal from Egypt, Hammarskjold sought only one concession from the Egyptian government on the status of Gaza, and that was that it not reintroduce its armed forces into the area. This was the maximum concession which he expected from that government.[57] On the question of free passage for Israeli ships and goods through the Gulf of Aqaba, Hammarskjold did not take any independent initiatives to support the Israeli claim, although one of his reports to the General Assembly in January had given support to the legal position of Israel.[58] He privately backed the Western assurances [59] during the first week of March 1957 that they would defend the free passage of Israeli ships through the Gulf, but he chose to say nothing publicly.

During February 1957 Hammarskjold remarked to Lester Pearson: "UNEF has no other function than that of acting as a buffer between the two armies while the heat cools down, and we look for a settlement." [60] By this statement the Secretary-General probably meant that he did not believe that the deterrent function which UNEF was playing between the two parties would be necessary for too long a time. He did not expect that a final peace settlement between Israel and Egypt would emerge, but he apparently believed that a *modus vivendi* would be achieved which would permit the departure of the force. As the major issues of the crisis were solved, he began to recognize that the continuation of UNEF might perform a valuable long-term role in deterring conflicts between Egypt and Israel. He seems to have concluded that its presence would deter armed aggression on both a minor and major level by the two states because they would fear the international repercussions of being observed by the United Nations force and perhaps of having to fire on it. He also appears to have felt that it would help the leaders of both sides to resist the advice of domestic factions for a limited or general armed attack because these leaders could point to the dangerous international repercussions of attacking a United Nations force.

The other occasion on which Hammarskjold and the United Nations representative organs sought to restore the *status quo ante* following an armed conflict was during the Bizerte crisis of 1961. In this case the Security Council's and the General Assembly's activities were confined to the passage of resolutions calling for a halt to military actions and a return to previous positions, and the Secretary-General was involved only in private negotiations to bring about these objectives. During this conflict their actions also did not meet the same success that they enjoyed during the Suez crisis.

The crisis began in June 1961 as a result of Tunisian demands that France withdraw from its naval base at Bizerte and that it accede to Tunisian claims to an area of Algerian territory along its southern borders. When France did not comply with either of these demands, Tunisia on July 19 began a siege of the French naval base at Bizerte and sent its troops into the territory which it claimed in Algeria. On July 20 the French troops in the Bizerte base broke the siege by capturing the town of Bizerte from the Tunisians. On July 22 a meeting of the Security Council was called to consider the crisis, and it passed a resolution, with France abstaining, calling for an immediate cease-fire and a withdrawal of all troops to previous positions.[61] At the meeting Hammarskjold added his personal authority to the resolution by recommending the cessation of all hostile action.[62]

On the day that the resolution was passed, Hammarskjold received an invitation from President Bourguiba to come to Tunisia to discuss the armed conflict, and he accepted.[63] There was a certain amount of political risk involved in his acceptance of the invitation, since he was going to the site of a conflict without the approval of the second party. Hans Engen, who knew Hammarskjold very well, said that the Secretary-General's actions were prompted by a desire to settle a conflict to which France was a party. He noted that one of Hammarskjold's greatest disappointments during his tenure as Secretary-General was France's general alienation from the United Nations, and that Hammarskjold hoped that a successful mediation of such a conflict would change French policy toward the United Nations and his office. After Hammarskjold arrived in Tunisia, he had long talks with President Bourguiba and his aides. Then he sent a letter to the French government asking for "the French attitude toward the necessary means of contact and its immediate goal" which was interpreted by most observers as a request for an invitation to come to Paris for talks with French authorities.[64] At about this time it was reported that Hammarskjold was trying to negotiate a French withdrawal from the city of Bizerte in return for a Tunisian withdrawal from the Saharan territory in Algeria which it had occupied.[65] Instead of an invitation by the French government, Hammarskjold received a stern rebuke for his efforts to restore the status quo. The French government published the Secretary-General's letter and Foreign Minister Couve de Murville's reply to him in which the Foreign Minister accused Hammarskjold of siding with Tunisia.[66] In addition, when Hammarskjold asked to speak with the French commander of the Bizerte base, Admiral Maurice Amman, he was refused, and French soldiers, contrary to standard diplomatic practice, were told to search the Secretary-General's car flying the United Nations flag when it passed through French checkpoints in Bizerte.[67] France's attitude in this instance caused one correspondent to recall a criticism of United Nations officials by President de Gaulle earlier in the year in which he disparaged their desire to "interfere in all kinds of things." [68]

Following this failure to become a channel of communication and a mediator between Tunisia and France, Hammarskjold stayed out of the public diplomacy of the crisis. He approved of the attempts of the emergency session of the General Assembly from August 20 to 25 to persuade the French to withdraw, but he did not participate actively in its proceedings.

> *5. In a situation of civil disorder outside the blocs where there is external intervention or the threat of external intervention (especially by bloc states), the United Nations organs should create peacekeeping forces which will maintain internal order and remove any foreign troops. In performing these tasks the peacekeeping forces will remove the need for foreign intervention to protect foreign nationals and deter foreign intervention on behalf of internal groups, thus reducing the possibility of a serious international war.*

This strategy constitutes an application of Hammarskjold's grand strategy of "preventive diplomacy" to situations where there has been a breakdown of civil order in a country outside the territorial sphere of the blocs. The outstanding example of such a disintegration of government during Hammarskjold's tenure was the Congo crisis of 1960, and it was actually in response to this crisis that he finally articulated the strategy of "preventive diplomacy" which had guided his policy prescriptions in many previous international conflicts. Prior to a detailed discussion of Hammarskjold's views toward the United Nations Operations in the Congo (ONUC), a distinction should be drawn between civil disorder and civil war, since this distinction is crucial to explaining his approach to such problems. By civil disorder is meant the collapse of the police and administrative organizations in a state, accompanied by sporadic violence, whereas civil war refers to a conflict between large and well-organized factions within a single country. As will be noted in the following discussion of the Congo crisis, one of the main causes of ONUC's difficulties in stabilizing the political life of that country was that the situation evolved from one of civil disorder to one approaching civil war.

Prior to the independence of the Congo on July 1, 1960, Hammarskjold anticipated the possibility of trouble in that African state. He recognized that as a result of the failure of the Belgians to prepare the Congolese for the political and technical problems of governing a modern state, the country would require extensive outside help if it were to become stable and prosperous. In order to provide the state with whatever technical and political assistance the United Nations might give it after independence, he sent one of the Organization's highest and most prestigious officials, Under-Secretary Ralph Bunche, to the Congo to represent the United Nations at the independence celebrations and to arrange with the new government a program of United Nations assistance.[69] His forebodings regarding the new state were proved accurate when on July 6 the Congolese army revolted against its Belgian officers and attacked some of the Belgian inhabitants of the Congo and when Belgium on July 8 responded by sending its troops into the Congo to protect its nationals. While in Geneva on July 10 Hammarskjold spoke to Under-Secretary Andrew Cordier nine times by telephone about the developing situation—once in a three-way conversation including Ralph Bunche in Leopoldville.[70] Hammarskjold realized that both the lack of internal order and the dispatch of Belgian troops to the country contrary to the wishes of the Congolese government posed grave threats to international peace since it was quite likely that outside countries would come to the aid of the Congolese government, Belgium, and perhaps different internal elements.

The problem which confronted the three United Nations officials on July 10 was: how would it be possible to stave off an international conflict from growing out of the Congolese situation? It was decided that the Congolese state required substantial assistance in maintaining internal order so that the Belgian troops could leave. They concluded also that the United Nations should provide the needed internal security forces for the Congo, since this would lessen the likelihood of outside states entering the country on behalf of political groups that they favored. While Hammarskjold believed that such a United Nations program was desirable, he did not think that he could suggest such a political initiative without considerable support from the Members. He believed that the most important step was to get the Members thinking in terms of a United Nations program of assistance instead of unilateral assistance. He did this by asking Under-Secretary Bunche to have the Congolese cabinet, whose meetings he had been attending, send a request to the United Nations requesting technical assistance. Since the Secretary-General was authorized by General Assembly resolutions to initiate small programs of technical assistance, a request from the Congolese government would allow him to introduce the idea of a United Nations program of assistance to the Members.[71]

When Hammarskjold arrived back at the United Nations on the evening of July 11, he immediately notified United Nations personnel at headquarters and in overseas missions to prepare themselves for possible service in the Congo. One of the men he alerted was Major General Carl Carlsson von Horn, the Swedish commander of the United Nations Truce Supervisory Organization in Palestine, who was later to become the first commander of ONUC. He then sent out invitations to the heads of nine African missions to meet with him in his office the following morning.[72] On the morning of July 12 Hammarskjold introduced to these diplomats his views on sending security personnel, specifically naming General von Horn and his UNTSO officers, to the Congo to give instructions to the ill-trained Congolese army, and he then asked the different African diplomats if their countries might also be able to send such instructors. One after another they spoke about the need to expel the Belgians and of the need for measures stronger than mere technical assistance.[73] They voiced the opinion that an actual military force was required. Out of this meeting, and without the urging of the Secretary-General, there had emerged what Joseph Kraft has called "an all-African lobby for United Nations military intervention."[74] These African diplomats then contacted their governments and urged them to persuade the Congolese government of President Kasavubu and Prime Minister Lumumba to request a military force from the United Nations, and the African governments complied with these requests from their United Nations representatives. While the support of these African countries was very important for the final approval of a United Nations force, it was not the crucial element which led the Congolese government to request a force from the United Nations. More important was the rejection of a Congolese request for military aid by the United States on July 11 and the United States' suggestion that it seek such assistance from the United Nations.[75] When the Congolese government made its initial request on July 12 for military aid "to protect the national territory of the Congo against the present aggression," [76] it probably had not yet received the suggestions from its fellow African states that it seek United Nations assistance. The main contribution of Hammarskjold's efforts with the African states was that they were already in favor of a United Nations force when the Congolese request came to the United Nations.

Hammarskjold's initial goal of obtaining African support for the force had been achieved, and it is important to understand why this support was the keystone of his strategy for creating the force. One of the primary tenets of his strategy for removing all threats to international peace which did not involve interests within the Western and Soviet blocs was to localize them and to isolate them from the Cold War. The best way he found of doing this was to obtain a consensus among the states in the area or among the Afro-Asian states as a whole on United Nations or non-United Nations measures for stabilizing the situation. He hoped that United Nations measures for isolating such conflicts from the Cold War could get substantial backing from the Western and Communist states as a result of their realization that their unilateral entry might spark an East-West confrontation and might seriously alienate the nonaligned states.

The strategy of initially obtaining the support of the African states in the Congo crisis was eminently successful because they then obtained the unanimous support of the Asian states at an Afro-Asian caucus on July 13, and this unified group then influenced the Western and Communist states to accept a United Nations operation.[77] At this time Hammarskjold and the United Nations were very fortunate that Africa was represented on the Security Council by the moderate nationalist state of Tunisia and its very adroit Foreign Minister, Mongi Slim. While Slim was a dedicated anti-colonialist, he was a cautious diplomat who, like Hammarskjold, set forth policies likely to receive very wide approval. This trait was important at this point because as the spokesman for the Afro-Asian states he was able to avoid any actions which would have led Britain and France to veto the creation of a United Nations force in the Congo in the Security Council. In his and other diplomats' efforts to persuade the two previously mentioned European colonial powers to accept the force, they were assisted by the United States, which viewed the force as the best means of keeping the Soviet bloc out of the Congo and of bailing Belgium out of a difficult predicament. By the time that the Security Council met at Hammarskjold's request on the evening of July 13, the Afro-Asian states and the United States had secured the approval of all the members of the Security Council for a United Nations force in the Congo. Britain and France did not vote for the resolution because of its implicit criticism of Belgium, but they abstained and let the resolution go through.[78] The Soviet Union balked at its creation for a while, but the pressure of the African and Asian states brought it around.[79]

At the Security Council meeting on the evening of July 13 Hammarskjold was the first person to address himself to the problem. He stated that he was not going to make a public judgment of the Belgian action, but he noted that he had to conclude from the telegrams from the Congolese government that the presence of the Belgian troops posed a threat to international peace.[80] He then went on to recommend a program of United Nations military assistance to the Congo to help it maintain internal order.[81] He noted prophetically that he was "fully aware of all the problems, difficulties and even risks involved" but that United Nations military assistance was "preferable to any other formula." [82] In respect to the principles which should guide the actions of the force, he recommended that the force should be guided by those rules which were set down in his UNEF Summary of 1958.[83] The most important of these were that the force should exclude the permanent members of the Security Council, that it should not interfere in the internal politics of the country in which it was operating, and that it should be allowed to use force only in self-defense. He also mentioned at this time that he was undertaking a program of technical assistance to the Congo to rebuild its security and administrative services so that in the future it would not need outside aid such as the United Nations would hopefully give to it.[84] In the early morning of July 14 the Security Council adopted a resolution which was submitted by Tunisia and which embodied the suggestions of the Secretary-General. It asked the Belgian government to withdraw its troops from the Congo, and it

decide[d] to authorize the Secretary-General to take the necessary steps, in consultation with the Government of the Congo, to provide the Government with such military assistance, as may be necessary, until through the efforts of the Congolese Government with the technical assistance of the United Nations, the national security forces may be able, in the opinion of the Government, to meet fully their tasks.[85]

At this time no one foresaw the agonies which the United Nations and the Congo were going to experience during the implementation of this mandate.

In the United Nations' efforts to restore peace and to prevent an international conflict in the Congo, Hammarskjold was depending on several pillars of political support. They were the willingness of the Belgian troops to leave the Congo, an Afro-Asian consensus supporting the force, the willingness of the Great Powers to stay out of the Congo, and the cooperation of the Congolese government itself. On July 15, the day following the creation of ONUC, several small cracks began to appear in several of these pillars. On that day President Kasavubu and Prime Minister Lumumba wired Premier Khrushchev that "we may have to ask the Soviet Union's intervention, should the Western camp not stop its aggression." The Soviet Premier replied soon afterward that his government "will not shrink from resolute measures to curb aggression." [86] Here were the first signs that both the Congolese government and the Soviet Union were not completely committed to solving the crisis through the United Nations and to isolating the conflict from the Cold War.

One problem which plagued ONUC throughout almost its entire existence, and which led to cracks in all of its four pillars of support, was the secession of the province of Katanga from the Congolese state, which had been announced on July 11. Katanga was the wealthiest of the Congolese provinces and was a necessary component in a viable Congolese state. During July and August

1960 this issue was to undermine the cooperation of Prime Minister Lumumba's Congolese government with the United Nations to a very serious degree. Almost from the time that ONUC's forces arrived in the Congo, Lumumba wanted to use them to subdue the rebel province. Hammarskjold and his aides explained to him and his representatives in New York that the use of ONUC for this purpose was contrary to the mandate of the force which had prescribed nonintervention in the internal affairs of the country. Initially Hammarskjold had felt that the Security Council's acceptance of his first report on the creation of the force which had set forth this principle was sufficient political backing for this principle, but as Lumumba's criticism increased, he finally sought and obtained on August 9 an explicit approval of the principle of nonintervention from the Security Council.[87] At the same time he obtained explicit backing of the Security Council to send United Nations troops into Katanga in order to maintain order. Although a United Nations force succeeded in entering Katanga on August 12, Prime Minister Lumumba's opposition to Hammarskjold and the United Nations' policy did not disappear, since he wanted ONUC to force Katanga back into the Central Government.[88]

During the summer of 1960 serious cracks also developed in Belgium's and the Soviet Union's support for ONUC. Belgium withdrew its troops from all of the Congo except Katanga by the end of July, but it dragged its feet on withdrawing from that province until the beginning of September. Even after the military withdrawal, many of the Belgian residents in the Congo with Belgium's approval were aiding the secessionist movement in Katanga which was led by its provincial president Moise Tshombe.[89] The loss of the Soviet Union's support for ONUC resulted from the refusal of the United Nations to aid Lumumba against his internal enemies and the opposition of the United Nations to the Soviet Union's unilateral aid to Lumumba. At the end of July Lumumba traveled to the United States and tried to obtain unilateral assistance to crush the Katangese secession and the new secessionist movement in Kasai. When the United States told him to seek all aid through the United Nations, Lumumba turned to the Soviet Union, which supplied him with trucks and planes. Hammarskjold called on the Soviet Union to halt this unilateral aid program,[90] but it was essentially Lumumba's removal from effective power in the Congo by President Kasavubu and General Mobutu in September 1960 which ended its assistance to the Congolese Prime Minister. With the overthrow of Lumumba and the imposed cessation of the Soviet aid program by the new Central Government, the Soviet government's opposition to ONUC and Hammarskjold, which had been growing in July and August, became increasingly vehement

The main pillar on which ONUC's political life depended during the worsening conditions of the summer of 1960 was an Afro-Asian consensus, although the political support of the United States was also crucial. Although the Afro-Asian states became impatient with the slow withdrawal of the Belgian army and although a few wanted ONUC to support Prime Minister Lumumba, they continued to support the presence of an impartial United Nations force. None of them attacked the Secretary-General as did the Congolese Prime Minister and the Soviet Union. During the last week of August Lumumba called a meeting of all of the African states in Leopoldville, at which time he tried to get them to create an all-African army to supersede ONUC and crush the opposition to the Central Government, but they unanimously refused. They even passed a resolution in support of ONUC and the Secretary-General.[91] During the heated debates which followed President Kasavubu's dismissal of Prime Minister Lumumba on September 5, 1960, Ghana, Guinea, the United Arab Republic, Morocco, and Ethiopia argued that ONUC should reinstate Prime Minister Lumumba,[92] but when it came to the question of whether they should continue to lend support to ONUC and the Secretary-General, all of them except Guinea lent their support when they voted for the General Assembly resolution of September 20, 1960.[93] This resolution supported the past Security Council resolutions on ONUC and Hammarskjold's plea that all states direct their aid to the Congo through the United Nations. The Afro-Asian states thus upheld Hammarskjold's strategy for keeping the Cold War out of the Congo and Africa.

The strategic nature of the Afro-Asian support for ONUC and the United Nations in general in Hammarskjold's thinking was

pointed up clearly by the manner in which he met Premier Khruschchev's attacks on him and the Soviet leader's demands that he resign. On the afternoon of October 3, following a blistering attack
by the Soviet premier that morning, Hammarskjold said:

It is not the Soviet Union or, indeed, any other big Powers who need the
United Nations for their protection; it is all the others. In this sense the
Organization is first of all *their* Organization, and I deeply believe in the
wisdom with which they will be able to use it and guide it. I shall remain
in my post during the term of my office as a servant of the Organization
in the interests of all those other nations, as long as *they* wish me to do
so.[94]

Hammarskjold in this statement struck a chord which almost all of
the Members and especially the Afro-Asians understood and deeply
approved, for, when he finished it, the Assembly broke into the
longest and most enthusiastic ovation that has taken place within its
halls. He had implicitly stated that it was by joint action through
the Organization that the great number of small and weak states had
the best opportunity to protect their independence and remain free
of the dangers of the Cold War.

Although the great majority of the Members had come to the
defense of ONUC and the Secretary-General during the General
Assembly meetings of late September and early October 1960, this
did not mean that ONUC had completely succeeded or that the
Secretary-General's policies were unchallenged to some extent by
many of the Members. In fact, ONUC was entering the darkest period of its very difficult history. Within the Congo President
Kasavubu and General Mobutu ruled the Central Government, but
Prime Minister Lumumba in his official residence and under United
Nations protection was trying to regain power. The Central Government was on very poor terms with ONUC and with the Secretary-General's Special Representative in the Congo, Ambassador
Dayal of India. The secessionist movements in Katanga and Kasai under these conditions were relatively free to go their own
way. With these conditions ONUC's pillars of support began to
crumble beyond what had happened to them during the summer of
1960. The Soviet Union was completely alienated from the operation although it was no longer able to provide aid to Lumumba since

its diplomatic mission had been expelled from the country by the Kasavubu-Mobutu government. Belgium refused to withdraw its officials from Katanga and other areas, and the Afro-Asians became seriously split. The split among the Afro-Asians was revealed by the vote on the resolution, which was put forward by the West, to recognize the Kasavubu government as the legitimate representative of the Congolese state at the United Nations.[95] The vote on this resolution on November 22, 1960, which accepted the credentials of the Kasavubu delegation, was 53 to 24, with 19 abstentions. Fourteen of the twenty-four who voted against the seating of the delegation were Afro-Asian states as were a large majority of the nineteen abstentions.

Hammarskjold during the latter part of 1960 was coming under more and more criticism from the radical nationalist Afro-Asian states about the conduct of the operation. They wanted him to restore the government of Prime Minister Lumumba, who at the end of November had been imprisoned by the Kasavubu-Mobutu government after he had tried to escape to Stanleyville, where his lieutenant, Antoine Gizenga, had established a government rival to the one in Leopoldville. Although Hammarskjold continued to support the doctrine of nonintervention, he urged in December 1960 that the Members pass a new mandate which would direct ONUC to promote the reconvening of Parliament and the reconciliation of internal Congolese factions.[96] The United Nations was already undertaking some work along this line through a United Nations Conciliation Commission which was composed of the members of the Congo Advisory Committee and which had been set up by the General Assembly in its September 20, 1960, resolution; [97] but the Committee did not go to the Congo until January and February 1961. The results of the Security Council and General Assembly meetings in December 1960 which tried to reformulate some new directives for ONUC were completely unproductive—much to the Secretary-General's discouragement. On top of this apparent collapse of the political consensus behind ONUC, ONUC and the Secretary-General received another setback when the governments of Ceylon, Guinea, Malaya, Morocco, the United Arab Republic, and Yugoslavia all decided to withdraw their troops from the U.N. force as a result of its failure to protect Prime Minister Lumumba and to support his government as the legal government for all of the Congo. With these occurrences the fortunes and the political support for ONUC reached their lowest ebb.

On February 14, 1961 there came an announcement which completely changed the political situation surrounding ONUC. This was the announcement by the provincial government of Katanga that Prime Minister Lumumba had been killed while trying to escape from imprisonment there. Although this news brought new accusations from the Soviet bloc and a few Afro-Asian states against ONUC and Hammarskjold, it permitted a new consensus to come into being regarding the direction of ONUC.[98] This consensus, which gained the support of both the Western and the Afro-Asian states, was based largely on the suggestions which Hammarskjold had set forth during the previous December. These proposals, which were finally embodied in a Security Council resolution of February 21,[99] were that ONUC should encourage Parliament to reconvene in order to form a new government; that the United Nations should try to bring the different parties together to agree on a constitutional order for the Congo; and that ONUC take more vigorous measures to expel the foreign personnel in the Congo who were supporting the secessionist movements. Between February 14, when the death of Lumumba was announced, and February 21, Hammarskjold made a special effort to persuade the Afro-Asians, but especially the Africans, to adopt a common policy along the lines of his above suggestions toward the Congo which would help ONUC achieve its original purposes. In a speech before the Security Council on February 15 he made a special appeal to the Africans based upon their strategic role in the crisis and upon their interest in excluding the Cold War from their continent. He remarked:

For seven or eight months, through efforts far beyond the imagination of those who founded this Organization, it has tried to counter tendencies to introduce the big Power conflict into Africa and put the young African countries under the shadow of the Cold War . . . . In the beginning the effort was successful, and I do not now hesitate to say that on more than one occasion the drift into a war with foreign power intervention of the Korean or Spanish type was avoided only thanks to the work done by the Organization, basing itself on African solidarity. . . . African solidarity within the United Nations was the reply to the threats last year; I am firmly convinced that it still is the only reply.[100]

Within the week following this speech all of the African states gave their backing to the new Security Council resolution which included many of Hammarskjold's suggestions. While the African states differed in their motives for supporting the new mandate for ONUC, almost all of them shared Hammarskjold's desire to prevent unilateral intervention by and conflict among the Cold War powers in the Congo.

Following passage of the February 21 resolution, Hammarskjold held numerous three-hour meetings with the Congo Advisory Committee, which was composed of all nations that had troops in the Congo, regarding the meaning and application of the resolution. Since the committee was overwhelmingly Afro-Asian, he wanted to mobilize the support of this group behind any action he might take. This was especially important for him since the Soviet bloc was still condemning him strongly and trying to plant seeds of distrust about his political integrity and impartiality in the minds of Afro-Asian states. The Soviet bloc states at this time also withdrew their recognition from Hammarskjold as Secretary-General.[101]

The first move upon which Hammarskjold decided in implementation of the resolution was to send two African United Nations officials, Robert K. A. Gardiner of Ghana and Francis Nwokedi of Nigeria, to the Congo in order to negotiate agreements with the Central Government concerning the removal of foreign military and political personnel not under the United Nations command and concerning the reorganization of the army.[102] On April 17, after about a month of negotiations, an agreement was signed between the United Nations and the Central Government of President Kasavubu in which President Kasavubu agreed to expel all foreigners not recruited by his government and to reorganize the army along the lines of the government's plan of March 5.[103] Hammarskjold and many Members did not particularly like the latter plan, but since he and the great majority of the Members did not believe that the Organization could force policies of an internal political nature on the government, they had to go along with the plan. Hammarskjold at this time also sent a representative to Belgium to try to enlist the cooperation of the new Belgian government and its new Foreign Minister, Paul Henri Spaak, in deporting the foreign personnel who were working for the Katangese government. The Belgian government said it would help with the Belgian government personnel there but not with the mercenaries in the Katangese "gendarmerie." [104] Since the presence of these mercenaries was perpetuating the Congo's threat to international peace by sustaining the secessionist movements and hence creating the possibility of external intervention on behalf of other internal factions, it was obvious that some kind of action to remove them would have to be taken in the future.

During the spring and summer of 1961 significant strides were taken to bring order to the political life of the Congo and hence to lessen its threat to international peace through the mediatory activities of the United Nations. These activities bore fruit in the convening of the national parliament by most of the major political groups in the Congo in July and in the establishment of a new national government under Cyrille Adoula on August 2, 1961. Apart from the Province of Katanga, all political factions in the country supported the new government.

Following the establishment of the Adoula government, plans got underway for ONUC to remove the foreign personnel in Katanga whose support was permitting the continued secession of that area. Hammarskjold was concerned that if the secession were not ended soon, the Central Government might call for foreign assistance and undermine all of the progress that had been achieved. According to Hammarskjold's associates he was optimistic about the possibility of removing these foreign mercenaries and advisers and about the likelihood of the crisis' termination in the near future.[105] During the latter part of August the ONUC forces in Katanga began to round up the foreigners in the service of the Katanga government. Hammarskjold, anticipating its successful completion, left for the Congo on September 12 with the expectation that he would be able to assist a peaceful reconciliation between the Central Government of Premier Adoula and the Katangese government of Moise Tshombe.[106] He felt that with the removal of Katanga's mercenaries its secessionist government would have to make peace with the

Central Government. This anticipated unification of all of the Congo would have largely ended the threat of an international war arising out of the internal politics of that country.

While Hammarskjold was on his way to the Congo, fighting broke out in Elizabethville in Katanga, and this completely changed the nature of his trip. There is some controversy as to the origin of the fighting between the United Nations force and the Katangese and mercenary troops, but there is little controversy as to how Hammarskjold thought that the United Nations force should act. It was always his view that ONUC should not intervene in the political disputes of the Congo. He believed that it was legitimate if ONUC affected the course of Congolese politics through its actions to maintain civil order and to secure the withdrawal of foreign personnel, but that it was not legitimate if it acted as an agent of any internal group—even the Central Government which it recognized as the legal government of the entire country. When Hammarskjold arrived in Leopoldville on September 13, he was distressed by the implication of a Reuters report that the United Nations representative in Elizabethville, Dr. Conor Cruise O'Brien, had announced that the secession of Katanga had ended.[107] The implication of this report was that the United Nations had acted to end the secession of Katanga as an agent of the Central Government. It is probable that there were some United Nations personnel in the Congo who favored a policy of United Nations action to end the secession, but neither Hammarskjold's past insistence on the principle of nonintervention nor the purpose of his trip to the Congo indicate that he favored or would have tolerated such a policy. As it turned out, the actual fighting in Katanga began as a result of a military challenge by the Katangese "gendarmerie" to the United Nations troops. Therefore, he was not placed in a position of having to explain a United Nations action of which he disapproved.[108] However, he had great difficulty in diplomatically explaining and justifying the United Nations action in the light of Dr. O'Brien's statement.

Soon after Hammarskjold arrived, it became obvious that the Katangese forces, because of previous planning and the use of several airplanes, had the upper hand in relation to the ONUC forces. Therefore, instead of trying to bring Tshombe to Leopoldville,

Hammarskjold was faced with the problem of having to negotiate a cease-fire with him. While flying to the agreed site of the negotiations in Ndola, Northern Rhodesia, the plane in which he was traveling crashed, and he was killed. Although it was almost another year and a half before the ONUC forces were able to expel or drive out the mercenaries who were fighting for the secessionist Katangese regime, the operation which Hammarskjold began in July 1960 did prevent another Spanish Civil War from taking place in the Congo. One of the prices that was paid for this accomplishment was his death.

> 6. *In a civil war (as opposed to a situation of civil disorder) outside the blocs where there is intervention or the threat of intervention by external states, the United Nations representative organs should establish observer forces whose presence and reports may be able to deter external intervention. At the same time a peacekeeping force should not be established, since it would probably come into conflict with one of the internal factions.*

The above strategy was prescribed by Hammarskjold and was accepted by the United Nations representative organs during the Lebanon crisis of 1958.[109] In making the statement that it was accepted by the representative organs, it should be mentioned that a number of states agreed to an observer force for reasons other than Hammarskjold's, and at certain times individual states opposed his prescriptions. For instance, most of the parties agreed to the force because they thought it would substantiate their viewpoint, and the United States, Britain, and Lebanon at one point opposed his recommendation that a peacekeeping force not be created.

On June 11, 1958 the Security Council passed a resolution which was submitted by Sweden and which requested the Secretary-General to dispatch an observer force to Lebanon "so as to ensure that there is no illegal infiltration of personnel or supply of arms or other material across the Lebanese borders." [110] Hammarskjold had actually suggested the observer force to the Swedish mission. He envisaged that it might be able to prevent armed conflict in Lebanon by deterring outside intervention on behalf of the internal Lebanese factions. More specifically, he hoped that it would deter any external infiltration of arms and men from the U.A.R. to the dissident Moslem faction by posing the possibility of public exposure and international criticism and that it would deter United States intervention on behalf of the Chamoun government by pointing up the essentially internal nature of the conflict—thus removing the rationale for intervention. He particularly feared that American intervention might provoke Soviet intervention on behalf of the Moslem faction and the U.A.R. and that a serious international conflict could ensue.[111]

Throughout its existence UNOGIL probably had a minor deterrent influence in the ways that Hammarskjold had envisaged. Its reports of negligible infiltration of men and weapons from the U.A.R. into Lebanon surely did not succeed in preventing the dispatch of United States forces to Lebanon, although it is possible that the reports did make the American government reluctant to intervene in the period prior to the Iraqi coup of July 14. In respect to deterring any infiltration of arms and men from the U.A.R., it is also probable that its effect was not very great—especially prior to July 15. On that date it was still limited to government-held territory; it had only 15 stations and 113 men throughout Lebanon; and it did not patrol at night.[112] Following the landing of the United States troops Hammarskjold decided to increase the size of the force despite a Soviet veto of a Japanese resolution which proposed its increase. Between July 31, when the selection of General Chehab as the next president was formally announced, and the middle of October, when a new cabinet was finally selected, he augmented the observer force to 591 men, but this was during the twilight of the crisis.[113] He obviously must have thought that as long as there was any tension between the Christian and Moslem communities in Lebanon, it was useful to try to ward off any intrusions from the U.A.R. or armed action by American forces by threatening the sanctions which impartial United Nations reporting would have invoked.

Hammarskjold at no time during the crisis appears to have thought that it would be useful to have anything more powerful than an observer force in Lebanon because of the nature of the crisis. Following the Iraqi coup on July 14 and the landing of the United States Marines on July 15, the United States proposed that a United Nations force should be created to defend the integrity of Lebanon and that it should be allowed to fire in self-defense.[114] Hammarskjold thought that such a UNEF-type force would be inappropriate because the tension in Lebanon was due primarily to a conflict between the two major political groups in the country and because the force would be forced to operate between the government and the rebel forces. In a Security Council meeting on July 21 he stated:

> The definition of the authority, here quoted, makes it clear that the delegate of the United States did not intend that a United Nations force in Lebanon, if established, should take military initiative against opposition or dissident groups. On this assumption such a force at present would find it quite difficult to operate outside government-held territory, if, as might well be, such operations were to meet with armed resistance. In these circumstances, and remaining as it must strictly within the terms of the Charter, it seems probable that a force would find itself restricted on the whole to a fairly passive role in government-controlled territory—a role which, if it has to be filled, could be provided for by simpler means.[115]

When conflicts within states were primarily between internal groups and when external involvement in these conflicts was of a minor nature, Hammarskjold apparently believed that the most the United Nations could do to deter external interference was to try to report objectively the extent of that interference. Beyond that, it would inevitably become entangled in the civil conflict, and in Hammarskjold's view this was illegal and politically unwise.

> 7. *In a civil conflict outside the blocs where intervention or the threat of intervention exists, the United Nations representative organs should initiate programs of economic and technical assistance to the country in order to remove those causes of the disorder which result from technical and economic deficiencies.*

While ONUC's military operations dominated the attention of most people throughout its life, ONUC carried on at the same time a less noticeable but very important Civilian Operation. While the military forces were supposed to prevent and to deter the entry of foreign troops by keeping internal order, the Civilian Operation was supposed to prevent an international conflict in the Congo by contributing to the immediate and long-run bases of social and economic order in the country. It was felt that only with social and economic progress and order would the threat of foreign intervention on behalf of competing domestic political factions disappear. In Hammarskjold's initial proposal of United Nations aid to the Congo on July 13, he stated his intention of establishing a technical aid mission to the Congo. He noted that the country had been stripped of many of its skilled personnel by the large exodus of Belgian citizens and that it was very poor in terms of skilled manpower.[116] In order to fill the immediate gap created by this mass departure, Hammarskjold dispatched personnel in fields such as education, health, agriculture, public administration, communications, and public works throughout the Congo to assume operational responsibilities.[117] Some men were assigned to the central Ministries as advisers, and in these capacities they assumed important decision-making powers. They contributed to the long-term stability of the country by helping to plan developmental programs in their respective fields. In addition they set up training programs and fellowships to train the personnel needed to run the country in the future. The large majority of United Nations personnel in the Congo came from the United Nations Specialized Agencies, and the Consultative Group which directed the Civilian Operation was composed primarily of representatives from these agencies.[118] During approximately the first year of its operation the Civilian Operation was limited to a budget of $18 million in the Congo,[119] but it went a long way toward promoting economic and social order in the Congo and hence reducing the conflict's threat to international peace.

Hammarskjold also sought to initiate a program of United Nations economic and technical assistance to Laos to ameliorate the conditions in that country which were encouraging civil strife and instability. He was of the opinion that if the economic and social standards of the Laotian people could be improved and if the country could be unified through the creation of a modern administra-

tive structure and a modern system of transportation, the strife between the conservative, neutralist, and Communist factions would
tend to disappear and hence the threat to international peace which
arose from the situation. In order to promote these developments he
sent Mr. Sakari Tuomioja, the Executive Secretary of the United
Nations Economic Commission for Europe, to Laos in November
1959 to draw up a detailed report of the country's economic and social needs.[120] Mr. Tuomioja submitted his report in December, and
in January 1960 Hammarskjold sent Mr. Roberto M. Heurtematte,
United Nations Commissioner for Technical Assistance, to Laos to
discuss with the government the ways in which the United Nations
and its Specialized Agencies might contribute to furthering the objectives set forth in Mr. Tuomioja's report.[121] Mr. Heurtematte did
make a number of suggestions for United Nations assistance, but an
increasing bipolarization of Laotian politics in 1960 and increasing
military conflict between the factions prevented a very active role
for the Organization in the field of technical and economic assistance. It should be mentioned that the Secretary-General viewed the
functions of the United Nations representatives in Laos as more political than economic,[122] but at the same time he did hope that with
a possible amelioration of the political situation the United Nations
would be able to undertake some of the tasks that Mr. Tuomioja
outlined.

> 8. *In a conflict over interests outside the blocs where technical
> and/or economic assistance is required at the locus of the con-
> flict, the United Nations representative organs should make the
> Organization the sole channel of aid in order to prevent national
> aid programs from permitting national interference in the area
> —with the possibility of an exacerbation of the conflict.*

In both the Suez and Congo crises Hammarskjold thought that
all economic and technical assistance to Egypt and the Congo should
be given through the United Nations since such assistance would
keep out national elements which might have undesirable political
effects on the crises. In the case of the Suez crisis the problem of the
clearing of the canal was raised in diplomatic circles even before all

the parties to the armed conflict had agreed formally to a cease-fire. This came about as a result of a request by President Nasser that the United Nations undertake the task.[123] He did not want Britain, which was the best equipped nation, to do so because it would have given Britain an opportunity to use the clearance of the canal as a lever against Egypt to make concessions concerning the future management of the strategic waterway. The General Assembly concurred with his wish when on November 7 it asked the Secretary-General to undertake a United Nations clearance operation.[124] The British and the French tried both at the time of their acceptance of the cease-fire and later to persuade Hammarskjold to delegate the clearance operation to them since they were best qualified to do the job, but Hammarskjold refused.[125]

Aside from the resolution of the Assembly there were several other grounds on which Hammarskjold favored a United Nations operation and opposed a British and French operation. First, he thought that the British should not be permitted to undertake such an operation without the consent of the state on whose sovereign territory it would have to operate. Second, he appears to have feared that any British and French attempt to put pressure on Nasser through a physical presence in Egypt risked the possibility that Egypt would call on foreign powers, probably Soviet bloc states, to come to its defense. Such an occurrence might have negated UNEF's efforts to isolate the conflict from the Cold War and to avoid a collision between the Cold War powers. After a month of resistance Britain and France gave in reluctantly to the United Nations operation which had the support of a great majority of Members. This operation, which was headed by Lt. General Raymond A. Wheeler, the former Chief of the United States Army Corps of Engineers, completed the clearance during the first four months of 1957.

In the Congo crisis the principle of having all aid directed through the United Nations was of strategic importance in Hammarskjold's plan to isolate the conflict from the Cold War and to keep the Congolese civil conflict from becoming another Spanish Civil War. In contrast to the Suez crisis he did not always have the support of the host government on this principle, and he never had the support of the secessionist government of Katanga. Although neither Hammarskjold nor the Security Council explictly requested at the time of ONUC's formation that the Members not undertake any unilateral aid programs to the Congo, he evidently believed that it was a premise on which ONUC was based and that it was implicitly set forth in the Security Council resolution of July 22, 1960. This resolution

request[ed] all States to refrain from any action which might tend to impede the restoration of law and order and the exercise by the Government of the Congo of its authority and also to refrain from any action which might undermine the territorial integrity and the political independence of the Republic of the Congo.[126]

Although Belguim and the Soviet Union carried on aid programs respectively to the province of Katanga and the Central Government during July and August, such unilateral aid did not become a critical political issue until September. During the first part of that month Hammarskjold sent notes to both Belgium [127] and the Soviet Union [128] asking them to please verify reports which he had regarding their aid shipments to the Congo. He noted that such shipments were in conflict with the July 22 resolution. Although Belgium replied that it would take measures to make sure that such occurrences did not take place in the future,[129] the Soviet Union replied that its shipments of trucks and its provision of aircraft and personnel were not in conflict with the Security Council resolutions.[130] Hammarskjold at this time informed the Belgian government that he had learned that it "had at least permitted persons connected with its military services under a 'technical assistance' program to give help to forces fighting the Central Government of the Congo." [131] He asked that these individuals be withdrawn immediately.[132]

Hammarskjold was concerned that the continuation of external assistance to different internal factions could undermine ONUC and its attempt to remove the threat to the peace which the Congo crisis posed. Therefore, he recommended to the Security Council that "it will achieve its aims only if it requests that such assistance should be channelled through the United Nations, and only through the United Nations." [133] The Security Council was unable to agree upon such a resolution because of the Soviet veto, but on September 20 the General Assembly passed a resolution which embodied the principle. The resolution

call[ed] *upon* all States to refrain from the direct and indirect provision of arms or other materials of war and military personnel and other assistance for military purposes in the Congo during the temporary period of military assistance through the United Nations, except upon the request of the United Nations through the Secretary-General for carrying out the purposes of this resolution and of the resolutions of 14 and 22 July and 9 August 1960 of the Security Council.[134]

This resolution strengthened Hammarskjold's hand in trying to get all Members to end unilateral aid measures, but it did not end them.

At about the time that this issue became a public one in September, the Soviet aid program was forcibly ended by the expulsion of the Soviet embassy from the Congo by the government of President Kasavubu and General Mobutu which assumed power in the first weeks of September. While the Soviet program ceased, the problem of Belgian aid increased. The Belgians refused to withdraw their program of "technical assistance" to the government of Katanga and its armed forces, and with the increasing political chaos in the latter part of 1960 more Belgians came to the Congo to assume both governmental and commercial positions.[135] Mercenaries of other nationalities also came into Katanga to bolster its regime. It was not until after the Security Council resolution of February 21, 1961,[136] which asked ONUC to expel all mercenaries and foreign political advisers, that real progress began to be made in cutting off all foreign aid programs to the Congo that were not directed through the United Nations. Following the resolution the Belgian government agreed to withdraw all military and political advisers who were in the Congo as a result of direct agreements between Congolese authorities and itself, but it said that it was not responsible for its citizens who had privately contracted to work in the Congo.[137] Hammarskjold's own belief appears to have been that once the foreign elements who were not working in cooperation with the United Nations operation were removed from the Congo, an internal reconciliation between competing Congolese elements would be more easily obtainable.

Tactics

CRITICISM OF ARMED ATTACKS

1. The Security Council, the General Assembly, and the Secretary-General should avoid harsh condemnations of states which commit breaches of the peace. Such condemnations are only likely to discourage cooperation by the parties with the United Nations at that time and in the future.

Although Hammarskjold felt that the United Nations should make its voice heard against all breaches of the peace and should demand their termination, he was strongly opposed to harsh condemnations since they were likely to discourage the cooperation of the aggressing parties. During the Suez Crisis his own statement of disapproval of the Israeli invasion and the announced intention of the British and French to occupy the canal zone on October 31 was understood by everyone, but the statement did not alienate them from Hammarskjold because it did not condemn them. In that statement he philosophized on the role of the Secretary-General, and the essence of his remarks was that the Secretary-General must "be a servant of the principles of the Charter and that its aims must ultimately determine what for him is right and wrong." He then went on to remark: "The bearing of what I have just said must be obvious to all without any elaboration from my side." [138] His disapproval of the policies of the three states was clear to everyone, but he had not offended their *amour propre* and thus undermined his ability to work with them.

During the General Assembly meetings on the Suez question Hammarskjold tried to prevent that body from making harsh or vindictive criticisms of the three parties, especially of Britain and France. Ambassador Hans Engen of Norway has said that

neither Pearson nor Hammarskjold was diverted from the conviction that Britain and France should at all costs remain untarnished by the brand of aggression. They were quite determined that the more vehement anti-colonialists who were gaining support should not succeed in persuading the Assembly to aggravate the crisis by adopting harshly worded resolutions.[139]

Aside from Hammarskjold's belief that such resolutions would make cooperation between the three parties and the United Nations very difficult in restoring the peace, the Secretary-General was concerned about the effect such resolutions might have on their future relationship to the Organization. According to Terrence Robertson, Hammarskjold used his personal influence with some delegations to prevent the initiation and the adoption of drastic proposals because he feared that the public reactions to them in Britain and France might be so adverse that both would have to withdraw from the Organization.[140]

During the Security Council meeting of July 13–14, 1960 concerning the Congo crisis Hammarskjold also abstained from any harsh criticism of Belgium and tried to prevent any such actions by the Council. In this case he did not even deem it desirable or necessary to make a judgment of the entry of Belgian troops in order to protect Belgian nationals. During his statement to the Security Council he noted:

It is not for the Secretary-General to pronounce himself on this action and its legal and political aspects, but I must conclude from the communication received from the Government of the Congo that the presence of these troops is a source of internal and potentially international tension.[141]

He probably thought that it was an unwise action, but he did not think that it was as serious a violation of United Nations principles as was the Suez invasion. He also knew that Belgian cooperation was going to be vital to the success of any United Nations operation, and he therefore did not want to alienate that country. Mr. King Gordon, a United Nations official at the time of the Congo crisis, has written since his departure from the United Nations that one of the reasons that Hammarskjold called the meeting himself was so that he "would be able to define the issue to the exclusion of certain factors which, if introduced, might make agreement difficult and defeat the possibility of achieving consensus on a firm mandate." [142] One of the issues that Mr. Gordon noted that Hammarskjold wanted to exclude was the question of "aggression" which had been raised by the Soviet Union and the Congolese government and which would have been strongly opposed by Belgium and her allies, especially Britain and France.[143] Hammarskjold only approved of criticism if it might serve a useful purpose in exerting pressure on a country to take a certain action, but he never condoned harsh condemnations which were only likely to hinder a restoration of the status quo and cooperation with the United Nations by the party or parties that had committed the breach of the peace.

PEACEKEEPING FORCES

During his tenure as Secretary-General, Hammarskjold left a very strong personal imprint on the principles which guided the United Nations' peacekeeping forces. Since these forces originated during his tenure and since their planning and direction was delegated to a great extent to his office, he was able to exert a strong influence on their character. The legacy of tactical principles which he left is likely to influence such United Nations operations for many years.

> *1. The establishment of peacekeeping forces in particular states should have the consent of those states, and the inclusion of national troops in the United Nations operations should require the permission of their national governments. Neither host and contributing states nor the overwhelming majority of the Members would give either political or physical support to the force without this consent principle which protects important areas of sovereignty.*

Since none of the United Nations peacekeeping forces which were created during Hammarskjold's tenure were intended to perform enforcement functions under Chapter VII of the Charter, he held that the consent of the states in which they were operating must be obtained. In his second and last report on the creation of UNEF on November 6, 1956, Hammarskjold wrote that

the Force, if established, would be limited in its operations to the extent that consent of the parties concerned is required under generally recognized international law. While the General Assembly is enabled to "establish" the Force with the consent of these parties which contribute units to the Force, it could not request the Force to be "stationed" or "operate" on the territory of a given country without the consent of the Government of that country.[144]

Hammarskjold also knew that the Members would not approve any force which did not require the consent of the host states since they were all sensitive to any steps which might undermine their own sovereignties. This was especially true of the Afro-Asian states which feared that such forces might be used by the West to re-establish some of their former control over them.

In the case of UNOGIL and ONUC this issue did not raise a very great problem since both Lebanon and the Congo came to the United Nations in search of such forces. When ONUC was formed on July 14, 1960, this principle was accepted implicitly by the Security Council when it approved Hammarskjold's proposal for the force. In the proposal he commented that if a force for the Congo were created, he would direct it in accordance with the principles set down in the UNEF Summary.[145]

Apart from feeling that peacekeeping operations required the consent of host states, Hammarskjold also believed that their establishment required the permission of a number of Member States to use their military personnel. He was of the opinion that since the Members had not intended that these forces be used for enforcement functions under Chapter VII of the Charter,[146] any contributions of troops to them had to be on a voluntary basis. Hammarskjold set forth this position in his UNEF Summary of 1958 when he wrote:

As the arrangements discussed in this report do not cover the type of force envisaged under Chapter VII of the Charter, it follows from international law and the Charter . . . that the consent of a Member nation is necessary for the United Nations to use its military personnel or material.[147]

This principle has never been challenged by a Member State after it was formally established for UNEF.

2. Peacekeeping forces should be under the ultimate authority of the Security Council or the General Assembly and the executive authority which these organs have created to direct

> *them because such an arrangement insures their conformity to the policy views of the majority of the Member States.*

This principle was directed at two issues which the peacekeeping forces faced. The first was the problem of who should be ultimately responsible for the force, and the second was the closely related problem of whether the forces should be required to act at the behest of the countries in which they were operating since their presence required the consent of those countries.

Hammarskjold discussed the first problem in his UNEF report of November 6, 1956, where he set forth three alternatives for organizing the force. He was opposed to two of the three alternatives. One was to charge a country or group of countries with the responsibility of organizing a force whose purpose was determined by the United Nations (for example, Korea), and the other was to allow a group of countries to set up a force which hopefully would be brought into a formal relationship with the organization at a later date (for example, the British and French suggestion that the United Nations charge them with certain functions).[148] His main reservation to the foregoing alternatives was that it would be very difficult to establish a real independence for such a United Nations force from the states which contributed troops to it.[149] The third alternative, and the one which he favored, was that the force be directly under the General Assembly and/or the Security Council.[150] He articulated his ideas on this model in his UNEF Summary of 1958 when he wrote that a United Nations force should be formed

on the basis of principles, reflected in the constitution of the United Nations itself. This would mean that its chief responsible officer should be appointed by the United Nations, and that he, in his functions, should be responsible ultimately to the General Assembly and/or the Security Council. His authority should be so defined as to make him fully independent of the policies of any one nation.[151]

It was his opinion that the states whose actions the force was trying to influence would be much more likely to comply with objectives of the force if it were truly international in character. Although he did not mention it, he probably doubted whether Egypt would have consented to the entry of any kind of force other than the kind he recommended.

The other problem, to which the foregoing principle addressed itself, is whether the state in which the force is operating can determine the nature of the force's activities. In both the Suez and the Congo crises this became a very serious issue. In the case of UNEF President Nasser at first demanded that Egypt's approval should be required for almost any step which the force took. It was only after considerable effort that Hammarskjold persuaded him that this could not be permitted. He explained that the General Assembly resolutions clearly set forth the nature of UNEF's tasks and that Egypt had accepted them. He made it clear that the General Assembly had accepted his report which had said that the executive officer of the force and the force itself should be "fully independent of the policies of any one nation." [152] Hammarskjold stated his thinking on this point very clearly in his UNEF Summary of 1958:

authority granted to the United Nations group cannot be exercised within a given territory either in competition with representatives of the host Government or in cooperation with them on the basis of any joint operation. Thus, a United Nations operation must be separate and distinct from activities by national authorities.[153]

In the Congo operation this principle came under an even more serious challenge than it did during the Suez crisis. First, Prime Minister Lumumba and later President Kasavubu wanted ONUC to subdue their internal enemies for them. Hammarskjold explained that such actions were not in conformity with the mandates of the force and that the Congolese government could not give directions to ONUC.

3. *Peacekeeping forces should remain until the completion of their task and should require the consent of the General Assembly or the Security Council for their termination. This prevents the termination of the force by the host state at a time when such an action might seriously endanger international peace.*

This particular tactical principle has recently been the object of a great deal of controversy as a result of the request of the United Arab Republic on May 16, 1967 that UNEF withdraw from its territory and the decision of the present Secretary-General, U Thant, to accede to this request. As a result of these occurrences a former associate of Hammarskjold's, Ernest A. Gross, has made public a private memorandum of the late Secretary-General which clearly sets forth the above principle and which describes the diplomacy surrounding its establishment.[154] The basic contents of this memorandum have been public since 1962 in a book which Mr. Gross authored.[155]

From November 10 to 13, 1956 Hammarskjold carried on a dialogue with the Egyptian government concerning the procedures for terminating the stay of UNEF in Egypt. During these negotiations Hammarskjold took the stand that since Egypt "had consented to the presence of U.N.E.F. for certain tasks," it "could not ask the U.N.E.F. to withdraw before the completion of the tasks without running up against their own acceptance of the resolutions on the force and its tasks." [156] This interpretation led him to take the stand that the withdrawal of the force would require the consent of the United Nations body whose resolutions had set up the force, namely, the General Assembly. Egypt rejected this viewpoint and said that the termination of the force should rest solely on its decisions. On November 13 Hammarskjold and the Egyptian government agreed to permit the entry of the force on the following day despite the fact that they had not come to an agreement on this issue. At that time the Secretary-General felt that after the force had arrived in Egypt, he could enter into private talks with President Nasser and "would be in a position to find a formula, saving the face of Egypt while protecting the U.N. stand. . . ."

On November 17 Hammarskjold flew to Cairo and held a seven-hour discussion with the Egyptian president in which an agreement which Hammarskjold had written the previous day was formally accepted by both parties. The Secretary-General has recorded very precisely what he sought to accomplish in his meetings with Nasser and what outcome was achieved. He noted that the best kind of agreement would have been one in which the Egyptians "declared, that withdrawal should take place only if so decided by the General Assembly"; but he realized that this was not feasible since it would have demanded a *volte-face* by Nasser. Likewise, he noted that an accord "to the effect that withdrawal should take place upon 'agreement of withdrawal' between the U.N. and the Egyptian Government" would be difficult for Nasser to accept. At the same time he felt that it might be possible to obtain an agreement very close to this latter one "according to which Egypt would declare to the United Nations that it would exert all its sovereign rights with regard to the troops on the basis of a good-faith interpretation of the tasks of the Force. The United Nations should make a reciprocal commitment to maintain the force as long as the task was not completed." Hammarskjold noted in the memorandum that such a mutual accord would mean that any request by Egypt for the withdrawal of the force would have to be approved by the General Assembly. It was exactly this accord that Hammarskjold and Nasser agreed to on November 17 and publicly announced on November 20 [157] and which was approved by the General Assembly on November 24.[158] In reflecting back on the specific character of the accord in his memorandum Hammarskjold wrote:

The device I used meant only that instead of limiting their rights by a basic understanding requesting an agreement *directly concerning withdrawal,* we created an obligation to reach agreement on the fact that the tasks were completed, and thus, *the conditions for a withdrawal established.*

Although it is not necessary to an exposition of Hammarskjold's views on this matter, a few words should be said about the authority of the views set forth in Hammarskjold's memorandum since Secretary-General U Thant has stated that it was not an "official document" and therefore had no authority.[159] In this author's view it should have been accepted as an official interpretation of the United Nations-Egyptian "good faith" agreement, unless it could have been ascertained that Hammarskjold's statement that Nasser clearly understood and accepted his views on the agreement was false. In the memorandum, he wrote concerning Nasser's understanding of the accord that the Egyptian president

very fully understood that, by limiting their freedom of action in the way I proposed, they would take a very serious step, as it would mean that the question of the extent of the task would become decisive for the relations between Egypt and the United Nations and would determine Egypt's freedom of action. He felt, not without justification, that the definition given of the task in the U. N. texts was very loose and that, tying the freedom of action of Egypt to the concept of the task—which had to be interpreted also by the General Assembly—and doing so in a written agreement, meant that he accepted a far-reaching and unpredictable restriction.

If this statement is accurate, Nasser acted contrary to a previous commitment when he demanded UNEF's immediate withdrawal, and U Thant did not follow one of the principles upon which the force was based. This does not necessarily mean that UNEF should not have been withdrawn when it was, but it does indicate that the procedures for initiating its withdrawal were contrary to those which were established by the United Nations and Egypt in 1956.

The reason why Hammarskjold supported this particular principle was that he feared that Egypt might either in the near or distant future request the withdrawal of UNEF when it had offers of foreign military assistance or when it sought to reactivate its struggle with Israel, and he felt that this could lead to a demise of the stability that the Members of the Organization had sought to create. He particularly feared at that time that Egypt might accept an offer of "volunteers" from the Soviet Union and its allies and that such an entry of Communist troops might lead to a conflict between the Cold War blocs in the Middle East.[160] In looking back at the recent June 1967 war in the Middle East, it is quite possible to judge that if UNEF had not been withdrawn from the Israeli-Egyptian border and the Straits of Tiran, the war might not have taken place. If the principles of the original Hammarskjold-Nasser accord had been called to Nasser's attention at the time and if the question had then been referred to the General Assembly, the United Arab Republic might have been temporarily deterred from taking up positions along the border and blockading the Straits of Tiran. While the United Arab Republic could probably have obtained the support of one-third of the General Assembly for its position, mediatory influence might have emerged in a meeting of the Assembly to change the Egyptian government's decision to request UNEF's withdrawal and/or to deter the Egyptian blockade and troop movements.

There was another United Nations-host state agreement which Hammarskjold negotiated for a peacekeeping force and which mirrored the United Nations-Egyptian accord. This was the accord which was created for ONUC with the Congolese government and which was formally signed on July 27, 1960.[161] During the Congo crisis it is highly likely that Premier Patrice Lumumba would have requested the withdrawal of the United Nations force in the summer of 1960 if he thought that it was his prerogative to do so. If he had been able to make such a decision and had invited Communist and radical nationalist Afro-Asians to replace the United Nations, a serious Cold War conflict might have ensued.

> 4. *The Secretary-General should obtain maximum and continual direction from the Members for his direction of peacekeeping forces (for example, through resolutions of the General Assembly and Security Council, advisory committees, consultations with delegations). At the same time, disagreement among the Members over the passing of the new mandates should not prevent the Secretary-General from applying previous mandates. Such continual direction lessens the likelihood that his decisions will seriously alienate the Members from himself and his office; and continued application of mandates in face of disagreement on their interpretation is a legal obligation and helps to reduce the threat of international violence.*

When Hammarskjold was given the responsibility of being the executive agent for the General Assembly and Security Council in several peacekeeping operations, he realized that he was risking his future efficacy as Secretary-General, since he might make a decision regarding a force which would seriously alienate important Members. While he was aware of these risks, he also felt that his role in these operations was important to the Organization's ability to promote international peace and that the risks could be minimized by constantly seeking the guidance of the Members through a number of channels. Regarding this last point, he noted that "experience has . . . indicated that the international civil servant may take steps to reduce the sphere within which he has to take stands on politically controversial issues." [162] The single step which he generally always took whenever he was faced with a difficult decision regarding how to interpret a previous mandate was to ask either the Security Council or the General Assembly for a clarification or amplification of its directives. While such formal mandates were the best political backing for him, they were often not forthcoming because of a lack of a consensus among the Members. It was also sometimes inconvenient to call a formal meeting if the decision was not of major importance or if he had to make a decision in a short period of time. In such circumstances he generally took one of two steps to obtain guidance from the Members. One was to create and then to seek guidance from special advisory committees composed of a select number of Member States, and the other was to carry on regular private diplomatic contacts with the national delegations at the United Nations.

Throughout the United Nations peacekeeping endeavors Hammarskjold urged states to make his mandates more precise, although he often knew that there was little likelihood of the Members' reaching very specific consensuses. During the Suez crisis he did not have to urge more specific resolutions very often since there was a fairly clear consensus regarding the policies which UNEF should follow. The one time that he did suggest explicitly that the Members might want to give him a new mandate was in a report on February 11, 1957, when Israel was refusing, contrary to the expressed will of the General Assembly, to leave Gaza and the western coast of the Gulf of Aqaba.[163]

During the first month that the observer force in Lebanon was in existence, there were no great problems concerning its political direction; however, the problem did arise after the American landings as to whether the group should be enlarged. At a Security Council meeting Hammarskjold supported a Japanese proposal to enlarge the group.[164] Then, when the Soviet Union vetoed the resolution, he announced that he would enlarge it on his own initiative.[165] Although this appeared to be contrary to his policy that the Secretary-General should always follow the guidance of the representative organs, it was not the case. In the debates concerning the resolution, the Soviet Union made it clear that it was not opposed to an increase in the number of United Nations observers but was opposed to the absence of a condemnation of the landing of American and British troops in Lebanon and Jordan.[166] Therefore, in taking the step to enlarge UNOGIL Hammarskjold apparently thought that he had the political support of all of the members of the Security Council.

The one peacekeeping operation in which he tried quite often to obtain clarifications of his mandate was ONUC, since there were numerous challenges to his policies both from inside the Congo and from some Members. The first and most striking instance where he sought a clarification of the Security Council's mandate was at the beginning of August 1960 when Katanga was balking at allowing the entry of the United Nations forces and when Lumumba was attacking ONUC more and more virulently for not crushing the Katanga secession. On August 9 he obtained explicit policy directives for ONUC that it should be allowed to enter Katanga and that it should not intervene in the domestic disputes of the Congo.[167] Again, in December 1960 when ONUC and the Secretary-General were under attack from many quarters, he asked the representative organs to clarify his mandate if they disagreed with ONUC's policies, and suggested several directions which a new mandate might take.[168] Both bodies were stymied at that time, but following the death of Lumumba in February 1961 the Security Council with African backing finally responded to his plea for a new mandate.[169]

Another means which Hammarskjold used to obtain continual guidance from the Members for his direction of peacekeeping operations was consultation with special advisory committees which were set up especially for each operation. The initial precedent for these committees was the UNEF Advisory Committee which was proposed by Hammarskjold in his November 6, 1956 report.[170] This committee was created by a United Nations resolution of November 7, 1956 "to undertake the development of those aspects of the planning for the Force and its operation not already dealt with by the General Assembly. . . ." [171] The General Assembly named the Secretary-General as the chairman and Brazil, Canada, Ceylon, Colombia, India, Norway, and Pakistan as the members of the committee. There were no votes taken during the meetings of this committee since it was purely advisory, but for the Secretary-General it often proved to be a source of ideas and a channel of communication with the thinking of the Members. Regarding the work of the committee Hammarskjold wrote in the UNEF Summary of 1958:

Meetings of the Advisory Committee have been held whenever matters have arisen requiring discussion, or whenever the Secretary-General has sought advice, or, at times, only to keep the Committee informed on current developments. The Advisory Committee has been consulted particularly on those questions which the Assembly had indicated should be the subject of consultation between it and the Secretary-General, such as the Regulations for the Force, the policy of the force, as regards self-defence and the issues of medals.[172]

The consensuses which developed during these meetings were very valuable for Hammarskjold in that they provided him with political protection from any criticisms which developed during the course of the operation.

When UNOGIL was created in Lebanon in June 1958, Hammarskjold did not suggest such a committee since he probably judged that its mandate would not require controversial political directives from his office. Then, on July 24, about a week after the American landing in Lebanon, he announced that he had set up an advisory committee for UNOGIL with the same composition as the UNEF committee. The most likely reason that he established the committee was that he foresaw the possibility at that very tense time that the United Nations group might find itself in a deteriorating situation; and he therefore wanted a group of Members with whom he could consult about its activities in such circumstances. As it turned out, such a conflict did not arise, and the advisory committee never met.

As occurred in the Lebanon operation, Hammarskjold did not create an advisory committee for ONUC until approximately a month and a half after the force had been in operation. He evidently thought at first that the resolutions of the Security Council and informal contacts with the Members gave him sufficient continual guidance in his direction of ONUC, but with the growing challenges to his policies in August 1960 he decided on August 21 to create a Congo Advisory Committee.[173] The committee was composed of the fifteen nations which had troops in the Congo. During the following thirteen months that Hammarskjold was Secretary-General, he met with this committee fifty-five times and usually for periods of three hours.[174] Like the UNEF committee its functions were only advisory, although the Congolese government[175] and the Soviet Union[176] at the time of its suggestion hoped that much of the political direction of the force would be given to it and that it would be stationed in the Congo. Hammarskjold apparently rejected these suggestions because they would have undercut the United Nations nature of the force and since they would have encouraged meddling by individual states in Congolese politics.

The most intensive series of meetings which the committee had was following the Security Council resolution of February 21 which directed ONUC to encourage the Congolese parliament to form a new government, to reorganize the army, and to expel the mercenaries and foreign advisors. Andrew W. Cordier has written about these meetings:

Despite the fact that the Committee was as deeply divided as the Council, the meetings were useful, and the Secretary-General's practice of formulating a consensus out of the discussion provided a chance for the members to dissent if they wished, and gave him a foundation, however weak at times, to carry out a specific policy in the Congo.[177]

Since the committee was heavily weighted with Afro-Asian states, it gave Hammarskjold an opportunity to mold a consensus within this group which he considered strategically important to the success of the operation. No doubt it was the support which he received from this group and the Afro-Asian states as a whole which kept the Soviet Union relatively quiet during the spring and summer of 1961.

A third means which Hammarskjold utilized in obtaining political direction from the Members was to communicate regularly with the national delegations at the United Nations. One aspect of this process of communication was the issuance of reports to the Security Council by the Secretary-General on the progress of peacekeeping operations. These reports discussed the policy decisions which he had made and why he had made them. They also presented the policy problems which the forces were facing. These reports kept the Members informed and thereby avoided criticisms by the Members due to lack of information. In addition they gave the Members the opportunity to express their views on the problems faced by the forces.[178] In general, the reactions of the Members were expressed privately in meetings between the Secretary-General and the national representatives.

In cases where the Secretary-General does not obtain clear political direction either formally from the political organs or informally through private consultation, Hammarskjold held that the Secretary-General should continue to apply the mandates which he had been given previously. In his speech at Oxford University in May 1961 he said:

the responsibilities of the Secretary-General under the Charter cannot be laid aside merely because the execution of decisions by him is likely to be politically controversial. The Secretary-General remains under the obligation to carry out the policies as adopted by the organs; the essential requirement is that he does this on the basis of exclusively international responsibility and not in the interest of any particular State or groups of States.[179]

Hammarskjold realized that there were political risks involved in such a course of action, but he thought that he would be undermining his responsibility for promoting international peace if he halted a previously approved peacekeeping operation.

5. *Peacekeeping forces* per se *should not try to influence the outcome of the dispute between the parties and should respect the legal status of the situations in which they are involved because any attempts to impose settlements on the host states would be strongly opposed by those host states and the majority of the members as being illegal, constituting intervention in internal politics, and perhaps rewarding aggression.*

This principle became a very important issue in the operation of UNEF. To a significant extent the purpose of the force was debated in terms of it. In his report on the creation of UNEF on November 6, 1956, Hammarskjold spelled out this principle very clearly when he wrote:

It follows from its terms of reference that there is no intent in the establishment of the Force to influence the military balance in the present conflict and, thereby, the political balance affecting efforts to settle the conflict.[180]

He then went on to mention that these terms had been clearly prescribed for the operation in the General Assembly resolution of November 2 which had asked all parties to withdraw behind the armistice lines. In the UNEF Summary of 1958 he explained that this was a necessary limitation on any United Nations forces which were not created under the enforcement provisions of Chapter VII of the Charter.[181] He also noted that this was a necessary limitation if the United Nations was going to be able to draw upon the men and materials of the Members for such operations.[182]

Challenges were raised to this principle first in relation to the British-French withdrawal and then in relation to the Israeli withdrawal. Initially the British and French hoped that UNEF would take its place along the canal until a new arrangement for the management of the canal had been negotiated between the users and Egypt. This question was settled very early in the history of the force since Hammarskjold, in order to get Nasser to let UNEF enter Egypt, had to promise him that it would not be used for this purpose. The problem of getting Israel to accept the principle was much more difficult. During the middle of January it had withdrawn its troops from all of the Sinai Peninsula except the west coast of the Gulf of Aqaba and the Gaza Strip. The Israeli government noted that it would remove the troops along the Gulf of Aqaba whenever it received assurances that it would be allowed free passage through the Straits of Tiran, and it announced that it intended to remain in an administrative capacity in the Gaza Strip.[183] Although the Secretary-General gave some support to the Israeli claim in relation to the Gulf of Aqaba, he stated specifically that it would not be allowed to remain in Gaza. In his report of January 24, 1957, he wrote:

The United Nations cannot condone a change of the "status juris" resulting from military action contrary to the provisions of the Charter. The Organization must, therefore, maintain that the "status juris" existing prior to such military action be reestablished by a withdrawal of troops, and by the relinquishment or nullification of rights asserted in territories covered by the military action and depending upon it. . . . Whatever arrangements the United Nations may now wish to make in order to further peaceful conditions, the Agreement must be fully respected by it . . . . These considerations exclude the United Nations from accepting Israeli control over the area, even if it were of a non-military character.[184]

In this position Hammarskjold had the support of the great majority of the Members.

When Israel saw that opposition to its position was too great to overcome, it then suggested that the United Nations assume complete administration of the Gaza Strip in order to prevent a recrudescence of *fedayeen* raids from that area.[185] Although Hammarskjold never rejected this possibility publicly, he did so privately. Also, his statement in his January 24 report that "deployment of the Force in Gaza, under the resolutions of the General Assembly, would have to be on the same basis as its deployment along the armistice lines in the Sinai Peninsula" implicitly ruled out his acceptance of the Israeli proposal. As a result of his insistence that UNEF honor the letter of the law, which in this case was the Armistice Agreement, Prime Minister Ben Gurion of Israel accused the Secretary-General of "legal pedantry" [186] and of a pro-Arab bias.[187] Premier Guy Mollet of France, after a conversation with Hammarskjold in February 1957, was also "appalled by the juridical formalism" of the Secretary-General in relation to this problem.[188] What both men did not recognize, intentionally or unintentionally, was that Hammarskjold's legalism was based upon a great deal of political realism. He knew that a large majority of the Members would never tolerate a change in the *status juris* which penalized Egypt, and he also knew that future United Nations operations of the same nature would never be accepted by the Members and especially by possible host states if this initial peacekeeping operation were used to impose a change in the law upon Egypt. As the situation turned out, the status of the Armistice Agreement was upheld, and Israel obtained some important benefits. Egypt acquiesced in the West's decision to protect Israel's right of free passage through the Straits of Tiran, and it complied with Hammarskjold's request that it not reintroduce military forces into the Gaza Strip.[189]

6. *Peacekeeping forces should not intervene in the internal politics of the states in which they are located. Most host states and the great majority of the Members would strongly oppose such violations of state sovereignty and any military clashes between the force and local troops which such interventions would cause.*

This tactical principle, which is taken from Article 2, paragraph 7 of the Charter, was closely tied to the political purposes of the United Nations peacekeeping operations. In the Suez crisis it reinforced the policy laid down for UNEF by the previous principle, namely, that the force could not impose any changes in the *status quo ante* on Egypt. In the case of UNEF, France, Britain, Israel, and several other states wanted the force at different times to assume responsibility for the temporary or permanent administration of different parts of Egypt until that state came to an agreement with them on certain problems or so that Egyptian military forces and government personnel would be excluded from certain sections of Egyptian territory.[190] Hammarskjold made it very clear that the Organization could not assume such internal political functions. In his November 6 report he wrote:

The Force obviously should have no rights other than those necessary for the execution of its functions, in cooperation with local authorities. It would be more than an observers' corps, but in no way a military force temporarily controlling the territory in which it is stationed.[191]

He elaborated upon another aspect of its relation to the internal politics of Egypt in his UNEF Summary when he wrote:

authority granted to the United Nations group cannot be exercised within a given territory either in competition with representatives of the host Government or in cooperation with them on the basis of any joint operation. Thus, a United Nations operation must be separate and distinct from activities by national authorities.[192]

Apart from a respect for the legal norms of the Charter, Hammarskjold believed that there were a number of very good political reasons for following this principle. First, he realized that the majority of the Members would not tolerate any action which imposed penalties on Egypt and rewarded Israel, Britain, and France. Second, he perceived that the great majority of Members were very sensitive about encroachments on their sovereignty and that they would not tolerate any United Nations forces at that time or in the future which made such encroachments. Third, he felt that any attempts to assume internal responsibilities would lead UNEF to come into conflict with Egyptian forces and citizens and that the Members would not contribute forces which were exposed to such attacks.[193]

While this principle of nonintervention in the internal politics of a state had important political implications for UNEF in that the force could not assume administrative and police responsibilities within Egypt against the will of its government, it assumed even greater importance in the Congo operation. When Hammarskjold proposed the creation of ONUC to the Security Council on July 13, he emphasized that any United Nations force which was sent to the Congo to help restore law and order should not interfere in the internal affairs of the country. Besides suggesting the approval of the principles contained in the UNEF Summary, he stated explicitly that the troops "may not take any action which would make them a party to internal conflicts in this country." [194] From the moment that ONUC arrived in the Congo, this principle or Hammarskjold's interpretation of it was challenged by the Congolese government and some Members. The first and most important challenge came from Prime Minister Lumumba, who wanted the Secretary-General to direct ONUC to suppress the secessionist province of Katanga. The challenge became so serious that by the beginning of August Hammarskjold felt compelled to ask the Security Council for explicit support of the principle of nonintervention.[195] It was his contention that the force was there to maintain civil order and to obtain the withdrawal of foreign troops but not to fight on behalf of any political faction in the country—even the Central Government. He stated the legal case for his position in a Security Council meeting on August 21:

in the light of the domestic jurisdiction limitation of the Charter, it must be assumed that the Council would not authorize the Secretary-General to intervene with armed troops in an internal conflict when the Council has not specifically adopted enforcement measures under Article 41 and 42 of Chapter VII.[196]

When President Kasavubu dismissed Prime Minister Lumumba in September 1960, he also called on the Secretary-General to direct ONUC to suppress his enemies such as Antoine Gizenga in Stanleyville, and Hammarskjold refused.

Some states, such as the Soviet Union and the radical nationalist states of Ghana and Guinea, accepted the doctrine of nonintervention, but they opposed Hammarskjold's interpretation of it. They took the position that the dispute between the Central Government and Katanga was not an internal dispute but one between a legitimate government and a foreign aggressor because Katanga was supported by foreign sources.[197] The two African states also argued that it was not intervention to support the legitimate government of the country. At one time Hammarskjold remarked that it could be "argue[d] in a purely theoretical way that the maintenance of law and order may embrace the enforcement of basic constitutional law," but he found it "hardly possible to reconcile this point of view with the actual decisions of the Security Council." [198] He also associated himself with those delegates who thought that "such forcible intervention in internal constitutional and political conflict could not be considered as compatible with the basic principles of Article 2 of the Charter relating to sovereign equality and nonintervention in domestic jurisdiction." [199]

Two implications which were derived from the principle of nonintervention were that ONUC could not force the Congolese army to submit to retraining and reorganization by United Nations personnel nor could it force the Congolese parliament to meet and choose a new government which could promote unity and stability in the country. Hammarskjold thought that both the retraining of the army and the convening of parliament were desirable, but he refused to use anything more than persuasion in pursuit of these goals in order to avoid intervention in internal Congolese politics. During the first month of the crisis Hammarskjold appointed General Kettani as the military adviser to the Congolese army with the hope that he could arrange for its retraining and reorganization by ONUC, and several ONUC commanders persuaded Congolese units to lay down their arms with the expectation that they would soon be reorganized. The hopes which were behind Hammarskjold's appointment of General Kettani and behind the actions of the ONUC commanders were soon dashed to the ground when first Prime Minister Lumumba and then President Kasavubu opposed the plans for reorganization. Even after the Security Council resolution of February 21, 1961,[200] which specifically requested ONUC to reorganize the army, Hammarskjold and the United Nations were forced to bow to President Kasavubu's refusal to go along with an ONUC plan for reorganization. The principle of nonintervention thus erected a barrier to ONUC's promoting the long-term stability of the Congo, but Hammarskjold felt that it was a legal and political limitation which the force had to accept.

As has already been mentioned, Hammarskjold also thought that ONUC did not have the prerogative to force the parliament to reconvene and choose a new government. He favored the use of "diplomatic means" and "political persuasion" [201] to encourage the creation of a new government by the conflicting factions, but he was adamant in his position that force should not be used. He resisted pressure to bring force to bear against Katanga, and as stated earlier, he died while on a mission to the Congo, the objective of which was to bring about a peaceful reconciliation between Premier Adoula and Katanga's President Tshombe.

The reasons why the Secretary-General upheld the principle of nonintervention in the Congo crisis are very similar to those which led him to support it in the Suez crisis, although in the former case the issue of "rewarding the aggressors" was not present. Along with the legal stipulation in Article 2, paragraph 7 of the Charter he perceived a large political consensus behind the doctrine of nonintervention, although his interpretation of the principle did not receive as large a backing as it did in the UNEF operation. The Members on the whole were unwilling that ONUC become the arbiter of the politics of a sovereign state, and they were unwilling that their troops undertake tasks which could have meant extensive losses of life.

7. *Peacekeeping forces should not be composed of any permanent members of the Security Council or any states having a special interest in the conflict which the forces are trying to stabilize*

because they might act so as to further the interests of their states. This could undermine the forces' functions and increase the conflicts' threat to international peace.

Hammarskjold thought that one of the most important political prerequisites for the creation and success of UNEF and ONUC was the exclusion from the forces of troops of the Great Powers and any states which had a special interest in the crisis.[202] He realized that the inclusion of troops from such states was likely to raise strong objections from the host states and might actually threaten international peace. One of Hammarskjold's major goals in both crises was to isolate the problems from the Cold War, and he was of the opinion that the inclusion of the Great Powers could open the door to their intervention. In taking this stand he knew that he had the strong support of the Afro-Asian states, which were very concerned that the introduction of Cold War forces into their regions might embroil them in a war and compromise their independence.

When it came to the inclusion of small states of the two blocs, Hammarskjold seems to have believed that it was safer to include those from NATO than from the Warsaw Pact. In both UNEF and ONUC he accepted the offers of Canada,[203] Denmark, and Norway, but he rejected the offer of Czechoslovakia for UNEF.[204] In the case of ONUC he made a point once of saying that the United Nations had requested personnel from Poland, but they were ordinance and veterinary personnel and not fighting troops.[205] It can be concluded therefore that he viewed the small Communist states as possessing special political ambitions in the conflicts which the small Western countries did not have. He probably feared that they would use their forces for their own political purposes.

In both large peacekeeping operations of the United Nations there were very few states outside the blocs which Hammarskjold publicly judged to have such a special interest that they should be barred from the forces. In organizing UNEF he decided, with Nasser's prodding, that it would not be wise to include Pakistan since its leaders had criticized Nasser recently.[206] He probably would have accepted their offer if it had not been for Nasser's objection. One group of states which he certainly would have excluded from UNEF, although it was not necessary because they did not offer troops, were the Arab states. Their political antagonism toward Israel would have made it politically unwise for them to supervise the withdrawal of Israeli troops and to be stationed along the Israeli-Egyptian border.

In the case of ONUC he decided to include radical nationalist African countries such as Ghana, Guinea, and the U.A.R. despite the fact that he knew they had a very strong interest in the internal politics of the Congo. He concluded that it was possible to include them in the force as long as there were enough other countries on whose loyalty to the United Nations he could count. At the beginning of the operation one of Hammarskjold's reasons for delaying the pickup of Ghanaian and Guinean troops and for sending in African troops from Tunisia and Ethiopia was that he knew that he could depend on the absolute loyalty of the latter troops, whereas he was concerned about the possible political activity of the former on behalf of Prime Minister Lumumba.[207]

> 8. *The opposition of host states to the inclusion of troops from certain countries should usually determine the action of the United Nations. On the other hand, host states should not be able to insist on the inclusion of troops from certain countries, and should not be able to determine the functions of or to expel certain national forces once they have accepted them as a part of a United Nations force. These policies respectively increase the acceptability of the forces to the host states, and allow the Secretary-General to determine its composition and the specific functions of different national contingents so as best to further the purposes of the force.*

Hammarskjold summarized this guiding principle for United Nations peacekeeping forces in his UNEF Summary:

It would seem desirable to accept the formula applied in the case of UNEF, which is to the effect that, while it is for the United Nations alone to decide on the composition of military elements sent to a country, the United Nations should in deciding on composition, take fully into account the view of the host Government as one of the most serious factors which should guide the recruitment of the personnel. Usually, this is likely to mean that serious objections by the host country in the United Nations operation will determine the action of the Organization.[208]

What this principle in fact did was provide both the United Nations and the host country with a veto over the inclusion of any country. In the case of UNEF Hammarskjold refused the offer of troops from Czechoslovakia which Egypt wanted him to accept,[209] and Hammarskjold agreed to accept Egypt's veto of troops from Pakistan and Canada.[210] It should be pointed out that as a result of Hammerskjold's pressure Egypt did accept the inclusion of an extensive number of noncombat Canadian troops. In the case of ONUC the Congolese government did not object to the inclusion of any troops prior to their arrival, but once they were there, it tried to get Hammarskjold to station troops of certain nationalities in certain areas and to expel the troops of certain other nationalities from the force. During the summer of 1960 Prime Minister Lumumba wanted the Secretary-General to use only African troops in Katanga,[211] and in September 1960 General Mobutu asked the Secretary-General to remove the troops from Ghana and Guinea from the United Nations force.[212] In both cases the Secretary-General refused to accede to the demands of the Congolese leaders. By these decisions he created an addendum to the principle in the UNEF Summary to the effect that once a host country has accepted the troops of another country in a United Nations force, it cannot determine their tasks, and it cannot revoke its acceptance of them.

9. Peacekeeping forces should use force only in self-defense since they are not supposed to have enforcement functions and since the contributing states would strongly oppose the use of their troops in enforcement operations.

This principle was a necessary limitation on peacekeeping forces such as UNEF and ONUC in Hammarskjold's view since they were not created to perform an "enforcement" function under Chapter VII of the Charter. The question which arose in both of the major peacekeeping forces was: when did a situation of self-defense arise? In the case of UNEF this was never defined precisely. General Burns wanted permission for the force to fire at anyone crossing the border since he thought that this would make the force a very effective deterrent against any resumption of hostilities as both sides would be reluctant to put themselves in the position of having to fire on an international force.[213] Hammarskjold took up this question with his Advisory Committee, and its members were hesitant to have their troops assume such a responsibility without the clear and explicit approval of the governments of Egypt and Israel. Without this explicit approval they feared that UNEF would be the object of attack from the governments and the local population.[214] Some of the governments also did not like the idea that their troops might become involved in conflicts in which many of them might be killed. Hammarskjold actually sought permission from Cairo and Jerusalem to shoot at any persons crossing the armistice lines, but they could not agree either on the conditions under which the United Nations troops could shoot or the places where they could shoot.[215] In practice what the ability to fire in self-defense has meant has been that the UNEF troops could fire only when their lives were threatened.[216]

In the case of ONUC the right to use force in self-defense became a more politically sensitive and relevant principle. In that peacekeeping operation the United Nations troops were often forced to fire on soldiers who were trying to win a military victory over them. At other times they had to use force to secure freedom of movement while trying to fulfill their mandates. By interpreting self-defense as permitting ONUC to use force when impeded from carrying out its mandates, the principle of self-defense bestowed upon the United Nations troops a very broad discretion in the use of force. All three major military actions in Katanga were justified as using force in defense of ONUC's freedom of movement while it was carrying out its mandates.[217] One important restraint which prevented ONUC from interpreting its power to use force in self-defense so as to secure its freedom of movement in a very liberal fashion was the attitude of the states whose troops composed the force. Although they all supported the purpose of the United Nations operation, most of them were not willing to see many of their soldiers die for it. Hammarskjold knew that many deaths were likely to occur if ONUC assumed an enforcement function within the society or if it invoked its right to use force in self-defense too freely. In his meetings with the Congo Advisory Committee following the February 21, 1961 resolution, he told the members that as contributing states they had a special voice in the interpretation of the mandate since their troops were going to have to bear the brunt of whatever policies were chosen. In general, they were opposed to any actions which would unnecessarily endanger their troops.[218]

Chapter Five

Hammarskjold's Strategies and Tactics for Promoting Arms Control and Disarmament

Strategies

1. In order to promote arms control and disarmament agreements between the Western and Communist states, the United Nations Members and the Secretary-General should arrange meetings of important scientists from these states in order to promote understanding and intensify collaboration between them.

While this strategy cannot be considered the most important one which Hammarskjold prescribed for the United Nations in the arms control field, it was the first one which he actively promoted. It was his feeling that the mistrust between the Western and Communist nations was one of the greatest barriers to progress in controlling the arms race, and that one of the best ways to remove this mistrust was to bring together those top scientists who made policy recommendations to the political leaders of their countries. In adopting this line of thinking he was greatly influenced by the Danish physicist Niels Bohr.[1] The major occurrences which can be regarded as implementing this strategy during Hammarskjold's years at the United Nations were the two Atoms-for-Peace Conferences in Geneva in 1955 and 1958 and the creation of the International Atomic Energy Agency in 1956. In both the convening of the conferences and the formation of the new organization the Secretary-General played very active roles. Concerning the relation of these occurrences to the above strategy Hammarskjold remarked in 1958:

The Atomic Conference of 1955 was the first great break in the wall which for so long had separated scientists in various countries and slowed down the progress which would have been possible if there had been full international cooperation . . . . It created contacts which served to promote the practical application of the findings of the scientists and a better international atmosphere in this vitally important field . . . . In doing so, the first Geneva Conference paved the way also for the creation of the new Atomic Agency, which after long negotiations was set up last year in Vienna. In both respects the United Nations proved to be a valuable instrument of negotiations and bridge building.[2]

Although Hammarskjold was disappointed in the tangible results of the conferences and the International Atomic Energy Agency in terms of their becoming a backdoor to disarmament, he continued to support such technical negotiations and agreements as one possible road to arms control and disarmament agreements. In the fall of 1958 he proposed to the General Assembly that it create and support technical study groups such as the Conference of Experts to Study the Possibility of Detecting Violations of a Possible Agreement on the Suspension of Nuclear Tests and the United Nations Scientific Committee on the Effects of Atomic Radiation, whose objectives were to create consensuses on certain technical matters in the disarmament field and to improve communications between experts from the two blocs.[3] Another technical body of which he was a very active supporter was the Committee on the Peaceful Uses of Outer Space. An initial body with this title was created in 1958,[4] but the Soviet Union refused to participate because the body did not reflect the principle of parity which it conceived then as equality of representation between the Western states on one hand and the Communists and the nonaligned states on the other. Hammarskjold sought to persuade the Western states to go along with the Soviet position and not to create a body which was destined for inactivity.[5] In 1959 the Western countries finally came around to the policy which Hammarskjold had been urging when they agreed to a new Committee on the Peaceful Uses of Outer Space [6] which reflected the Soviet notion of parity. As it turned out, during Hammarskjold's tenure the committee never met, and the official conference on outer space, which was to bring together leading scientists working on space exploration, never took place because the two blocs could not agree on the chairman for the committee and on different positions at the anticipated conference. Hammarskjold tried privately to mediate between the different parties—but to no avail.[7]

> 2. *In order to promote arms control and disarmament negotiations and agreements, the Secretary-General and nonaligned states should try to arrange arms control conferences (preferably in which they are permitted representation) and should put forward proposals which might gain the acceptance of the Great Powers.*

Soon after Hammarskjold became Secretary-General in 1953, the General Assembly created a subcommittee of the Disarmament Commission which was composed of the four Great Powers, and it requested these states to try to come to some arms control and disarmament agreements.[8] All disarmament talks were conducted in this group until 1957. Hammarskjold commented very little on their proceedings and privately did not play a significant role in them. One reason for his failure to intervene was that he was quite reluctant to mediate important disputes between the superpowers unless they seriously threatened international peace or unless there was a high level of consensus on which to base a particular proposal. His lack of activity was influenced also by his ideas regarding the needed steps in the disarmament field at that stage of history (for example, increased contact between scientific personnel).

By 1958 the organizational context for arms control negotiations changed, and so did Hammarskjold's activities in this field. The United Nations Disarmament Commission, which had been the organ for all disarmament talks since 1953, collapsed because the Soviet Union refused to participate in it after the Western states had violated a tacit agreement not to seek approval of its policies from the General Assembly. After this occurrence the Soviet Union said that it would take part only in a disarmament negotiating organ in which all United Nations Members were represented or in which there was parity between Communist and Western states.[9]

During the years 1958–1960 Hammarskjold was active in trying to persuade the parties to reconvene their meetings. Throughout 1958 his activities were confined primarily to supporting the technical conferences in Geneva on the cessation of nuclear testing and the prevention of surprise attacks, but following the stagnation of these meetings in 1959 he became very active in trying to promote general arms control and disarmament negotiations. His activities during this year revolved primarily around trying to arrange for the creation of a negotiating subcommittee of the new United Nations Disarmament Commission which was created on November 4, 1958 [10] and which included all Members of the Organization. By May 1959 he observed that the Great Powers themselves were not on the verge of creating a new committee so he approached their foreign ministers at their meeting in Geneva. Soviet Foreign Minister Gromyko insisted that the composition of any new subcommittee be based on "hard parity" or on an equivalent number of NATO and Warsaw Pact countries. Hammarskjold proposed "soft parity," by which he meant the infusion of two neutralist states along with an equal number of Communist and Western states.[11] He evidently hoped that the neutralist states would serve as mediators representing the interest of the larger international community and thereby encourage Great Power agreement. Although the United States agreed to this proposal if no votes were taken, it did not push very hard for it. In fact, both the Communist and Western states were reluctant to allow the participation of any neutralist states. They preferred to deal with the problem strictly between themselves so that it would be easier to protect their national interests.[12]

In August 1959 Hammarskjold took another initiative to reactivate general disarmament negotiations. He proposed that a three-member directorate for the Disarmament Commission be appointed with a neutralist as chairman and that this body should try to arrange for the resumption of negotiations. The Great Powers again rejected this private mediatory effort by the Secretary-General.[13]

In September 1959 the Foreign Ministers of the Four Powers announced in a surprise move that they had agreed to establish a Ten-Nation Commission on the basis of parity between the two blocs.[14] No formal links were announced between this organ and the United Nations although they did say that the United Nations had primary responsibility in the area of general disarmament matters.[15] In creating this commission the Great Powers for the first time since the war placed general disarmament negotiations outside the United Nations framework. Hammarskjold was distressed by their move to evade the United Nations and the influence of the rest of the world community. Therefore, he contacted the four Great Powers and requested that they convey formally their decision to the General Assembly. Before its presentation he recommended to the Members that they give their official approval to the new commission and that they request that the Secretary-General provide conference services for the discussion. He suggested these actions because they would give the talks a formal tie to the United Nations and its Disarmament Commission and would impress upon the Great Powers their responsibility to the other Members and the legitimate interest of the Members in their proceedings.[16] On November 20, 1959 the General Assembly acknowledged the receipt of the communiqué of the four Great Powers and passed a resolution in accordance with the recommendations of the Secretary-General.[17] It should be mentioned that in Hammarskjold's private attempts to influence the Great Powers and the General Assembly he worked in close coordination with several governments which had an interest in seeing the new Ten-Nation Commission integrated into the United Nations system.

Apart from urging the Members to hold arms control talks and suggesting certain procedural formats for the discussions, Hammarskjold also tried to persuade the negotiating parties to accept certain agreements. During both the test ban talks in 1958 and 1959 and the general arms control talks in the Ten-Nation Commission from March to June 1960, he intervened on numerous occasions through private talks, written communiqués, and representations of his representatives. He also made two public statements in which he proposed certain agreements—one in the Security Council in April 1958 and another at the meeting of the Ten-Nation Commission in April 1960.

His first attempt at public mediation occurred in the Security Council on April 29, 1958. At that time he welcomed an American proposal for an Arctic inspection zone, and he recalled that earlier in the month at a press conference he had welcomed the announcement by the Soviet Union that it would cease all testing of nuclear weapons.[18] By supporting proposals of both the Soviet Union and the United States he was obviously trying to attain a position of impartiality and thus bring the influence of his impartiality to bear on the decisions of the Great Powers. In his statement he stressed that he was taking this initiative "in support of the purposes of this Organization and the principles laid down in the Charter" and because "the stalemate in the field of disarmament has been permitted to last for far too long." [19] Following this public initiative, Hammarskjold made several statements in which he elaborated on the motives for his action. In a speech he said that he hoped it would contribute to "the breakdown of the walls of distrust" among the Great Powers and would "check fatal tendencies in the direction of stale conformism and propaganda" [20] on the part of these states. Then, in a press conference he remarked:

What I said was what I felt about the sense of urgency at the present state of disarmament efforts and talks to explore to the full the positive results which may be derived from this or that initiative. An appeal for that, irrespective of the substance of the specific initiative and, of course, irrespective from where it comes, does not involve a taking of stands as to the substance. It involves in a very serious way an evaluation of the situation and an evaluation of what may come out of this or that initiative . . . .

That sense of urgency, that sense of responsibility, in the face of every new opening, was what prompted me, what made me feel that it was one of those occasions where public statements by the Secretary-General are very much a part of his duty and a very adequate supplement to private diplomacy.[21]

His attempt did not succeed. The Soviet representative, Sobolev, criticized his statement strongly,[22] and the United States representative did not show any overt enthusiasm for it. It should be noted, however, that several weeks after the sharp criticism by the Soviet representative, the Soviet government made several obvious moves which showed that its criticism did not mean that it questioned Hammarskjold's impartiality, nor that it wanted to curtail its cooperation with the Secretary-General.[23]

The second public intervention occurred on April 28, 1960 in a speech before the Ten-Nation Commission on Disarmament, when he opposed a Western proposal for the establishment of an international disarmament organization which would be independent of the United Nations.[24] While this intervention will be described in greater detail in a following tactical principle, it should be mentioned that this attempt at public mediation was a bit different from the previous one. Instead of trying to persuade the negotiating states to agree on a specific arms control agreement, he was seeking to influence the nature of any agreement which they might make in the future.

During his last several years as Secretary-General, Hammarskjold used every possible means at the United Nations' disposal to promote agreements in the arms control and disarmament field. He urged a sense of obligation on the Great Powers to respect their commitment in the Charter to seek disarmament accords. He promoted communication between experts from the two sides by urging technical negotiations both within and outside United Nations structures. He tried to persuade the Great Powers to enter into negotiations and to accept negotiating arrangements through which the other Members could make their views heard and their influence felt. He intervened privately and publicly on behalf of various formulas of agreement in order to exert whatever influence his own office and personality might have had. Some of the negotiating arrangements and substantive points of view which he proposed have been accepted since his death, so it is possible to conjecture that his views on both procedural and substantive matters have had some influence on the evolution of the disarmament issue.[25]

Tactics

DISARMAMENT NEGOTIATING BODIES

> *1. All arms control and disarmament negotiations should be organized under United Nations auspices, and some nonaligned states should be included in the negotiating bodies since such arrangements will allow these states to make their views heard on a*

*matter which affects their security and to put pressure on
the Western and Communist states to sign agreements.*

Hammarskjold's philosophy on the importance of organizing
disarmament negotiations within the United Nations framework
was set forth following the decision of the Great Powers in September 1959 to create a Ten-Nation Commission for disarmanent
talks outside the United Nations. This was the first time since the
war that general disarmament negotiations had been set up outside
the United Nations. The Great Powers did state that the United
Nations had primary responsibility for disarmament,[26] but this was
more of a token gesture to the Organization and the majority of its
membership than a serious statement that they intended to involve
these parties in the negotiations. As has been previously mentioned,
Hammarskjold finally managed to obtain some recognition of the
Western and Communist states' responsibility to the United Nations
and its membership by getting the Great Powers to convey their intentions to the General Assembly, having the Assembly give their
official blessings to the talks, and having the United Nations provide
the conference services in Geneva. In a review of the fouteenth session of the General Assembly later in 1959 Hammarskjold noted
that "the full endorsement by the other seventy-two of the step
taken by the ten" was just as important as the formation of the commission by the ten.[27] In making this statement he was implicitly in-
forming the Great Powers that their decisions were subject to review by all Member States since such accords affected the interests
of the less powerful states in the world and since disarmament questions fell within the legal purview of the Organization. Because the
United Nations was providing the conference services for the Ten-
Nation talks at its Palais des Nations in Geneva, Hammarskjold took
the liberty of making a statement to them on the above points at
their first meeting on March 15, 1960. He reminded them:

In creating this new forum as 'a useful means of exploring through
mutual consultations avenues of possible progress,' the four powers explicitly recognized that 'ultimate responsibility for disarmament measures
rests with the United Nations' and expressed the hope that 'the results
achieved in these deliberations would provide a useful basis for consideration of disarmament in the United Nations.[28]

Promoting Arms Control

In his 1961 Introduction Hammarskjold reflected on the United Nations' relationship to past disarmament negotiations and expressed both a realistic acceptance of the special role of the Great Powers and a dissatisfaction with the extent of their domination of the negotiations. He wrote in that document:

in recent years these efforts of the Organization have been running parallel to other efforts which are either outside of it or only loosely tied to the work of the United Nations. This may be justified on the basis that a very limited number of countries hold key positions in the field of armaments, so that any effort on a universal basis and by voting, to reach a decision having practical force, would be ineffective, unless founded on a basic agreement between those few parties most concerned. Therefore, direct negotiations between those countries are an essential first step to the solution, through the United Nations, of the disarmament problem, and do not in any way derogate from the responsibilities or rights of the Organization.

The situation may serve as an example of a problem, which has become increasingly important in the life of the Organization: the right way in which to balance the weight of big Powers and their security interests against the rights of the majority of member nations. Such a majority naturally cannot expect the big Powers, in questions of vital concern to them, with their superior military and economic strength, automatically to accept a majority verdict. On the other hand, the big Powers cannot, as members of the world community, and with their dependence on all other nations, set themselves above, or disregard the views of, the majority of nations.[29]

He went on to note that both the Charter provisions regarding the Security Council and the General Assembly and past forums for disarmament negotiations reflected the special position of the Great Powers. He then remarked that "no fully satisfactory or definite formula has been found."[30] He did not offer any specific formulas of his own, but from this statement and his past positions one can presume that he wanted to have some states which did not belong to either bloc in the negotiating body and to have this organ more closely integrated into the United Nations structure.

This previous discussion leads into the second part of this tactical principle—namely, that the disarmament negotiating bodies should contain a number of nonaligned nations along with the Western and Communist states. Hammarskjold believed that, as with the establishment of negotiations within the United Nations, the inclusion of nonaligned states allowed the great majority of United Nations Members to express their views on matters that affected them and to mediate between the disputing Western and Communist nations. During the talks on the establishment of a negotiating body prior to September 1959 he urged the acceptance of the principle of "soft parity," which he defined as an equal number of Western and Communist states and two nonaligned nations. Even after the establishment of the Ten-Nation Commission he privately expressed the view that states from outside the two power blocs be included, but he was not optimistic about the possibility.[31] It is interesting that within three months after Hammarskjold's death a new disarmament negotiating committee was established where for the first time the nonaligned states were represented and where their representation was equal to that of each of the Cold War blocs.[32]

MEDIATION BY THE SECRETARY-GENERAL

1. In seeking to promote arms control and disarmament agreements, the Secretary-General should make a public proposal when he perceives that his views might have a crucial influence, that an agreement might have important influence on the maintenance of peace, and that his statement will be viewed as impartial by the parties concerned.

This tactical principle can be considered as an extension of the principle presented in Chapter III, which deals with the advisability of attempts at public mediation by the Secretary-General.[33] Hammarskjold's reasons for abstaining from public pronouncements in most situations will not be repeated here since they can be found in the discussion of that principle; instead, this section will concentrate on why he felt that he could intervene in the two disarmament discussions in which he made public judgments of national positions.

His first public intervention occurred on April 29, 1958, when he welcomed the American proposal for an Arctic inspection zone and recalled that several weeks beforehand he had welcomed the

Soviet announcement of the cessation of nuclear tests.[34] While he undoubtedly knew that in taking these positions he was risking being attacked by the governments of the superpowers, he evidently felt that the risk was not too great and that what risk existed was worth it. He probably thought that his impartiality would not be impugned because he was supporting one proposal of each party and that the minor risk which existed was worth the possibility of obtaining some initial agreement in the long stalemated area of arms control negotiations. In the end his intervention did not bear fruit, and he was attacked by the Soviet representative as "praising an American propaganda manoeuver." [35] At the same time it is important to note that the Soviet Union soon made clear that it had not taken undue offense by the intervention and that it still wished to cooperate closely with the Secretary-General.[36]

The other attempt by the Secretary-General to influence the disarmament dialogue occurred in April 1960 when he opposed the Western proposal for an international disarmament organization outside the framework of the United Nations.[37] In this case it is possible to surmise that he did not view the likelihood of attacks on his impartiality and discretion as very great because there was not a popular expectation that such an organization would be created in the near future and because he was defending the position of the Organization of which he was executive officer. While he regarded the issue at stake as an important one in the long-term development of the Organization, it was not the type of question where states would be likely to take offense if their viewpoint was criticized. In fact, the whole nature of the question was such that the intervention was probably viewed more as an initiation of a dialogue than a criticism of policy.

A DISARMAMENT CONTROL ORGANIZATION
AND AN INTERNATIONAL POLICE FORCE

> *1. If future arms control and disarmament agreements require inspection and policing, the United Nations Members and the Secretary-General should promote the creation of a disarmament control organization and an international police force under the authority of the United Nations in order to obtain the most effective international security system and in order*

*to secure a voice for non-Great Powers on matters which would
strongly effect their security.*

Hammarskjold's ideas regarding the relationship of a disarmament organization and an international police force to the United
Nations were set forth very clearly following the proposal by the
Western states in March 1960 for the creation of an International
Disarmament Organization (IDO) and an international police force
independent of the United Nations.[38] There were a number of reasons why he opposed the Western plan and why he thought that an
IDO should be under the authority of the United Nations, and more
specifically the Security Council. First, an independent IDO and the
United Nations would conflict with each other since their functions
would be closely interrelated, if not overlapping. Second, a disarmament organization would basically have to mirror the United Nations in its membership, and therefore no advantages would be
gained by creating a new organization. Third, the Members had bestowed upon the Organization the legal authority over the function
of international enforcement, and this function was recognized as a
part of any disarmament program.

Hammarskjold believed that an independent IDO and the
United Nations would conflict with and undermine each other because the Organization's functions in the peaceful settlement and
enforcement fields could not be separated from the functions of
arms control and disarmament. He spoke of this matter in a speech
before the Ten-Nation Commission on Disarmament on April 28,
1960, when he said:

disarmament, pacific settlement of disputes and action in view of
breaches of the peace . . . are inseparable and integrated elements of the
policies of Member Governments within the framework of and through
the United Nations. Just as efforts towards preservation of peace through
negotiation and similar means and through action, if necessary, in face of
a breach of the peace need the support of action in the field of disarmament, so disarmament must be integrated with effective machinery in the
other two respects.[39]

In other words, he thought that the United Nations and such an independent disarmament control organization would tend to undermine each other if they did not have a common source of political

direction. An individual who discussed these matters with Hammarskjold remarked that the Secretary-General also was disturbed at the
large budget which was envisaged for the independent IDO. He felt
that such a well-financed disarmament institution would deflect attention from the United Nations as a peace and security organ and
would thus tend to initiate a process of atrophy within the Organization.

Hammarskjold did not oppose the idea that a separate organ
should be set up to administer a disarmament agreement, but he
thought that ultimate political control of it should rest with the
Security Council. In a press conference on April 8, 1960, he said:

I believe that it is necessary to see to it that such an organ, although administratively autonomous, is tied in with the United Nations in such a
way as to provide for integration—I mean real integration—of disarmament policies in the broader sense of the word, one end being these practical arrangements which might be the responsibility of a special organ,
the other end, of course being, finally what is the responsibility of the
Security Council . . . . I believe that we must find a form which in fact
makes the organ an organ of the United Nations, because all experience
up to date seems to indicate that it is extremely difficult indeed to get the
proper kind of policy integration when an organ is independent not only
administratively, but also politically.[40]

Throughout Hammarskjold's tenure he had been bothered by the
problem of coordination between the United Nations and the Specialized Agencies, and he thought that once a disarmament control
organization was given a similar or greater degree of independence
from the United Nations, it would be very difficult to coordinate its
work with that of the United Nations in the peace and security
field. He was therefore concerned at that very early stage on the
long road to disarmament that an IDO should be integrated within
the United Nations framework.

Another reason that Hammarskjold favored the IDO's integration into the United Nations was that he believed that the voting
rules for its governing organ would have to mirror those of the
Security Council of the United Nations. In his estimation no Great
Power would agree to a political organ in which it did not have a
veto over important policy questions. Some of the Great Powers
argued with Hammarskjold that their plan would allow the IDO to

escape the veto in the Security Council, but Hammarskjold retorted that they would never create the organ of ultimate authority without a veto for themselves.[41] In his speech to the Ten-Nation Commission he said:

The United Nations, like other international organizations, of course reflects only the political realities of the moment. Important though organizational arrangements are, they are subordinated in the sense that they do not change realities; what at a given time politically is attainable on one organizational basis is equally attainable on another one. Essential difficulties encountered with the United Nations are based on realities and not on the specific constitution of the Organization.[42]

He told the Great Powers in private discussions that the actual administrative organization which policed the agreements could be given a different voting formula from that in the Security Council, but that major decisions should rest with the Security Council. He also noted that at any time they were prepared to forego their veto over major political decisions in the disarmament field, they would also be ready to change the rules for the Security Council.[43]

Hammarskjold also objected to several other justifications by the Great Powers for the establishment of the IDO outside the United Nations. One put forth by the West was that it would allow the entry of Communist China into a future disarmament agreement without its having to be a Member of the United Nations. Hammarskjold replied that Communist China would never enter into such an agreement if the West did not first allow it to become a Member of the United Nations.[44] Another justification was that it would permit the Great Powers to avoid the influence of the small states in the United Nations. To that argument Hammarskjold said that any long-run disarmament program had to include non-Great Powers and that they would surely not accept any voting arrangement in an IDO which was less favorable than the one which they have in the United Nations.[45]

Hammarskjold also believed that an IDO should be under the authority of the United Nations because most plans for it envisaged some enforcement functions and because the Members had given the Organization the legal responsibility for international enforcement measures. In a press conference on May 5, 1960, he stated that the creation of an international police force apart from the United Nations would be "by-passing" legal obligations in the Charter. He went on to comment:

We have eighty-two Member nations, which are all, as Member nations, signatories to the Charter. All of them have accepted the obligations under Chapter VII. For that reason, if and when the parties to disarmament were to reach the conclusion that there is a need for some kind of international policing, it should, in my view, first of all, call for the reconsideration of Chapter VII, in the first instance of course in order to give effect to Chapter VII. If there is considered to be any snag in Chapter VII which makes it impossible to reach implementation, one should of course study whatever revisions of Chapter VII might meet the new situation.[46]

Although Hammarskjold probably did not expect that an international force to police a disarmament agreement would be created for some time, he was concerned with putting future discussions about it on what he considered to be the right track. He explained that the Members had a legal obligation to place the IDO under the authority of the United Nations, and he argued that such an arrangement would be the most politically effective one in the long run. It is possible that Hammarskjold's intervention in the spring of 1960 did have some effect on the thinking of the Great Powers because on September 20, 1961—just three days after the Secretary-General's death—the United States and the Soviet Union signed an agreement concerning principles for disarmament negotiations in which they stated that "an international disarmament organization including all parties to the agreement should be created within the framework of the United Nations." [47]

Chapter Six

Hammarskjold's Strategies and Tactics for Building a More Peaceful World Order

Political Equality and Equal Economic Opportunity

Of the five objectives which Hammarskjold said that the United Nations should pursue in order to secure international peace, the relevance of three of them to the maintainance of peace—namely, the peaceful settlement of disputes, the control of the use of force, and the rule of law—is quite obvious. In the case of the other two—political equality and equal economic opportunity—the connection is not immediately obvious. For this reason Hammarskjold's philosophy on their relevance to international peace will be described before an elucidation of the strategic and tactical principles which he formulated in order to promote them. The import of the two objectives is being presented in a single discussion since Hammarskjold often linked and intermingled his perceptions on the importance of political and economic equality in the modern world.

Hammarskjold viewed the historical movement toward political and economic equality both within and among nations as one of the dominant political movements in the modern world, and he feared that unless this movement was both furthered and directed through orderly channels, it could result in serious international violence. His fears were based upon his own perception of the effects which this movement has had in recent history both within and between nations. In the context of a speech during his first year in office he attributed "the dictatorships of the few—and the dictatorships of the masses—the devastating wars and the great revolutions that have characterized our generation" [1] as being due primarily to failures to guide and control the progress of these movements. In taking this position he was voicing the opinion that violence is the result of the frustration of peoples who are denied equality, and dictatorships are the product of societies which are set on rapidly achieving equality —either within their own borders or within the world, or within both contexts. He elaborated on these points in his first report to the United Nations Members in 1953 when he wrote:

International equality and justice are prerequisites of the domestic social development of all the people of the world and, together, they are the decisive factors if we are to build a world of peace and freedom. No system of collective security can be built with sufficient strength unless the underlying pressures are reduced—and those pressures can be mastered only to the extent that we succeed in meeting the demands for international justice and internal social justice.

He continued:

An analogy with the life of a nation may serve as an illustration. No police force can be of sufficient strength to maintain internal security, at least without excessive costs, both financial and social, unless the government meets its basic responsibility to guide the economic and social development of the nation.[2]

He stressed again in 1956 this point regarding the potential for violence resulting from economic disparities when he said:

Whatever may be our political philosophy we all recognize that it is impossible within any nation today to defend for long an inequality of economic conditions which the majority of people believe to be unjust. What is a cause for unrest within a nation may become just as much a cause of unrest and instability in the international community.[3]

It was Hammarskjold's understanding that the United Nations and the League of Nations before it were the products of men who "surmised at least the basic trends of the twentieth century at its inception and sought in the international field to channel them within a peaceful framework of law and orderly development." [4] He felt that both organizations were "first steps towards the establishment of an international democracy of peoples" [5] and that a major purpose of both was to direct and control the movements toward political and economic equality on a world-wide basis so as to minimize physical violence. In terms of present-day international politics the specific problem which he felt faced the United Nations was the gap in political power and economic standards between the developed Western states and underdeveloped countries in Asia, Africa, and Latin America, and he noted that the Organization's activities to ameliorate these inequalities "should be recognized as contributions to world peace which are just as basic as its efforts in the field of collective security." [6]

Strategies

1. In order to promote both political equality and equal economic opportunity, the United Nations Members and the Secretary-General should seek to increase the amount of technical and economic assistance being channeled through the United Nations since such a multilateral aid program both reduces economic differences between nations and avoids the political pressures inherent in bilateral programs.

The reasons why Hammarskjold favored increased United Nations economic assistance in order to further equal economic opportunity in the world are quite obvious; what is not so immediately obvious is why he viewed such multilateral assistance as a means of promoting political equality. His basic reasoning on this latter point was that multilateral aid through organizations such as the United Nations avoided the possibility that aid would be used as a tool of political pressure or that national aid programs would impose an inferior-superior relationship between the receiver and the granter of the aid. He perceived that in the past bilateral aid programs had often been used by the developed states to pressure less-developed states into adopting certain policies and that they had almost always imposed a feeling of dependency on the weaker states, and he thought both such pressure and dependency were inimical to the ideal of political equality among nations. In 1955 in Oslo he spoke about this question:

In the case of a Great Power . . . it is difficult to avoid giving a political overtone to its technical assistance, even though all such conditions may be expressly waived. The beneficiary tends to feel his economic dependence as a political liability. Political considerations apart, the fact remains that the beneficiary country—often a newcomer on the world scene—feels the burden of maintaining relations of indebtedness and gratitude to another country.

If aid is channeled from the giver country to the beneficiary country through the United Nations or one of the specialized agencies within the United Nations framework, a political accent is avoided and psychological pressure is eased in other ways at the same time. It is not my contention that the multilateral form should supplant the bilateral one. Both are needed. What I want to stress is that bilateral forms are insufficient and face difficulties which make it urgent to pursue the multilateral course further and fully utilize its potentialities.[7]

Although Hammarskjold once admitted that "aid through the United Nations will always be only a fraction of aid received from big Powers," he noted that "from the point of view of what I call moral support it may be used in such a way as to carry greater weight." [8] By this statement he evidently meant that since the new states had a governing voice in administering United Nations aid and since there were no political strings attached to it, it gave them a sense of independence and dignity which helped them resist pressures from the Great Powers, and which hence improved their status as equal members of the international community.

Although Hammarskjold in 1960, in the above-quoted statement, noted that "aid through the United Nations to countries will always be only a fraction of aid received from big Powers," his 1961 Introduction intimates that he aspired to have this fraction increased considerably. He wrote:

While receiving countries should have full freedom to take assistance from whatever source they find appropriate, they should not be barred, if they so wish, from getting all the assistance they need through United Nations channels or under United Nations aegis.[9]

He then went on to relate the question of bilateral vs. multilateral aid to the question as to whether the Members wanted the Organization to be a "static conference machinery" or a "dynamic instrument of government." On this matter he wrote:

With the conference approach to the work of the Organization a choice is made also in favor of bilateral assistance, while the alternative approach opens the door to a development under which international

assistance, in implementation of the principle of equal economic opportunities for all, would be channelled through the Organization or its
related agencies to all the extent that this is desired by the recipient
countries and is within the capacity of the Organization.[10]

Hammarskjold hoped for an increasing expansion of the program
and thought that such an expansion was a part of the natural evolution of the Organization. His statement that the less-developed states
should be able to obtain all of the aid they wanted through multilateral channels was both an evaluation that these states would prefer the more egalitarian status that this form of aid would afford
them in international politics and a request to the developed states
that they use the Organization in a more dynamic fashion in the
economic field.

During Hammarskjold's term as Secretary-General from 1953–
1961 the United Nations' aid program increased from $30.6 million to
$93.9 million,[11] and several new forms and programs of aid were
initiated. The dominant forms of United Nations aid were technical
assistance, surveys of resources, and economic evaluations of development projects. The latter two forms of aid increased a great deal
during Hammarskjold's tenure as a result of the creation of the
United Nations Special Fund in 1958. This fund was created specifically for the purpose of making preinvestment surveys. Hammarskjold was pleased when he was able to recruit Paul Hoffman, the
former head of the United States Marshall Plan, to be the director
of the Special Fund. Not only was Hoffman a very capable man, but
he also lent a prestige to the United Nations' economic aid program
which was a prerequisite for its increasing use by the Members.[12]
One new aid program originated by Hammarskjold himself was the
experimental program for the provision of operational and executive
personnel (OPEX). Under it skilled personnel were recruited from
the developed countries to serve in governmental positions in the
new states. By the end of 1961 ninety men had been placed in positions through the OPEX program.[13] Apart from this formal program the United Nations also helped governments of less-developed
states locate experts for particular technical jobs on an informal basis.

During Hammarskjold's tenure the United Nations never engaged in the field of capital investment, although he suggested the

217

creation of a Special United Nations Fund for Economic Development (SUNFED) from 1956 on.[14] In 1960 he suggested that the Members give the United Nations the resources to undertake such investment activities without setting up a separate organization like SUNFED.[15] Since there was major opposition from many of the developed states to a separate United Nations development program with a sizeable budget, he hoped that he might be able to introduce the Organization into such activities by having either the Expanded Technical Assistance Program or the Special Fund initiate small programs in this field; but the determination of the wealthier states not to lose the political influence which their bilateral programs provided prevented even this minor step. Since Hammarskjold perceived that this opposition could not be overcome, he strove to improve the standards of the existing programs to such a level that the developed states might view it as a desirable and efficient channel of aid in the future when their political calculations might undergo some modifications.

> *2. In order to promote equal economic opportunity, the United Nations Members and the Secretariat should strive to make the Organization a center for the sharing and dispersal of information pertinent to the problem of economic development and for the coordination of national aid programs to certain countries or regions.*

Hammarskjold perceived a number of opportunities for the United Nations to assist in improving the rate of economic development in the less-developed countries apart from the actual dispersal of technical assistance or economic aid. One major opportunity was for the elucidation of the lessons of past economic development. During his years at the United Nations Hammarskjold observed countries making the same mistakes in their economic development which others had made in the past and which could have been eliminated if the past experience of others had been brought to their attention. He also thought that insufficient attention had been given to studying the novel problems of economic development for the less-developed states and that increased work in this field was urgently needed. In both analyzing past economic policies and prescribing future policies, Hammarskjold felt that the Secretariat could play a very active role through the issuance of reports. He desired that the Secretariat become a center of intellectual innovation in the area of economic development and international trade,[16] and he proposed that the Members use it as "a clearing house" for the thought and experience of governments in these fields.[17] More specifically, he called for it to undertake "the formulation of operationally meaningful goals for economic growth" and "the definition of priorities for the proper phasing of policies of countries at various stages of development and under different social systems." [18] Although the Secretariat could only recommend certain courses of action and bring before the Members the experience of other nations with problems which they were facing, he thought that these functions could have a significant influence. He noted that they could "have a direct practical impact by shortening the process of trial and error and [could] help to create a body of collective knowledge and wisdom on problems of development and administration." [19] He felt that the secretariats of the regional economic commissions could also play an active part in providing governments with data and analyses of problems which were relevant to their own development,[20] but he was of the opinion that the center of analysis and policy research should be at United Nations headquarters in New York.[21]

Apart from the issuance of reports, Hammarskjold also felt that the Secretariat could expedite the development process by assisting the developed states in coordinating their aid programs to the less-developed countries. In his view this would maximize the value of the aid by coordinating the aid projects and avoiding duplication or conflict among individual projects. Regarding this "clearing house" function, he wrote:

the need will be increasingly felt for more systematic information on aid activities if the waste or misdirection which may result from many unrelated initiatives are to be avoided and if opportunities for investment are to be at all times known to potential aid-giving governments. . . . Possibilities for this kind of action are inherent in the structure of the United Nations.[22]

He noted that this function could be performed often by the United Nations' regional economic commissions since countries in different regions usually have similar problems. Along with a general coordination of aid programs, Hammarskjold proposed that the Members might also delegate the actual administration of a particular national or regional aid project to the United Nations personnel. This would allow both joint financing and efficient cooperation, and he pointed to the cooperation which took place between the Secretariat and a number of governments in planning the development of the Lower Mekong basin as an example of what could be accomplished.[23]

> *3. In order to promote political equality, the United Nations Members should seek to utilize United Nations organs for the settlement of international problems as much as possible because such procedures allow the less powerful states greater influence over international events than do traditional procedures.*

One of the major strategies which Hammarskjold prescribed for the promotion of greater equality among states in the world was the increased use of the United Nations where the smaller and less-developed countries were represented in the decisionmaking bodies. In his opinion this held true for the Security Council, where the less-developed states were in a minority, as well as in the General Assembly, where they held a majority of the votes. In his 1955 Introduction Hammarskjold remarked that the need to reconcile the drive for equality on the part of the non-Western states was one of the two reasons why the Members should seek to use the Organization as much as possible in solving their problems. Regarding this question he wrote:

We are still in the early stages of this development, but its direction, in one respect at least, is clear enough. The people of Asia today, of Africa tomorrow, are moving towards a new relationship with what history calls the West. The world organization is the place where this emerging relationship in world affairs can most creatively be forged.[24]

Hammarskjold's thinking regarding the role of the Organization in providing small and less-developed states with a greater voice in international decisionmaking was revealed most clearly during the Congo crisis, and especially following Premier Khrushchev's "troika" proposal and his attack on the Secretary-General. The main strategy which Hammarskjold used at that time to rally the majority of Members to the cause of the Congo operation and the cause of an effective United Nations executive was to point out that the Organization and its executive afforded them the greatest opportunity to influence international politics. On this point he wrote in his 1960 Introduction:

The United Nations has increasingly become the main platform—and the main protector of the interests—of those many nations who feel themselves strong as members of the international family but who are weak in isolation. . . . They look to the Organization as an agent for the principles which give them strength in an international concert in which other voices can mobilize all the weight of armed force, wealth, an historical role and that influence which is the other side of a special responsibility for peace and security.[25]

In October 1960, following the attack of Premier Khrushchev on the Secretary-General and the United Nations Operation in the Congo, Hammarskjold made even more explicit his judgment of the importance of the Organization to the drive of the developing nations to protect their independence and to lift themselves to positions of equality with the developed states. He then remarked: "It is not the Soviet Union, or, indeed, any other big Powers who need the United Nations for their protection; it is all the others. In this sense the Organization is first of all *their* Organization. . . ."[26] Hammarskjold regarded some Western states which wanted to reduce the role and the influence of the United Nations in international politics as reactionary in their desire to undermine the movement toward more political equality among world states. He was of the opinion that such policies were likely to bring about cataclysms similar to those of the past which resulted from efforts to thwart the egalitarian currents in the world. He appears to have felt that the greater the amount of international decision-making that took place within the United Nations organs, the less likely were the chances that antagonisms and eventual hostilities would occur between the historic West and the new nations of Africa and Asia. In this movement toward greater international democracy Hammarskjold realized that there would be some resistance from the established powers. At the same time he apparently thought that a growing realization on the part of the developed states that this movement toward greater political equality among nations was inevitable and that their future security and economic well-being depended on their gradual acceptance of it would lead to their acceptance of a larger role for the United Nations.

> 4. *In order to promote political equality, the United Nations Members should retain the existing one-nation one-vote formula in the General Assembly and the unitary executive in the Secretariat. They permit the less powerful states respectively to obtain greater influence and more equal status in United Nations councils and to influence the creation and direction of military and nonmilitary operations in international politics.*

Throughout his tenure as Secretary-General, Hammarskjold supported the voting arrangement in the General Assembly and opposed any attempts by certain parties in the West to have the Organization adopt a system of weighted voting. In his view this arrangement was a foundation of the Organization's policy to realize the political equality of all nations in the world and was somewhat comparable to the adoption of the one-man one-vote formula in the attempts of nation-states to establish democracy within their own jurisdictions. On this matter he wrote that the United Nations

tries to find forms in which the ancient nations which are now gaining or have gained their freedom, may find their new place without frictions. It accords them all an equal voice in the councils, independent of race, history and physical or economic power. The latter respect is one in which, in particular, one encounters a skepticism similar in nature to that which once formed an obstacle to universal suffrage. One may be conscious of the hazards of such an experiment and yet be convinced that it is necessary and has to be carried out.[27]

In supporting the present voting arrangement, Hammarskjold also disagreed with those individuals who thought that the new states—especially the Afro-Asian states—were irresponsible in their judgment of international problems. In a press conference in April 1959 he noted:

I do not believe that the small nations have less of an understanding of central political problems of concern to the whole world than those who are more closely related to them and who traditionally wield greater power in the international councils. For that reason, I cannot . . . share the view of those who regard the possible influence of smaller powers as a danger—I would add, in any context.[28]

It can be assumed that Hammarskjold knew that most of the developed states were not ready to bestow any significant authority on any body in which the developing countries had a ruling voice, but he probably surmised that the one-nation one-vote provision would be accepted by the developed states as long as the General Assembly could only pass recommendations.

Another structural aspect of the United Nations which Hammarskjold felt supported the Organization's promotion of political equality was the unitary executive in the Secretariat. This position was based on the judgments that the Organization would only be able to initiate executive actions which directly influenced situations if there were a single decisionmaker at the head of such operations, and that it was largely through such operations as the United Nations Force in the Congo that the weaker states could directly influence international problems. In Hammarskjold's opinion, greater influence for these states brought greater equality in that it gave them increased status and the ability to protect their independence. He voiced these opinions in his last written report to the Members when he wrote: "A weak or non-existent executive would mean that the United Nations would no longer be able to serve as an effective instrument for active protection of the interests of those many Members who need such protection." [29]

5. In order to promote political equality, the United Nations Members and the Secretariat should seek to prevent the use of force, except when it is employed in the common interest, because the less powerful states will seldom be able to influence the outcomes of disputes when force becomes the arbiter.

The interdependence of the major objectives which Hammarskjold prescribed for the United Nations is illustrated very well by this principle. In his 1961 Introduction, where he set forth the five objectives or principles which the Organization should seek to realize, he remarked:

Obviously, the Charter cannot, on the one side, establish a rule of law and the principle of equal rights for 'nations large and small,' and, on the other hand, permit the use of armed force for national ends, contrary to those principles and, therefore, not 'in the common interest.' Were nations, under the Charter, to be allowed, by the use of their military strength, to achieve ends contrary to the principle of the equality of Members and the principle of justice, it would obviously deprive those very principles of all substance and significance.[30]

The logic behind this linking of these objectives of equality and the prohibition of the use of force is that when the use of force is allowed, it is impossible for smaller states to achieve significant equality with (or independence from) larger states. It is only with the shift of decisionmaking from the battlefield to the parliamentary assembly and the conference table that the smaller and less powerful states can gain a significant voice in international politics and hence some kind of real equality with their larger and wealthier brethren.

> *6. In order to promote political equality, the United Nations Members and the Secretariat should further self-determination and independence for all peoples because political control of one people by another is by definition the antithesis of political equality.*

Throughout Hammarskjold's tenure the process of decolonization in Africa and Asia took place at a very rapid pace,[31] and he strongly supported the process and the United Nations' promotion of it since it was realizing the principle of the political equality of peoples throughout the world.[32] While he did not believe that the Organization was a major force in and of itself in the decolonization process, nevertheless he held that it was "inevitably a focal point" [33] for international efforts to influence the march of former colonies to independence. His reason for holding this opinion was probably that the United Nations was the one organization where both African and Asian states and European colonial powers were represented. He also believed that there was much to be gained by having negotiations regarding decolonization conducted in the United Nations both because the goals for the talks were established by the Charter and because the Organization offered formal and informal procedures of settlement to the parties. As he remarked in his 1956 Introduction:

I believe that such negotiations gain by being conducted against the background of the purposes and principles of the Charter and that the results can usefully be brought within the framework of the United Nations. If the negotiations prove unsuccessful, they should then be followed up on the basis laid down and in the forms prescribed by the Charter.[34]

Among the means that the Organization used to promote self-determination of dependent territories, Hammarskjold had a special respect for the United Nations trusteeship system. He believed that such an international arrangement, which encouraged the establishment of terminal dates for the dependent status of colonial territories and which gave the dependent people a forum for airing their grievances, avoided a great deal of the conflict between administering countries and nationalist movements which usually occurred during the decolonization process in nontrusteeship territories. He also was of the belief that the obligation of the administering trusteeship powers to account for their policies to the United Nations often led them to pursue more progressive policies.[35]

The Rule of Law

STRATEGIES

1. In order to promote the rule of law, the United Nations representative organs and the Secretary-General should base their policy positions on legal accords whenever it is possible.

In his first formal report to the United Nations in 1953, Hammarskjold wrote: "No organized international development can take place unless it is founded on a respect for international law and an acceptance of the obligations which that law imposes."[36] During his tenure Hammarskjold sought on many occasions to support a respect for the law by urging parties to settle their differences along the lines of established legal rules or norms and by urging the representative organs to base their proposals on such legal strictures. Some examples of his reliance on international legal agreements, which have already been cited in this study, were his positions on the Arab-Israeli conflict, where he supported on numerous occasions the General Armistice Agreements, and the Laotian crisis, where he upheld the Geneva Agreements of 1954. Another example was his support of Israeli "free passage" through the Straits of Tiran on the basis of the general international law of the sea. His purpose in supporting such legal norms was not only a desire to obtain compliance with some specific legal agreements or rules but also to strengthen the habit of compliance with the law and states' perception of the value of international law in regulating international relations. He was quite cognizant of the fact that the international legal system was not a well developed one, and he realized that the movement toward a more developed legal system must be made by small steps on many fronts.[37]

> 2. *In order to promote the rule of law, the United Nations Members and the Secretary-General should use the Organization as a framework to discuss the possibilities of establishing new international legal norms and to conclude new accords.*

Throughout his tenure Hammarskjold urged the Members to use the United Nations as a framework for negotiating and creating new international legal agreements. On the Organization's role in contributing to the creation of law which did not directly bear on the powers of the United Nations (for example, the law of the sea), he wrote in 1955:

The systematic examination within the United Nations of the practice of States can bring to light areas of agreement and divergence in the law and stimulate efforts to seek a reconciliation of opposing views. To some extent this process is taking place through the work of the International Law Commission and through the adoption of conventions by the Economic and Social Council and the General Assembly.[38]

Several of the most notable attempts on the part of the Organization to undertake such work were the the 1958 and 1960 conferences on the law of the sea which had their initial stimulus in the International Law Commission and the formation of a committee of the General Assembly to arrange for a conference on the law of outer space. Hammarskjold was especially active in promoting the conference on outer space and in trying to obtain an agreement banning military weapons from outer space. He also hoped during his tenure that the Economic and Social Council would become an important organ for negotiating multilateral economic agreements on matters such as the stabilization of commodity prices and the setting of tariffs, but this never materialized. One of the main reasons for this was the existence of the General Agreement on Tariffs and Trade (GATT) and the reluctance of most Western states to abandon this framework.

As Secretary-General, Hammarskjold did not try to force new legal agreements upon states, and especially upon the Great Powers. Rather, he sought to identify the growing areas of common interest which are emerging in our increasingly interdependent world and tried to persuade states to compromise their differences on these questions. As Oscar Schachter has written:

He did not attempt to set law against power. He sought rather to find within the limits of power the elements of common interest on the basis of which joint action and agreed standards could be established. In the area of advancing technologies, such as atomic energy and outer space, he pursued efforts to develop new normative arrangements based on the acknowledged factors of interdependence.[39]

While the actual accomplishments in the field were modest during his years in office, Hammarskjold foresaw that the role of the Organization in promoting such agreements was likely to be greater in the future. He thought that this role rested on the inevitable increase in international interdependence and cooperation and on the fact that the United Nations was the only universal political organization in the world. He explained his ideas on this matter to the American Bar Association in 1955 when he said:

As international cooperation increases, so necessarily will the development of the law, by which international cooperation is organized and given a stable framework. . . . I expect that the United Nations as the only permanent instrument for cooperation on a world-wide scale in dealing with major political problems will play a large part in these developments.[40]

While he thought that a growing interdependence would lead to international legal agreements, he appeared to believe that the United Nations through pressure from the Members and the Secretariat could be a spur to as well as a framework for such agreements. This was certainly true in the matter of the regulation of weapons in outer space, where both Hammarskjold and some of the Members tried to bring the United States and the Soviet Union together on the convening of a conference and on the signing of an actual agreement.

> *3. In order to promote the rule of law, the United Nations Members should gradually augment the role of the United Nations in world politics through increasing use of its organs and its means of action and through greater compliance with its decisions. Such developments represent a greater willingness to settle disputes in accord with legal procedures and greater agreement on the norms which should govern certain issues.*

Hammarskjold thought that the law with which the United Nations should concern itself most actively was the United Nations Charter itself. While the Charter constitutes existing law, he did not view its contents as static legal rules. He viewed it as "a framework within which the governments can, by trial and error, build up traditions of world community and mutual responsibility that will over a period of years gradually acquire the force of world law. . . ." [41] While Hammarskjold never actually predicted the extent to which "traditions of world community" and "world law" would develop in the future, some of his statements do reflect several aspects of his thinking on the constitutional development of the Organization. First, he believed that "the traditions of world community" at the present time are weak and that consequently it is unrealistic to expect a sudden development of "world law" or a sudden strengthening of world political and legal institutions. The extent to which he believed that the world was unready for any drastic augmentation in the United Nations' authority was reflected in a report of Andrew W. Cordier that Hammarskjold "often said that international organization as expressed in the United Nations, was more advanced in this stage of world history than the sense of world community which supported it." [42] While emphasizing this latter point, it should also be stressed that he did think that the United Nations would undergo an expansion in its political practices and its legal powers over a long period of time. Second, he believed that some small but significant developments in "world law" were occurring as a result of perceptions of interdependence and nascent sentiments of world community during our present era and that they could be recognized in the changing practices of the United Nations organs.

During his tenure Hammarskjold made a number of statements which indicated both his assessment of the very modest level of international organization which the world would support and an implicit appraisal that gradually the future would bring stronger world political institutions. While these statements are a bit lengthy, they are very pertinent to an understanding of the way in which he thought the strategy of increasing the political role of the United Nations should be pursued. In June 1955 in a speech at Stanford University he remarked:

We undoubtedly need world organization, but we are far from ripe for world government. Indeed, even modest attempts at regional "integration" have met with considerable difficulties, not because of any superstitious respect for national sovereignty, but because the people want to know in whose hands they put their fate, if they are to surrender part of their self determination as nations. . . .

Such expression of national feelings is both an asset and a liability. It is an asset to the extent that it reflects the determination to shape one's own fate and to take the responsibility for it. It is an asset as a brake on immature experiments in international integration. But it is a liability when it blinds our eyes to the necessity of that degree of international organization which has become necessary to national life. [43]

In May 1956 he said to a New York audience:

true collective security in the sense of an international police power engaged to defend the peace of the world, is to be found at the end, not at the beginning, of the effort to create and use world institutions that are effective in the service of the common interest.

The spirit and practice of world community must first gain in strength and custom by processes of growth. It is to the helping along of these processes of growth that we should devote all our ingenuity and our effort.[44]

In July 1958 he said:

It is difficult to see how a leap from today's chaotic and disjointed world to something approaching a world federation is to come about. To attain such a goal, elements of organic growth are required. We must serve our apprenticeship and at every stage try to develop forms of international coexistence as far as is possible at the moment, if we are to be justified in hoping some day to realise the more radical solutions which the situation may see fit to call for.[45]

In his last Introduction in 1961 Hammarskjold made another statement which also reflects the opinion that the United Nations will be the center for the construction of more highly developed political institutions in the future. In that report he wrote that the principles of the Charter were those generally accepted as "binding for life within States" and that as such their inclusion in the Charter constituted "a first step in the direction of an organized international community." [46]

While Hammarskjold was not very specific about future constitutional powers and institutional forms which the United Nations might attain, he did discuss in some detail the nature of the developmental processes which were taking place and which were transforming the Organization. At different times he described this development as being from "institutional systems of international coexistence" to "constitutional systems of international cooperation" [47] and from "a static conference machinery" to "a dynamic instrument of governments." [48] The bases of this evolution which Hammarskjold observed were the departure of the United Nations from a solely diplomatic conference organ to an operational organ which created different kinds of cooperative enterprises, an increasing use of United Nations organs by the Members to solve problems, and an increasing "weight" or influence of United Nations decisions on the behavior of states.[49] Although he did not say so, he probably imagined that this increasing influence of United Nations decisions would someday be given a formal legal recognition which would increase the probability that they would be respected and enforced.

It is important to point out that Hammarskjold in analyzing this evolution and in calling for its further development was not calling for states to make any sudden grants of legal authority to the United Nations. He was solely asking states to respond to international problems in a creative and cooperative manner and to use the possibilities which the United Nations offered for multilateral cooperation. As Oscar Schachter, the Director of the United Nations General Legal Division, wrote: ". . . he always was conscious that he was nurturing an organic growth, not designing an ideal pattern." [50] Hammarskjold expressed his belief that the United Nations must develop slowly and within the realistic limits of what the pattern of common and conflicting interests will allow at any single period of history when he wrote:

The dynamic forces at work in this stage of human history have made world organization necessary. The balance of these forces has also set the limits within which the power of world organization can develop at each step and beyond which progress, when the balance of forces so permits, will be possible only by processes of organic growth in the system of custom and law prevailing in the society of nations.[51]

Hammarskjold believed that the bases of this evolving body of United Nations custom and law were an increasing sense of obligation on the part of the Members to resolve their problems through the use of United Nations organs, an increasing sense of obligation to abide by United Nations decisions, and the creation of more varied and influential operations by the United Nations. In this development he thought that each organ of the United Nations could play an important role.

The one organ of the United Nations which Hammarskjold did not view as very important in the legal development of the Organization during the years that he was Secretary-General was the International Court of Justice. On several occasions he urged states to submit more disputes to it and to accept its compulsory jurisdiction,[52] but he never personally urged that a specific dispute be referred to the Court.[53] In one statement in which he did urge greater use of the Court and an acceptance of its compulsory jurisdiction, he commented on a number of reasons why such courses of action were not generally accepted by states.[54] One was the fact that international law at this stage of history is still quite fragmentary and sometimes very vague. Another reason was that states generally are not willing to submit their fate to judicial institutions because of a rather pervasive judgment in the world that more satisfactory results can be achieved through negotiations and different forms of political pressure.[55] He obviously lamented these facts, but he was realistic in his appraisal of them. He probably envisioned that the judicial organ of the United Nations would play a greater role in the future when substantive international law became more developed and when the habit of resorting to international institutions for the settlement of disputes became stronger, but he did not see a very important role for the Court in the rather underdeveloped international legal system of the period 1953–1961.

In the present world Hammarskjold looked more to the Members' cooperation within and outside the United Nations' quasi-legislative organs, the Security Council and the General Assembly, and to actions by the Secretariat as the main vehicles through which the rule of law could be furthered. His primary aspirations in both the legal and political realms during his years as Secretary-General were to persuade states to resort more often to the United Nations for the settlement of their disputes, to cooperate with any attempts which the United Nations might initiate to solve their disputes, and to abide by any of the decisions of the representative organs. He apparently felt that such voluntary use of community institutions and compliance with their decisions constituted the foundations of an evolving international legal system. He hoped that as the United Nations organs were used and their decisions complied with more often, states would feel a greater obligation to seek solutions for their disputes within their framework and to respect their decisions. He explained his thinking on the legal development of the United Nations in 1954 when he said:

We need to think of the institutions of the United Nations not as parliamentary in character but as a framework within which the governments can, by trial and error, build up traditions of world community and mutual responsibility that will over a period of years gradually acquire the force of world law built upon the only sure foundation for any law—well established and generally accepted customs and traditions.[56]

In this statement he was saying that the legal development of international institutions is not likely to be a dramatic one nor is it apt to be marked by any great leaps forward. Rather, it will come about as a result of numerous cooperative endeavors from which a habit of cooperation and a feeling of obligation will ensue. He envisioned that as this feeling of obligation and a consequent legal commitment came into being the United Nations would pass from "institutional systems of international co-existence" to "constitutional systems of international cooperation." During his own tenure in office he thought that this development in "international constitutional law" was still in its "embryonic state." [57]

During Hammarskjold's term in office he felt that this legal development was being promoted most actively by the Members through two different forms of action. One was the formation of positions on different conflicts or problems, and the other was in the initiation of different kinds of "executive actions," [58] especially in the peacekeeping field. Concerning the development of consensuses on issues he remarked that although the positions which are formulated formally by the representative organs and informally by the Members are not enforced on the parties to the disputes, it is impossible for the parties to ignore these positions which constitute "something like an independent position for the Organization. . . ." [59] He remarked further on the influence of positions which emerge from the United Nations diplomatic process:

Granted that States are far less inclined than individuals and groups to be affected by the fact that negotiations are taking place and by the way they are going; still, they are affected. Therefore, it means something essential that membership in the United Nations forces all States to subject themselves to such an influence.[60]

He continued:

The roots of this development are, of course, the existence of an opinion independent of partisan interests and dominated by the objectives indicated in the United Nations Charter. This opinion may be more or less articulated and more or less clear-cut, but the fact that it exists forms the basis for the evolution of a stand by the Organization itself, which is relatively independent of that of the parties.[61]

In his 1961 Introduction he spoke of the possibility that positions on conflicts which emerge from the General Assembly might someday be considered legally binding after a period of growing use of

United Nations organs and an increasing compliance with their decisions. Regarding such an evolution from their present legal status as recommendations, he wrote:

such a formula leaves scope for a gradual development in practice of the weight of the decisions. To the extent that more respect, in fact, is shown to General Assembly recommendations by the Member States, they may come more and more close to being recognised as decisions having a binding effect on those concerned, particularly when they involve the application of the binding principles of the Charter and of international law.[62]

He thought that all decisions of the Security Council, except those explicitly designated as recommendations, were binding on the Members, but he noted that the practice of states fell short of the intended legal weight of the Charter in respect to the resolutions of the Security Council.[63] He urged that the Members bring their practices in consonance with "the pattern established by the Charter." [64] One can surmise that he expected this to take place under the same circumstances that he envisioned a change in the weight of General Assembly decisions. These circumstances are a growing habit of states to solve their problems through United Nations organs and to abide by United Nations decisions and a growing sense of interdependence and mutual responsibility among the Members.

In his 1961 Introduction Hammarskjold also elaborated on the importance of "executive actions" in the legal development of the United Nations. He stated that debates in the United Nations during the previous year, which had revolved primarily around the Congo operation and the Soviet Union's challenges to that operation and the office of the Secretary-General, had brought forth two different concepts of the Organization. He labeled those concepts as "a static conference machinery" and "a dynamic instrument of governments." [65] He felt that the crux of their differences lay in whether the Organization should or should not embark on new and varied forms of "executive action" such as the United Nations Operation in the Congo. He wrote of the differences between the two concepts:

The first one is firmly anchored in the time-honored philosophy of the sovereign national States in armed competition of which the most that may be expected in the international field is that they achieve a peaceful co-existence. The second one envisages possibilities of inter-governmental action overriding such a philosophy, and opens the road towards more developed and increasingly effective forms of constructive international cooperation.[66]

He also remarked:

Naturally the latter concept takes as its starting point the conference concept, but it regards it only as a starting point, envisaging the possibility of continued growth to increasingly effective forms of active international cooperation, adapted to experience, and served by a Secretariat of which it is required that, whatever the background and the views of its individual members, their actions be guided solely by the principles of the Charter, the decisions of the main organs, and interests of the Organization itself.[67]

For Hammarskjold, the legal development of the Organization was dependent upon its ability to take actions in pursuit of its stated goals in a particular conflict or situation. Without this power its ability to influence a problem would be greatly diminished, and it would not be able to assume operational responsibilities which are prerequisites for effective political control over situations. A stable government has never been established upon fiat alone, but has required the power to control numerous activities within its territorial domain, especially that of the maintenance of order. Hammarskjold realized this, and he viewed operations such as UNEF and ONUC as the very beginnings of the United Nations' attempts to assume direct responsibilities for the maintenance of order between nations or within nations. He knew that the evolution of its activities in the security field would be a long one, but he hoped that the Organization would begin "to press against the wall that hides the future." [68]

Apart from the achievement of consensuses on conflicts and the creation of "executive actions," Hammarskjold believed that the Members furthered the development of the Organization through all cooperative endeavors within the multilateral diplomatic setting at the United Nations. He believed that every successful cooperative undertaking within the context of the United Nations, even on the most simple of technical matters, was another building block in the constitutional development of the Organization. As he remarked in Oslo in 1958:

Building a More Peaceful World Order

The road toward more satisfactory forms of organization for a world community of states . . . leads through a series of good or bad experiences with the specific techniques made possible by the United Nations. It goes via the conclusions we are able to draw, in action, about these experiences. In this respect, the continuous, but unsensational and therefore little-known, work on current tasks which is conducted within the United Nations is also of importance. Each conquest of new ground for diplomatic activity and international cooperation is a lasting gain for the future.[69]

Here his attitude approaches somewhat the theory of "functionalism" which was initially put forward by David Mitrany.[70] Mitrany foresaw the gradual development of a world government through the creation of many international functional (that is, economic and technical) organizations which would bring all peoples into a closely interdependent society. He believed that a world government would emerge naturally from this economically and technically interdependent society. While Hammarskjold appears to have agreed with Mitrany's thinking on the importance of functional cooperation in the constitutional development of the international organization, he thought that political and diplomatic cooperation had to develop *pari passu* with cooperation in the economic and technical fields and that political and diplomatic cooperation might actually be more important. In his University of Chicago speech of May 1960 Hammarskjold spoke of the possibility that within the present framework of international organizations states, through the practice of cooperation in different areas, would gradually feel an obligation to cooperate on certain matters and to abide by the decisions of community organs. He said that the present "institutional system for coexistence, stage by stage, may be developed and enriched until, on single points or on a broad front, it passes over into a constitutional system for cooperation." [71] He never ventured to predict the day when different facets of international life would pass over into a constitutional system of cooperation, or which facets would come first, but he believed that the feeling of obligation to act through international organizations and to abide by their decisions was developing.

> *4. In order to promote a larger role for the United Nations in world politics, and hence in order to encourage the rule of law,*

the Secretary-General should seek to become an active agent of the Members in the pursuit of peace, and the Members should support such a role and the unitary character of his office. Such policies support the development of an executive agency in the international community.

In Dag Hammarskjold's thinking about the legal development of the United Nations, the office of the Secretary-General occupied an important role. Its primary importance in this development was that it afforded the Members of the Organization an impartial agency to which they could delegate responsibilities in both the diplomatic and operational spheres. In discussing the development of the Organization and the office of the Secretary-General, Hammarskjold commented that "the main significance of the evolution of the office of the Secretary-General . . . lies in the fact that it has provided means for smooth and fast action, which might otherwise not have been possibly open to the Organization." [72] Without an organ like the Secretariat he thought that the Organization would have had a very difficult time in being anything more than a "static conference machinery" since it would not have had an agent to which it could delegate diplomatic and operational responsibilities. While all of his efforts as an agent of the representative organs and as an independent agent on behalf of the Organization were directed toward promoting peace in individual circumstances, they were also directed at furthering the legal and political growth of the Organization. Ambassador Adlai Stevenson of the United States described this contribution of Hammarskjold's to the growing influence and constitutional development of the United Nations when he said:

Hammarskjold . . . understood that the machinery not only needs lofty goals and high principles but it has to work in practice . . . .
    Understanding all this, Dag Hammarskjold—himself a key part of the machinery—helped make the machinery more workable, more adaptable, more relevant to the immediate political needs. By doing so, he helped expand the capacity of the machinery to act effectively. This, I think, was his greatest contribution to the United Nations, and thus to world peace.[73]

During his tenure in office the new kinds of operations which Hammarskjold was influential in initiating were diplomatic missions by

237

the Secretary-General at the behest of the representative organs, new kinds of independent diplomatic initiatives by his office, diplomatic missions by his personal representatives, and United Nations peacekeeping operations.

Hammarskjold attached considerable importance to having a unified executive in the office of the Secretary-General for the constitutional development of the United Nations. This was demonstrated clearly during the aftermath of Premier Khrushchev's proposal in 1960 for a three-member executive (a "troika") which was to be composed of members of the Western, Soviet, and neutralist blocs and which could act only with the unanimous consent of the three members.[74] On a number of occasions Hammarskjold stated unequivocally that such a constitutional change of the character of the Secretariat's executive would be disastrous to the future development of the United Nations operations. He once said that it would be tantamount to a "Munich of international cooperation." [75] In a speech to the United Nations Secretariat just nine days before his death he set forth his reasoning very clearly:

At stake is a basic question of principle: Is the Secretariat to develop as an international Secretariat, with the full independence contemplated in Article 100 of the Charter, or is it to be looked upon as an intergovernmental—not international—secretariat providing merely the necessary administrative services for a conference machinery? This is a basic question and the answer to it affects not only the working of the Secretariat but the whole future of international relations.

If the Secretariat is regarded as truly international, and its individual members as owing no allegiance to any national government, then the Secretariat may develop as an instrument for the preservation of peace and security of increasing significance and responsibilities. If a contrary view were to be taken, the Secretariat itself would not be available to member governments as an instrument, additional to the normal diplomatic methods, for active and growing service in the common interest.[76]

In his last Introduction on August 17, 1961, he stated dramatically what the executive structure and the international impartiality of the Secretariat meant for the constitutional development of the United Nations: ". . . the choice between conflicting views of the United Nations Secretariat is basically a choice between conflicting views on the Organization, its function and its future." [77]

Hammarskjold also believed that the Secretary-General influenced the constitutional development of the United Nations insofar as he assumed an independent influence in international politics. He thought that this occurred in two kinds of situations. The first was where the Secretary-General voluntarily voiced his views on a conflict between Members either privately or publicly and thereby influenced the resolution of the conflict, and the second was where the Security Council or the General Assembly gave the Secretary-General mandates with a certain amount of independent decision-making authority. In respect to the effect of the Secretary-General's independent initiatives, he wrote: "Step by step, he . . . builds up a practice which may open the door to a more generally recognised independent influence for the Organization as such in the political evolution." [78] On the Security Council's and the General Assembly's delegation of responsibilities to the Secretary-General, he said: ". . . the development reflects an incipient growth of possibilities for the Organization to operate in specific cases within a latitude of independence in practice given to it by its Member governments for such cases." [79] Hammarskjold was never very clear as to why such assertions of an independent influence by the Secretary-General were important in the legal development or "political evolution" of the United Nations, but his ideas on this matter can be deduced from his general train of thought on this topic. He most likely viewed such independent practices by the Secretary-General as contributing to the legal development of the Organization because they represented a greater willingness among the Members to delegate powers to institutions of the international community at the United Nations and because they strengthened the habit of the Members to resort to United Nations organs in solving their problems. He also probably viewed the Members' acceptance of such independent influence by the Secretary-General as nurturing the development of an executive authority within the United Nations and the international community. Actual delegations of responsibility to the Secretary-General are comparable to a legislature's giving authority to the executive within a state, and states' acceptance of independent diplomatic activities of the Secretary-General are equivalent to a national constitution's bestowal of independent powers upon the head of the executive branch of the government. These were very modest developments in the constitutional development of the United Nations' executive branch, but Hammarskjold viewed them as hopeful signs.

Before closing this discussion of Hammarskjold's ideas on the Secretary-General's role in the development of the United Nations, some further clarification should be made regarding his views on how an incumbent could further the development of the Organization through his assumption of independent responsibilities. It is especially important to be fairly precise about this matter because a number of students of the United Nations have criticized Hammarskjold's views on the role of the Secretary-General as an independent agent for the Organization, and others have interpreted his views in a very radical manner. One criticism of Hammarskjold's viewpoint was made by Professor Jean Siotis:

In law and practice, the manifestation of the international organization's "own will," which is distinct but not "independent" of the wills of its composing elements, is actually subordinated to the wills of the states which are expressed, tacitly or explicitly in its midst. For not having taken account of this reality, Dag Hammarskjold met a political death, before dying physically; and perhaps the second death was only the consequence of the first.[80]

Another criticism was made by Dr. Conor Cruise O'Brien, the former Irish delegate and former member of the United Nations Secretariat during the Congo crisis. Writing of Hammarskjold's approach he said:

roughly speaking the theory was this: the Secretary-General represented the general will of the international community as a whole, independent of the will of any individual member or group of members; where the other organs of the Charter, the Security Council and the General Assembly, had failed to reach agreement or, as more often happened, had reached only ambiguous agreement, the Secretary-General, and under him the Secretariat, could be, and ought to be, trusted to act in the general interest of all. In this way, and through such situations, the authority of the Secretary-General and the Secretariat were to be gradually built up in the direction, it was hoped, ultimately of a genuinely supranational authority—a world government. . . .

I do not believe however that we are helping the tendency in that direction by pretending that we have already reached a stage which we have not in fact reached: a stage where the Secretary-General and the Secretariat can be implicitly relied on as an impartial instrument in the service of the international community as a whole, influenced by no national policies.[81]

Although Joseph Lash did not criticize Hammarskjold's views on the independent influence of the Secretary-General, his interpretation of Hammarskjold's thought on this matter could be used as a basis for attacking the late Secretary-General's outlook, and for this reason should be mentioned. He wrote:

In his 1959 Copenhagen speech, he came close to enunciating a "vox populorum" concept of the Secretary-Generalship. The Secretary-General was the spokesman of the Organization "in its capacity as an independent opinion factor." There was such an "independent opinion" building up, he insisted. It reflected the reaction, judgment and evaluation of that vast majority of member nations not directly involved in a dispute for which the principles of the Charter weighed more heavily than direct or indirect partisan interests.[82]

In trying to judge the validity of these men's interpretations and to clarify what Hammarskjold meant by the Secretary-General's assuming an independent influence in international politics, it is well to recall the ways in which he thought that this influence might be exerted. They are: (1) when private or public statements by the Secretary-General have an influence on a particular conflict; and (2) when the Secretary-General is given a certain amount of discretion or independence by the Security Council or the General Assembly in the execution of a mandate. Within a discussion of each of these means of influence, both Hammarskjold's ideas on them and the previously quoted authors' perceptions of Hammarskjold's ideas will be described and compared.

Although Hammarskold's support for private and public statements by the Secretary-General as a means of solving conflicts and of building the authority of the Organization was not criticized directly in the three previous statements, Lash's interpretation of this support as reflecting a "vox populorum" concept of the office does deserve some comment. Hammarskjold did think that the Secretary-General could exert an influence on behalf of the Organization independent of its Members through private and public statements on conflicts and that the success of such exertions of influence might lead to an increasing influence for the Organization as a whole; but during his tenure as Secretary-General he viewed this ability as very limited and far from anything that one could describe as a "vox populorum." He described the limited extent to which the Secretary-General could be an "independent opinion factor" when he said that the Secretary-General "had to accept the limitation of acting mainly on inner lines without publicity," and that "in nine out of ten cases, the Secretary-General could destroy his chances of exerting an independent influence on developments by publicly appealing to opinion over the head of governments." [83] At another time earlier in his career as Secretary-General he spoke of the problem of public statements on international conflicts, and he noted that "clearly . . . a relationship of mutual confidence and trust would be impossible in an atmosphere of publicity. . . . He [the Secretary-General] should not permit himself to become a cause of conflict unless the obligations of his office under the Charter and as international civil servant leave him no alternative." [84] Hammarskjold's practice followed this pattern very closely too. Aside from his statements at the time of the Suez and Hungarian crises, his criticism of the United Arab Republic's barring Israeli ships from passing through the Suez Canal, and his intervention in the Security Council disarmament debate of April 1958, it is difficult to recall any occasions on which he publicly voiced his judgment on national policies in an international conflict. Thus, both his statements and his actions make it very difficult to accept Lash's view that Hammarskjold held "a 'vox populorum' concept of the Secretary-Generalship." Such a concept implies that the Secretary-General speaks out on many problems facing the Members rather than only on those problems in which he feels that the principles of the Charter are seriously threatened or in which a tactful statement might influence the policies of the Members toward a peaceful settlement. While Hammarskjold was very interested in building the executive prerogatives of his office, he was extremely cautious neither to alienate Members nor to sacrifice his reputation for tactfulness and impartiality.

The second way in which the Secretary-General can assume an independent influence in international politics is in carrying out a mandate with some discretionary authority given him by the Security Council or the General Assembly. It was Hammarskjold's views on this matter that O'Brien attacked and that are at the heart of Siotis's criticism too. Both questioned whether the Secretary-General could interpret such delegations of authority in an impartial manner in today's world, and they viewed such assumptions of power by the Secretary-General as politically unwise. On the question of the Secretary-General's ability to make impartial interpretations of Security Council and General Assembly mandates, Siotis said that Hammarskjold believed that the Organization had its "own will" apart from that of its Members, and O'Brien remarked that Hammarskjold believed that "the Secretary-General represented the general will of the international community as a whole, independent of the will of any individual member or group of members. . . ." In other words, they both thought that Hammarskjold saw himself as embodying some transcendent international will and thereby leading the Organization on to higher stages of constitutional development. Dr. O'Brien said explicitly about Hammarskjold's aspirations in this regard: ". . . the authority of the Secretary-General and the Secretariat were to be gradually built up in the direction, it was hoped ultimately to be a genuinely supranational authority—a world government."

Hammarskjold neither thought that he embodied the will of the international community, as these critics suggest, nor did he think that he and the Secretariat should be or were such ambitious and independent agents on behalf of the legal development of the Organization as their statements imply. He was of the opinion that the Secretariat could contribute to the legal growth of the United Nations, but he saw increasing multilateral cooperation among the Members as the most important factor in this development.[85] In respect to their charges that he thought that he embodied the will of the international community, one need only look at his actions and statements to discount them. In his speech at Oxford University in May 1961 he remarked that the Secretary-General was not "a kind of delphic oracle who alone speaks for the international community," and he then went on to describe means by which he could maintain international impartiality and remain responsive to the wishes of the

Members. These means were guiding his actions by the principles of the Charter and United Nations legal precedents and obtaining maximum direction from the Members through formal resolutions and informal consultations with advisory committees and individual delegations.[86] He continued:

> Even if all of these steps are taken, it will still remain as has been amply demonstrated in practice, that the reduced area of discretion will be large enough to expose the international Secretariat to heated political controversy and to accusations of a lack of neutrality.[87]

This remark, as well as his concern for obtaining maximum support from the Members and his opposition to over-reliance on the Secretary-General, illustrates that he did not have any illusions as to his embodying the general will of the Members. He realized that even with his seeking guidance from the Members and the Charter there were discretionary decisions that would be controversial and would be criticized. He reckoned that if the representative organs asked him to undertake the administration of a United Nations operation, he could make decisions "on the basis of his exclusively international responsibility and not in the interest of any particular State or group of States" [88] and that the decisions would be respected as such by the great majority of Members. He viewed the Secretary-General's ability to make such decisions as "a question of integrity," [89] and he believed that most Members were prepared to accept the decisions of a Secretary-General whose integrity they trusted and who made a maximum effort to elicit directives from the Members.[90] It is very difficult to conceive of any other policy that he could have pursued toward United Nations "executive actions," given the fact that he had been asked by the representative organs to direct them in conformity with the resolutions of those organs.

Whether impartiality is possible for an individual who is educated within a national culture must be judged by every person, but the overwhelming support which Hammarskjold received from the Members in the face of Communist attacks does give some indication of the support of the Members for the possibility of basically impartial decisions and of their willingness to bestow some discretionary authority on the Secretary-General.[91] Secretary-General U

Thant expressed his belief in Hammarskjold's impartiality and complete loyalty to the principles of the Organization when he said:

I admired his principles even more than his remarkable personal qualities. To him the provisions of the Charter were so important—almost sacred—that he was willing to forego any temporary advantage that could be gained by following the easier path of expediency.[92]

In this statement U Thant was reflecting a widely felt judgment of his predecessor and implicitly of the possibility of such impartiality in the office of the Secretary-General.

Tactics

SPECIALIZED INTERNATIONAL ORGANIZATIONS

1. In molding the legal relationships among organizations within the United Nations system of agencies and in creating new international organizations, the United Nations Members and the Secretariat should seek to place them under the authority of the United Nations or at least to support coordination of their activities with those of the United Nations and other international organizations.

Hammarskjold's ideas on the relationship which should exist between the United Nations and more specialized international organizations was set forth in his comments on the proposed creation of an International Disarmament Organization (IDO) and in his comments on the nature of the ties between the United Nations and the Specialized Agencies and the International Atomic Energy Agency. In all of these cases Hammarskjold wanted the organizations more closely integrated into the United Nations framework, and in the case of the IDO, with a United Nations organ constituting its highest political authority. His motives for this policy were that the particular organizations would be most effective and that they were most likely to contribute to the building of a stronger and more stable world order if their work were closely coordinated with that of the United Nations.

The single event which prompted Hammarskjold to make several statements setting forth his disapproval of the tendency to create international organizations independent of the United Nations was the Western proposal of March 1960 for the creation of an International Disarmament Organization with complete organizational independence.[93] Although this proposal was responsible for his public proclamations, he had been concerned for almost two years about this problem in the disarmament field because of an agreement among the Great Powers that an independent organization be established in Vienna to administer and police any future test ban treaty.

Hammarskjold's ideas regarding the relationship between the Specialized Agencies and the United Nations are less clear than his ideas concerning the IDO's relationship to the Organization. It can be stated that he wanted more cooperation among the Specialized Agencies and between them and the United Nations, but it is difficult to say precisely what form he hoped that the cooperation would take. In his speech at the University of Chicago in May 1960 he said:

There are provisions for cooperation among the various organizations within the United Nations family. However, this group of organizations as a whole has no organ, which through a majority decision, can lay down a common line of action. A committee of the administrative heads of the various organizations established for cooperation functions on a basis of unanimity which is made necessary by the autonomy or the organizations.[94]

While the above statement does indicate that he wanted the Specialized Agencies to sacrifice some of their autonomy and to accept a system by which they could be bound to a common line of policy, Luther H. Evans, who as Director-General of UNESCO was a member of the Administrative Committee on Coordination (ACC) during most of Hammarskjold's years as Secretary-General, remarked that he never thought that Hammarskjold was trying to persuade the agencies to accept a binding voting system. Evans noted that Hammarskjold wanted the Directors-General to agree to more cooperation among their agencies than the Directors-General were willing to accept, but that he did not try to pressure them to make any legal grants of authority to the ACC or another body.

Both Evans and Andrew W. Cordier mentioned that Hammarskjold was very pragmatic regarding the nature of the coordination that the Specialized Agencies would accept. They said that he tried to get the agencies to accept common courses of action but that the compliance which he sought was of a voluntary nature. Whether Hammarskjold hoped that in the near future the Specialized Agencies would sacrifice some of their autonomy and accept decisions of the Administrative Committee on Coordination, the Economic and Social Council, or the General Assembly as binding, as his University of Chicago speech intimates, is difficult to say. All that one can say positively is that he wanted greater coordination within the United Nations system because the lack of it was economically inefficient and was impeding the legal and political development of that system. He made this very clear in his last report to the Economic and Social Council in July 1961 when he remarked:

It is a fact that dispersion of responsibilities, uncoordinated initiatives, complexity of procedures and a certain degree of administrative "Byzantinism" are used as an argument against the strengthening of action through the United Nations family, and in favor of new, more homogeneous and centralized institutions outside the framework of the United Nations . . . . The role of the United Nations family is surely far too crucial to allow this challenge to go unanswered, and to meet it should be first priority for the ACC as well as for this Council.[95]

In his speech at the University of Chicago Hammarskjold linked his preference for a greater integration of an IDO and the Specialized Agencies with the United Nations specifically to the problem of the development of the international political system. On this matter he questioned whether the tendency to create independent organizations might "not prove to be a deviation leading us away from the most fruitful direction for an evolution of a framework for international organization."[96] This attitude clearly indicates that he viewed the United Nations as the keystone upon which a more stable and more organized world order might be built. Although he commented that "if this tendency is accepted and continued, it should be counterbalanced by an effort to evolve new forms for integration of the work of the various international agencies,"[97] it is quite clear that he preferred to have the United Nations as the ultimate political authority for all these agencies. Although Hammarskjold was a pragmatic individual not prone to formulate ideal plans, he had a general vision of the political evolution of the world, and he wanted to set the world on the shortest and soundest path to its final goal. He thought that a proliferation of international organizations with the consequent problem of integrating their activities would only slow down the inevitable march of world politics toward its logical destination. Although he viewed this evolution to be in line with his own ethical predispositions regarding men's political relationships, he did not regard his ideas to be outside the realm of realism. On the contrary, he viewed the growing acceptance of the principles of the Charter throughout the world and the growing interdependence of all peoples as encouraging the growth of a more integrated world political system and increasingly stronger community institutions. It was his purpose to make this evolution as peaceful and efficient as possible.

Chapter Seven

Conclusion

One point which Dag Hammarskjold's colleagues at the United Nations often made about him was that he was usually ahead of everyone in his thinking about individual crises and about the course of international politics in general. The British economist Barbara Ward has also commented on the presence of this trait when she noted that "he was a man of the next generation." [1] Since Hammarskjold's death and the advent of a serious constitutional crisis in the United Nations, a number of individuals have criticized this forward-looking or visionary characteristic. They have noted that Hammarskjold was unrealistic about what could be accomplished at this time and that his conception of the Organization was too ambitious for this present stage of history. These critics have also usually pointed out that we are now witnessing the demise of a number of unrealistic developments in the United Nations which Hammarskjold helped to build during his years as Secretary-General. One American scholar, Professor Hans J. Morgenthau, has felt that the reaction to Hammarskjold's policies has been so great that he has pronounced that "the U.N. of Dag Hammarskjold is dead." [2]

The conclusion of this study is perhaps a good place to recall the major kinds of action by the United Nations which Hammarskjold supported and helped to develop and to examine briefly their realism and appropriateness at this stage of history. The kinds of activity which he supported for his own office on one hand and the

Conclusion

Security Council and the General Assembly on the other are closely linked in that the expansion in the activities of the two representative organs rested significantly on the initiation of new forms of activity by the Secretary-General. In specific terms, the Security Council's and General Assembly's delegation of mediatory activities to the Secretary-General and their creation of peacekeeping operations rested on the Secretary-General's willingness to serve as a mediator and as an executive director of the peacekeeping forces.

In looking at the expansion of the Secretary-General's practices which Hammarskjold encouraged, it should first be noted that very little criticism has arisen regarding his willingness to undertake mediatory tasks at the behest of the representative organs or on his own initiative. The peaceful settlement activities of Hammarskjold seldom stirred any opposition since states were never bound to accept the Secretary-General's suggestions and since Hammarskjold was generally very careful not to offend them in public. His numerous successes, in fact, made most of the Members enthusiastic supporters of an active mediator in the office of the Secretary-General.

While Hammarskjold's encouragement of the expansion of the mediatory activities of his office escaped a great deal of criticism, his policies of encouraging the creation of United Nations peacekeeping operations and the choice of the Secretary-General as their executive director have not enjoyed the same fate. Instead, they have stirred up a storm of protest and debate. Probably the most vehement criticism has concerned the assumption by the Secretary-General of independent decisionmaking powers over United Nations peacekeeping operations. This criticism has been based on judgments that states would not accept such independent power by an international executive and that Hammarskjold or any other individual could not make decisions in a manner which was sufficiently impartial to the interests of the Member States to be acceptable to them. His answers to these charges, which are set forth in the previous chapter,[3] were that the areas of independent decisionmaking power could be narrowed through the use of various means of guidance, that the Member States—in creating the peacekeeping forces—were stating their willingness to accept a certain amount of independent decisionmaking authority, and that the Secretary-General could make decisions without partiality to the interests of particular Members. While Hammarskjold presented a good case for his viewpoint, it is true that in some of his statements he perhaps overstressed the civil service character of his post at the expense of its political character. Unlike a civil servant the Secretary-General in his role as executive agent for peacekeeping operations has ultimate political authority over certain matters. Hammarskjold stressed the bureaucratic nature of his post in order to elucidate his role as an impartial servant of the representative organs and in order to encourage precise mandates by the representative organs, but this had the effect of covering the independent political roles of the office.

It is likely that some of the independent powers which Hammarskjold enjoyed as the executive officer of peacekeeping forces will be curtailed as a result of the opposition of a number of Member States. While the Members will probably be willing to provide some latitude of discretionary authority to the Secretary-General, it is unlikely that they will allow him the freedom which Hammarskjold possessed at times during the Congo operation. In the future there will be a great deal of reluctance to create forces if detailed directives cannot first be agreed upon. It is also quite possible that peacekeeping operations will only be established for periods of three or six months, as has been the case with the United Nations Force in Cyprus, in order to prevent the Secretary-General's direction of such forces over a long period of time in the face of dissension about the force's mandate among the Members. Looking back, one can judge that Hammarskjold had to make too many independent decisions concerning the United Nations Force in the Congo, but given the lack of specific mandates, the substantial support for the Secretary-General's position at that time, and the implications of withdrawal for the Congo and international peace, it is difficult to be critical of Hammarskjold. In making individual decisions he was always very careful to seek a consensus among and maximum support from the Member States. That consensuses did not exist among the Members and especially among the Great Powers in respect to mandates which these states had themselves originally passed cannot be blamed on Hammarskjold.

While criticisms of Hammarskjold's views on peacekeeping operations have centered on the Secretary-General's direction of them, there has also been a more general opposition to the actual creation of certain kinds of peacekeeping forces. This criticism has primarily been a result of reflection on the United Nations' experience in the Congo crisis. The main point of men who have challenged certain types of forces has been that the United Nations should never allow itself to become involved in a conflict in a peacekeeping capacity where its functions are not precisely defined and thus where it could become an object of attack by different domestic groups and/or states. These critics have generally been in favor of military observation groups or small armed border forces such as those in Kashmir and Lebanon and along the Arab-Israeli armistice lines. But the United Nations Operation in the Congo, which demanded executive decisions which affected the interests of the civil factions and a number of states, is anathema to them. Their fear is that all of the functions of the United Nations will be harmed by excessively ambitious operations which seriously alienate some states from the Organization.

It is true that Hammarskjold was willing to take some risks of alienating important Members when he supported the establishment of peacekeeping forces. At the same time it should be mentioned that he tried to calculate very carefully whether the Organization had the support to succeed. He was willing to take calculated risks, but he was not reckless. He expressed his overall approach very well in 1959 when he said:

The policy line, as I see it, is that the United Nations simply must respond to those demands which may be put to it. If we feel that those demands go beyond the present capacity, for my point of view, that in itself is not a reason why I, for my part, would say no, because I do not know the exact capacity of this machine. It did take the steep hill of Suez; it may take other and even steeper hills. I would not object beforehand unless I could say, and had to say in all sincerity, that I know it cannot be done.[4]

In retrospect, one can conjecture that Hammarskjold was probably a bit optimistic regarding the ability of the Organization to solve the Congo problem in a manner acceptable to all Members, but it should be stressed that he did not stray far from what the great majority of

Members favored or thought possible. If he were Secretary-General today, it is very likely that the experience of the Congo crisis would have significantly molded his ideas regarding what "cannot be done" at this time. Hammarskjold's critics, who urge the Organization to avoid any operation which might incur some attacks upon itself, are probably more unrealistic about the role of the Organization in international politics than Hammarskjold ever was. Their predictions that doom would befall the Organization as a result of its controversial operation in the Congo have just not come to pass. It has brought to the fore problems of the management and financing of United Nations forces, but it has by no means debilitated the Organization. In fact, a number of new United Nations peacekeeping operations have been created since the crisis over the force in the Congo. While Hammarskjold was perhaps a bit optimistic about the potentialities of the United Nations at this stage of history, one's overall judgment of his activities must be admiration for his understanding of how the United Nations could be used creatively to promote international peace. What misjudgments he did make were usually shared by most statesmen and observers at the time. His own realism about the role of the United Nations was probably exceptionally high if one takes into account an understanding of what the Organization could do as well as what it could not do.

It is very likely that in the future Dag Hammarskjold will be considered as one of the most important individuals in the development of international organizations which are dedicated to promoting international cooperation and peace. If his belief that increasing political and economic interdependence and gradual acceptance of the Principles and Purposes of the Charter will occur and will lead consequently to stronger political institutions in the world community, he may be remembered as a great visionary and theoretician as well as a great tactician and diplomat. Even if the United Nations should some day crumble under the forces of nationalism and conflicting ideologies, and if therefore the world would be forced to start anew its attempt to establish peace and order through international organization, it is likely that his thought and practice would still be regarded as both a guide and a beacon.

During our own times Hammarskjold has already become a

beacon and legend for men who are seeking the road to international peace and security. The British scholar Peter Calvocoressi has perhaps overstated the importance of Hammarskjold's thought and work when he wrote that "it can be said—as perhaps only of Pericles in the whole course of history—that when he [Hammarskjold] died, mankind faltered";[5] but at the same time his statement does illustrate Hammarskjold's impact on a serious and knowledgeable student of international politics. Perhaps a more modest and fitting evaluation of the political legacy which he left was voiced by the economist and political analyst Barbara Ward when she remarked:

He truly belonged to the whole world. He had passed beyond so many of our local tribal differences . . . . I do not think anyone, looking back on the enormous contribution he made in such a relatively short time to the conception of a genuine world society, can ever feel that his work will be wasted, or that in any sense he lived in vain. All of us who knew him had the feeling that he was pointing the way which we must never, can never abandon.[6]

Notes

Notes to Introduction

1. Michel Virally, "Le Rôle Politique du Secrétaire Général des Nations-Unies," *Annuaire Français De Droit International,* IV (1958), 381.
2. See particularly Myres S. McDougal and Florentino P. Feliciano, *Law and Minimum World Public Order: The Legal Regulation of International Coercion* (New Haven: Yale University Press, 1961), Chapter IV; also see Harold D. Lasswell, *The Future of Political Science* (New York: Atherton Press, 1963). While the McDougal and Feliciano volume focuses on the regulation of international coercion by international law, the basic framework employed is just as applicable to political science studies. Also, the fact that their study is specifically directed at the regulation of international violence makes it particularly appropriate for policy-oriented studies of the United Nations.
3. Wilder Foote (ed.), *Servant of Peace; A Selection of the Speeches and Statements of Dag Hammarskjold, Secretary-General of the United Nations 1953–61* (New York: Harper and Row, 1962), pp. 354–75.

Notes to Chapter One

1. Joseph P. Lash, *Dag Hammarskjold: Custodian of the Brush-Fire Peace* (New York: Doubleday and Co., 1961), p. 17.
2. Ernst Wigforss, *Minnen,* III (Stockholm: Tidens Forlag, 1954), 198.
3. Lash, *Dag Hammarskjold,* p. 40.
4. Remarks by Paul G. Hoffman following his Dag Hammarskjold Memorial Lecture at Columbia University, January 23, 1964.
5. Interview with Sven Ahman, November 12, 1964.

Notes

6. Dag Hammarskjold, "Statstjanstemannen och samhallet," *Tiden,* XLII (1951), 396.
7. *Ibid.*
8. *Foote* (ed.), *Servant of Peace,* p. 158. Fred Charles Iklé, in *How Nations Negotiate* (New York: Frederick A. Praeger, 1964), has also noted the tendency of Westerners "to transend their national interests by using their insight and wisdom in behalf of a larger unity. . . ." (p. 145).
9. *Ibid.,* p. 23.   10. Lash, *Dag Hammarskjold,* p. 23.
11. Wigforss, *Minnen,* III, 198.   12. *Ibid.,* 198–99.
13. Foote (ed.), *Servant of Peace,* p. 29.
14. Lash, *Dag Hammarskjold,* p. 17.
15. Dag Hammarskjold, "Statstjanstemannen och samhallet," *Tiden,* XLII (1951), 391.
16. *Ibid.,* 393.   17. *Ibid.,* 393–94.
18. *Ibid.,* 395.   19. *Ibid.*
20. Interview with Sven Ahman, November 12, 1964.
21. Foote (ed.), *Servant of Peace,* p. 74.
22. Interview with Per Lind, January 23, 1965.
23. Foote (ed.), *Servant of Peace,* p. 74.
24. Dag Hammarskjold, *To Choose Europe* (Copenhagen: United Nations, Information Center for Denmark, Iceland, Norway and Sweden). A translation of an article which Hammarskjold wrote in 1952.
25. Dankwart A. Rustow, *The Politics of Compromise: A Study of Parties and Cabinet Government in Sweden* (Princeton: Princeton University Press, 1955), p. 8.
26. Interview with Oscar Schachter, October 30, 1964.
27. Oscar Schachter, "Dag Hammarskjold and the Relation of Law to Politics," *American Journal of International Law,* LVI (January 1962), 1.
28. Foote (ed.), *Servant of Peace,* pp. 75–76.
29. Lash, *Dag Hammarskjold,* p. 44.
30. Walter Lippmann, "Dag Hammarskjold, United Nations Pioneer," *International Organization,* XV (Autumn 1961), 548.
31. Andrew W. Cordier, "Motivations and Methods of Dag Hammarskjold," *Paths to World Order,* Andrew W. Cordier and Kenneth Maxwell, eds. (New York: Columbia University Press, 1967), pp. 20–21.
32. Dag Hammarskjold, *To Choose Europe* (Copenhagen: United Nations, Information Center for Denmark, Iceland, Norway and Sweden).

33. *Ibid.*, p. 7.   34. *Ibid.*   35. See p. 238.
36. Dag Hammarskjold, "Politik och ideologi," *Tiden*, XLIV (1952), 14.
37. *Ibid.*   38. *Ibid.*

Notes to Chapter Two

1. Foote, (ed.), *Servant of Peace*, p. 358.
2. *Ibid.*, pp. 356–61.
3. *Ibid.*, p. 184.
4. *Ibid.*, p. 355.   5. *Ibid.*, pp. 360–61.
6. Andrew W. Cordier, "The Political Role of the United Nations Secretary-General," Speech to the International Fellows Program at Columbia University, April 20, 1964.
7. Foote (ed.), *Servant of Peace*, p. 47.
8. The financial resources to support the administrative costs of the Organization will not be discussed in this chapter since there is no need for an elaborate description of them. A discussion of the modest resources to support its program of technical assistance can be found on pp. 217–18.
9. Foote (ed.), *Servant of Peace*, p. 355.
10. Security Council, *Official Records,* 751st meeting (October 31, 1956), para. 4.
11. Foote (ed.), *Servant of Peace*, pp. 361–65.
12. *Ibid.*, p. 364.
13. *Ibid.;* see also *Ibid.*, pp. 361–62. A discussion of Hammarskjold's ideas regarding the legal weight of different United Nations decisions occurs on pp. 27–29 and 32–33.
14. *Ibid.*, p. 222.
15. Dag Hammarskjold, "United Nations—The Way Ahead," *United Nations Bulletin*, XVI (January 1, 1954), 8.
16. U. N. Doc. A/2911, July 8, 1955, p. xi.
17. United Nations: Office of Public Information, Press Services, Press Release SG/376, February 24, 1954, p. 2.
18. Foote (ed.), *Servant of Peace*, p. 312.
19. *Ibid.*, p. 173.
20. *Ibid.*, p. 225.   21. *Ibid.*, p. 229.
22. *Ibid.*, p. 362. Article 25 reads: "The Members of the United Nations agree to accept and carry out the decisions of the Security Council in accordance with the present Charter.
23. *Ibid.*, p. 363.

24. *Ibid.*   25. *Ibid.*, p. 364.
26. Security Council, *Official Records*, 676th meeting (June 25, 1954), paras. 65–81.
27. Interviews.
28. U. N. Doc. A/2663, July 21, 1954, p. xi.
29. Foote (ed.), *Servant of Peace*, p. 222.
30. *Ibid.*, p. 370.
31. U. N. Doc S/3721, October 31, 1956; Interviews.
32. Foote (ed.), *Servant of Peace*, p. 142.
33. G. A. Res. 337 (V), November 3, 1950.
34. Foote (ed.), *Servant of Peace*, p. 145.
35. *Ibid.*, p. 362.   36. *Ibid.*, p. 361.
37. *Ibid.*, p. 251.   38. *Ibid.*, p. 361.
39. *Ibid.*, pp. 361, 364.
40. U. N. Doc A/3383 and Rev. 1, November 21, 1956.
41. General Assembly, *Official Records*, 15th Session, Plenary meeting 977 (April 5, 1961), paras. 33–34.
42. Foote (ed.), *Servant of Peace*, pp. 345–46.
43. *Ibid.*, p. 335.   44. *Ibid.*
45. Michel Virally, "Le Rôle Politique du Secrétaire Général des Nations-Unies," *Annuaire Français de Droit International*, IV (1958), 370. Hammarskjold admired this article so much that he had it translated and circulated throughout the Secretariat.
46. United Nations: Office of Public Information, Press Services, Note No. 657, May 12, 1953, p. 15.
47. Foote (ed.), *Servant of Peace*, p. 150.
48. Security Council, *Official Records*, 751st meeting (October 31, 1956), para. 4.
49. *Ibid.*   50. *Ibid.*, p. 223.
51. U. N. Doc. A/2404, July 21, 1953, p. xi.
52. Foote (ed.), *Servant of Peace*, pp. 339–40.
53. Ernest Gross, *Dag Hammarskjold as Secretary-General* (New York: Oral History Project, Columbia University, 1964), p. 36a.
54. See Georges Langrod, *The International Civil Service* (Dobbs Ferry, New York: Oceana Publications, 1963), Chapter IX.
55. Interview with Luther H. Evans, former Director-General of UNESCO, April 23, 1965.
56. Virally, "Le Rôle Politique du Secrétaire Général des Nations Unies," pp. 385–86.
57. Conor Cruise O'Brien, *To Katanga and Back* (New York: Simon and Schuster, 1962), pp. 14–15.
58. Foote (ed.), *Servant of Peace*, p. 329.

59. *Ibid.,* p. 369.   60. *Ibid.,* pp. 346–47.
61. Ralph J. Bunche, "The United Nations Operation in the Congo," *The Quest for Peace,* Andrew W. Cordier and Wilder Foote, eds. (New York: Columbia University Press, 1965), p. 122.
62. Interviews.
63. General Assembly, *Official Records,* 15th Session, Plenary meeting 869 (September 23, 1960), paras. 272–285.
64. Foote (ed.), *Servant of Peace,* p. 349.
65. *Ibid.,* p. 368.   66. *Ibid.,* p. 349.
67. Andrew W. Cordier, "Dag Hammarskjold." Speech to the Scandinavian Society of Columbia University, December 17, 1964.
68. Remarks by Paul G. Hoffman following his Dag Hammarskjold Memorial Lecture at Columbia University, January 23, 1964.
69. Interviews.   70. Interviews.
71. Dag Hammarskjold, *Markings* (New York: Alfred A. Knopf, 1964), p. 14.
72. Interviews.
73. Andrew W. Cordier, "Motivations and Methods of Dag Hammarskjold," *Paths to World Order,* Andrew W. Cordier and Kenneth Maxwell, eds. (New York: Columbia University Press, 1967), p. 16.
74. Henry P. Van Dusen, *Dag Hammarskjold: The Statesman and His Faith* (New York: Harper and Row, 1964), p. 109.
75. *Ibid.,* p. 89.
76. Interview with Per Lind, January 23, 1965.
77. Interviews.
78. Foote (ed.), *Servant of Peace,* p. 224.
79. *Ibid.,* p. 209.
80. *Ibid.,* p. 145.   81. *Ibid.,* p. 365.
82. Dag Hammarskjold, "Politik och ideologi," *Tiden,* XLIV (1952), 14.
83. Foote (ed.), *Servant of Peace,* p. 224.   84. *Ibid.,* p. 94.
85. Interview with Andrew W. Cordier, April 21, 1965.
86. Foote (ed.), *Servant of Peace,* p. 222.
87. *Ibid.,* pp. 222–23.
88. Emery Kelen (ed.), *Hammarskjold: The Political Man* (New York: Funk and Wagnalls, 1968), p. 14.
89. His statements from 1953 to 1955 could be interpreted as alluding to the general impasse in admitting new members which was finally broken by the "package deal" of 1955. At the same time the point that the Organization would not be immobilized

by a state which frequently employed the veto in the Security Council (which is cited later in this paragraph) could only be relevant to the case of Communist China.

90. Interviews. He also specifically told Chinese Communist officials in Peking in 1955 that he favored their admission.
91. Foote (ed.), *Servant of Peace*, p. 44.
92. *Ibid.*   93. *Ibid.*   94. *Ibid.*

Notes to Chapter Three

1. His views on the role which he hoped the I.C.J. would assume in the future can be found on pp. 231–32.
2. U. N. Doc. A/2404, July 21, 1953, p. xi.
3. Interview with Hans Engen, December 3, 1964.
4. U. N. Doc. A/2911, July 8, 1955, p. xi.
5. U. N. Doc A/2911, July 8, 1955.
6. U. N. Doc. A/3137/Add. 1, October 4, 1956.
7. Alexander Dallin, *The Soviet Union at the United Nations* (New York: Frederick A. Praeger, 1962), p. 39.
8. Foote (ed.), *Servant of Peace*, p. 302.
9. *Ibid.*, p. 370.
10. U. N. Doc. A/2830, December 5, 1954.
11. Richard I. Miller, *Dag Hammarskjold and Crisis Diplomacy* (Dobbs Ferry, N. Y.: Oceana Publications, 1961), p. 24.
12. *The New York Times*, November 28, 1954, p. 1.
13. *The New York Times*, December 8, 1954, p. 1; *The New York Times*, December 28, 1954, p. 6.
14. G. A. Res. 906 (IX), December 10, 1954.
15. U. N. Doc. A/2888, December 10, 1954. In this telegram Hammarskjold did not request that he come under the authority of the General Assembly resolution since he knew that Communist China could not accept the authority of a resolution which condemned it. Rather, he suggested that he come under his own authority as Secretary-General. This legal arrangement for the Secretary-General's conducting talks with a state which had been criticized by a multilateral organ became known as the "Peking Formula." For a more detailed discussion of Hammarskjold's reasoning behind and use of the "Peking Formula," pp. 128–30.
16. Interview with Hans Engen, December 3, 1964.
17. Interviews. All of the following information regarding the discussions between Hammarskjold and Chou En-lai has been derived from interviews.

18. Interviews.
19. Some of the international conflicts which Trygve Lie tried to influence were the dispute over the presence of Soviet troops in Iran in 1946, the future of Palestine in 1947 and 1948, the Soviet blockade of Berlin in 1948 and 1949, the dispute over Communist China's admission to the United Nations, and the Korean War. See Trygve Lie, *In the Cause of Peace* (New York: The Macmillan Co., 1954).
20. Foote (ed.), *Servant of Peace*, p. 203.   21. *Ibid.*, p. 273.
22. Lash, *Dag Hammarskjold*, p. 162; Interview with Andrew W. Cordier, April 21, 1965.
23. *The New York Times*, July 20, 1958, p. 1.
24. *The New York Times*, July 23, 1958, p. 1.
25. *The New York Times*, August 5, 1958, p. 1.
26. Walter Z. Laqueur, *The Soviet Union and the Middle East* (New York: Frederick A. Praeger 1959), p. 338; Boyd, *United Nations*, p. 39; Fahim Issa Qubain, *Crisis in Lebanon* (Washington, D.C.: Middle East Institute, 1961), p. 96. For an interpretation rejecting the idea that it was the Chinese Communists who persuaded the Soviet Union to reject the summit conference, see A. Doak Barnett, *Communist China and Asia: A Challenge to American Policy* (New York: Vintage Books, 1961), p. 367.
27. Foote (ed.), *Servant of Peace*, p. 202.
28. U. N. Doc. A/2404, July 21, 1953, p. xi.
29. U. N. Doc. A/2911, July 8, 1955, p. xi.
30. *Ibid.*, p. xiv.   31. Foote (ed.), *Servant of Peace*, p. 120.
32. Emery Kelen, *Hammarskjold* (New York: G. P. Putnam's Sons, 1966), p. 84.
33. Foote (ed.), *Servant of Peace*, p. 303.   34. *Ibid.*
35. *Ibid.*, p. 302.   36. *Ibid.*
37. This excludes colonial conflicts between nationalist movements and metropolitan powers.
38. Lash, *Dag Hammarskjold*, p. 69.
39. *Ibid.*, pp. 68–69; John C. Campbell, *Defense of the Middle East* (New York: Frederick A. Praeger, 1960), p. 95.
40. Lash, *Dag Hammarskjold*, p. 69.
41. U. N. Doc. S/3575, April 4, 1956.
42. U. N. Doc. S/3596, May 9, 1956, paras. 21, 40, 44, and 46.
43. E. L. M. Burns, *Between Arab and Israeli* (New York: I. Oblensky, 1962), pp. 143–44.
44. United Nations: Office of Public Information, Press Services, Press Release SG/478, May 6, 1956.

45. U. N. Doc. S/3596, May 9, 1956, para. 107.
46. Lash, *Dag Hammarskjold*, p. 74.
47. *Ibid.;* Burns, *Between Arab and Israeli*, p. 149.
48. *Ibid.*   49. Lash, *Dag Hammarskjold*, p. 74.
50. U. N. Doc. S/3605, June 10, 1956.
51. Interview with Andrew W. Cordier, April 21, 1965.
52. Herman Finer, *Dulles Over Suez* (Chicago: Quadrangle Books, 1964), p. 344.
53. Terence Robertson, *Crisis: The Inside Story of the Suez Conspiracy* (New York: Atheneum, 1965), pp. 141–43.
54. Qubain, *Crisis in Lebanon*, pp. 10–71.   55. *Ibid.*, p. 171.
56. U. N. Doc. S/4007, May 22, 1958.
57. Interview with Andrew W. Cordier, September 6, 1966.
58. G. A. Res. 1237 (ES-III), August 21, 1958.
59. Foote (ed.), *Servant of Peace*, pp. 190–93.
60. United Nations: Office of Public Information, Press Services, Note No. 1862, August 22, 1958, p. 1.
61. U. N. Doc. A/3934/Rev. 1, September 29, 1958.
62. *Ibid.*, paras. 31–37.   63. *Ibid.*, para. 16.
64. Interview with Andrew W. Cordier, April 21, 1965. Mr. Cordier described Mr. Spinelli's role in Jordan as that of a "grand seigneur" to the government.
65. Miller, *Dag Hammarskjold and Crisis Diplomacy*, pp. 218–19.
66. *Ibid.*, p. 219; Interview with Andrew W. Cordier, April 21, 1965.
67. U. N. Doc. A/3934/Rev. 1, September 29, 1958, para. 39.
68. Lash, *Dag Hammarskjold*, p. 77.   69. *Ibid.*
70. See Terence Robertson, *Crisis: The Inside Story of the Suez Conspiracy* (New York: Atheneum, 1965), pp. 141–43.
71. *Ibid.*, p. 143.   72. U. N. Doc. S/3675, October 13, 1956.
73. Security Council, *Official Records*, 11th year, 743rd meeting (October 13, 1956), para. 106.
74. Robertson, *Crisis: The Inside Story of the Suez Conspiracy*, p. 144.
75. U. N. Doc. S/3728, November 2, 1956.   76. *Ibid.*
77. United Nations: Office of Public Information, Press Services, Note No. 1947, February 26, 1959, p. 39.
78. Foote (ed.), *Servant of Peace*, p. 175.   79. *Ibid.*
80. United Nations: Office of Public Information, Press Services, Note No. 1947, February 26, 1959, p. 37.
81. United Nations, *Treaty Series*, XLII, No. 656.
82. Andrew Boyd, *United Nations: Piety, Myth and Truth* (England: Penguin Books, 1962), p. 110.

83. United Nations: Office of Public Information, Press Services, Note No. 1693, December 7, 1957.
84. Interviews.
85. United Nations: Office of Public Information, Press Services, Press Release SG/635, December 5, 1957.
86. Campbell, *Defense of the Middle East,* p. 315.
87. United Nations, Treaty Series, XLII (1949), No. 653.
88. U. N. Doc. S/2322, September 1, 1951.
89. Gabriella Rosner, *The United Nations Emergency Force* (New York: Columbia University Press, 1963), pp. 8–9.
90. United Nations, Treaty Series, CCLXIV (1957), No. 3821.
91. United Nations: Office of Public Information, Press Services, Note No. 1571, April 4, 1957, pp. 5 and 16.
92. United Nations: Office of Public Information, Press Services, Note No. 1590, April 25, 1957, pp. 6–7.
93. *Ibid.,* p. 8.
94. United Nations: Office of Public Information, Press Services, Note. No. 2026, September 3, 1959, p. 1.
95. Lash, *Dag Hammarskjold,* pp. 131–32.
96. United Nations: Office of Public Information, Press Services, Note No. 2038, September 10, 1959, p. 21.
97. Lash, *Dag Hammarskjold,* pp. 131–32.
98. United Nations: Office of Public Information, Press Services, Note No. 2113, February 18, 1960, p. 20.
99. *Ibid.,* p. 21.
100. Lash, *Dag Hammarskjold,* p. 133.   101. *Ibid.,* p. 135.
102. U. N. Doc. A/4121, June 15, 1959.
103. Campbell, *Defense of the Middle East,* p. 331.
104. U. N. Doc. A/4121, June 15, 1959.
105. Lash, *Dag Hammarskjold,* p. 135.
106. U. N. Doc. A/4121/Annex, para. 22.
107. Lash, *Dag Hammarskjold,* p. 134.
108. Lash, *Dag Hammarskjold,* p. 115; Interview with Andrew W. Cordier, April 21, 1965.
109. *The New York Times,* June 24, 1958, p. 1.
110. Interviews.
111. Sven Ahman, "Mr. Hammarskjold's Not-So-Quiet Diplomacy," *The Reporter,* XIX (September 3, 1958), 12–13.
112. Foote (ed.), *Servant of Peace,* p. 190.
113. *Ibid.,* p. 191.   114. *Ibid.,* p. 192.
115. General Assembly, *Official Records,* Third Emergency Session, 733rd Plenary meeting (August 13, 1958), paras. 2–58.

116. Sven Ahman, "Mr. Hammarskjold's Not-So-Quiet Diplomacy," *The Reporter*, XIX (September 4, 1958), 13.
117. G. A. Res. 1237 (ES-III), August 21, 1958.
118. Interview with Ambassador Hans Engen, December 3, 1964; Interview with Andrew W. Cordier, April 21, 1965.
119. Interview with Hans Engen, December 3, 1964.
120. General Assembly, *Official Records,* Third Emergency Session, Plenary meeting 746 (August 21, 1958), paras. 4–43.
121. U. N. Doc. A/4132, August 20, 1959, p. 22.
122. *Ibid.*   123. *Ibid.*
124. United Nations: Office of Public Information, Press Services, Press Release SG/658, February 17, 1958.
125. Miller, *Dag Hammarskjold and Crisis Diplomacy*, pp. 214–15.
126. U. N. Doc. S/4121, December 2, 1958.
127. U. N. Doc. S/4126, December 8, 1958.
128. Boyd, *United Nations: Piety, Myth and Truth*, p. 115.
129. United Nations: Office of Public Information, Press Services, Note No. 1934, February 11, 1959, p. 7.
130. Foote (ed.), *Servant of Peace*, p. 210.
131. All of the information about this peaceful settlement action was obtained in an interview with Ambassador Hans Engen on December 3, 1964.
132. For the background of this dispute, see J. B. Kelly, *Eastern Arabian Frontiers* (London: Faber and Faber, 1964).
133. Interviews.
134. Kelly, *Eastern Arabian Frontiers*, pp. 266–67.
135. Interviews.
136. Kelly, *Eastern Arabian Frontiers*, p. 268.
137. U. N. Doc. S/4023, June 11, 1958.
138. Interview with Andrew W. Cordier, April 21, 1965.
139. *Ibid.*   140. U. N. Doc. S/4040, July 4, 1958.
141. Interview with Andrew W. Cordier, April 21, 1965.
142. Security Council, *Official Records,* 13th year, 837th meeting (July 22, 1958), paras. 10–15.
143. Interview with Hans Engen, December 3, 1964.
144. General Assembly Resolution 1237 (ES-III), August 21, 1958.
145. General Assembly, Official Records, Third Emergency Session, 746th meeting (August 21, 1958), paras. 30–59.
146. *Ibid.*, paras. 71–77.
147. Interview with Andrew W. Cordier, April 21, 1965.
148. Interviews.
149. Russel Fifield, *The Diplomacy of Southeast Asia, 1945–1958* (New York: Harper and Brothers, 1958), pp. 280–81.

150. United Nations: Office of Public Information, Press Services, Note No. 2020, August 13, 1959, p. 21; Interviews.
151. United Nations: Office of Public Information, Press Services, Note No. 2027/Rev. 1, September 4, 1959.
152. *Ibid.*
153. United Nations: Office of Public Information, Press Services, Note No. 2038, September 10, 1959, p. 26.
154. Lash, *Dag Hammarskjold*, p. 142.
155. *The New York Times*, November 10, 1959, p. 1.
156. Lash, *Dag Hammarskjold*, p. 143.
157. For a legal justification of this mission, see General Assembly, *Official Records*, 5th Committee, 769th meeting (October 18, 1960), paras. 10–12.
158. See Donald S. Zagoria, *The Sino-Soviet Conflict, 1956–1961* (Princeton, N. J.: Princeton University Press, 1962).
159. United Nations: Office of Public Information, Press Services, Press Release SG/871, November 15, 1959.
160. Interviews with Andrew W. Cordier and others.
161. *The New York Times*, January 9, 1960, p. 3.
162. Interview with Andrew W. Cordier, April 21, 1965.
163. United Nations: Office of Public Information, Press Services, Note No. 2339, May 29, 1961, p. 45.
164. U. N. Doc. S/4300, April 1, 1960.
165. Interview with Andrew W. Cordier, April 21, 1965.
166. Interviews.
167. Security Council, *Official Records*, 920th meeting (December 13, 1960), para. 97; General Assembly, *Official Records*, 15th year, Plenary meeting 953 (December 17, 1960), paras. 184–90.
168. U. N. Doc. S/4741, February 21, 1961.
169. Ernest W. Lefever, *Crisis in the Congo: A U. N. Force in Action* (Washington, D. C.: Brookings Institution, 1965), pp. 52–53.
170. King Gordon, *United Nations in the Congo: A Quest for Peace* (New York: Carnegie Endowment for International Peace, 1962), pp. 118–20.
171. Conor Cruise O'Brien, *To Katanga and Back* (New York: Simon and Schuster, 1962), pp. 186–90.
172. Ralph J. Bunche, "The United Nations Operation in the Congo," *The Quest for Peace*, Andrew W. Cordier and Wilder Foote, eds. (New York: Columbia University Press, 1965), p. 134.
173. Dag Hammarskjold, "The Element of Privacy in Peace-Making," *United Nations Review*, IV (March 1958), 10.
174. Foote (ed.), *Servant of Peace*, p. 53.

175. *Ibid.*, p. 95. Some interesting insights into both the disadvantages and advantages, which support and supplement those of Hammarskjold, can be found in: Fred Charles Iklé, *How Nations Negotiate* (New York: Frederick A. Praeger, 1964), pp. 85–86, and 133–34; and Thomas C. Shelling, *The Strategy of Conflict* (New York: Oxford University Press, 1963), pp. 29–30.

176. Andrew W. Cordier, "Methods and Motivations of Dag Hammarskjold," *Paths to World Order*, Andrew W. Cordier and Kenneth Maxwell, eds. (New York: Columbia University Press, 1967), p. 19.

177. Foote (ed.), *Servant of Peace*, p. 95.

178. *Ibid.*, p. 54.

179. General Assembly Resolution 906 (IX), December 10, 1954.

180. U. N. Doc A/2888, December 10, 1954.

181. Ernest A. Gross, *The United Nations Structures for Peace* (New York: Harper and Brothers, 1962), p. 29.

182. *Ibid.*

183. Max Ascoli, "The Price of Peacemongering," *The Reporter*, XV (November 29, 1956), 12.

184. Interview with Andrew W. Cordier, April 21, 1965.

185. Max Ascoli, "The Future of the U. N.—An Editorial," *The Reporter*, XXV (October 26, 1961), 22.

186. Foote (ed.), *Servant of Peace*, p. 271.   187. *Ibid.*

188. Schachter, "Dag Hammarskjold and the Relation of Law to Politics," 5–6.

189. See pp. 125–27.

190. General Assembly, *Official Records*, 5th Committee, 769th meeting (October 18, 1960), paras. 10–12.

191. Interview with Andrew W. Cordier, September 6, 1966.

192. For additional information and documentation on this mediation, see pp. 102–106.

193. For additional information and documentation on this mediation, see pp. 70–73.

194. For additional information on this mediation, see pp. 94–97.

195. Interviews; see pp. 97–98.

196. Foote (ed.), *Servant of Peace*, p. 27.

197. Andrew W. Cordier, "The Role of the Secretary-General," *Annual Review of United Nations Affairs, 1960–1961*, Richard N. Swift, ed. (Dobbs Ferry, N.Y.: Oceana Publications, 1961), pp. 6–7.

198. Interviews.

199. United Nations: Office of Public Information, Press Services, Note No. 2113, February 18, 1960, p. 3.

200. Sven Ayman [Ahman], *Impressions of Dag Hammarskjold* (New York: Oral History Office, Columbia University, 1963), p. 6.
201. *Ibid.* 202. Foote (ed.), *Servant of Peace*, p. 209.
203. *Ibid*, p. 208. 204. See pp. 80–82.
205. *The New York Times*, September 20, 1961, p. 10.
206. United Nations: Office of Public Information, Press Services, Note No. 2113, February 18, 1960, p. 6.
207. Foote (ed.), *Servant of Peace*, p. 209.
208. For text of these statements, see Security Council, *Official Records*, 751st meeting (October 31, 1956), paras. 3–4; Security Council, *Official Records*, 754th meeting (November 4, 1956), para. 76.
209. Security Council, *Official Records*, 751st meeting (October 31, 1956) para. 4.
210. *Ibid.* 211. *Ibid.* 212. See pp. 85–87.
213. See pp. 209–10. 214. Foote (ed.), *Servant of Peace*, p. 209.
215. See pp. 202–203. 216. See pp. 92–93. 217. See pp. 89–90.
218. Interview with Sven Ahman, November 12, 1964.
219. Foote (ed.), *Servant of Peace*, p. 355. 220. *Ibid.*, p. 346.
221. Schachter, "Dag Hammarskjold and the Relation of Law to Politics," p. 3.
222. *Ibid.*, p. 4.
223. United Nations: Office of Public Information, Press Services, Services, Press Release SG/912, April 28, 1960.
224. Emery Kelen, *Hammarskjold* (New York: G. P. Putnam's Sons, 1966), p. 131; Sven Ayman [Ahman], *Impressions of Dag Hammarskjold* (New York Oral History Office, Columbia University, 1963), p. 44.
225. Kelen, *Hammarskjold*, p. 131.
226. U. N. Doc. A/2888, December 10, 1954.
227. Joseph L. Lash, "Dag Hammarskjold's Conception of His Office," *International Organization*, XVI (1962), 548.
228. *Ibid.*
229. "Chou En-lai Receives Hammarskjold for Peace, Says Indian Press," *Survey of the China Mainland Press* (Hong Kong: United States Consulate General), No. 966, p. 2 (January 12, 1955), From New China News Agency, New Delhi, January 11, 1955.
230. U. N. Doc. A/2889, December 17, 1954.
231. U. N. Doc. S/4300, April 1, 1960.
232. U. N. Doc. S/4305, April 19, 1960, para. 5.
233. All information regarding the negotiations between Hammarskjold and Chou En-lai has been obtained from interviews.

234. Interviews.   235. Lash, *Dag Hammarskjold*, p. 64.
236. *Ibid.*   237. See pp. 99–100.
238. Interview with Hans Engen, December 3, 1964.
239. Dag Hammarskjold, *Markings* (New York: Alfred A. Knopf, 1964), p. 114.

Notes to Chapter Four

1. United Nations: Office of Public Information, Press Services, Note No. 1995, May 1, 1959, p. 6; see also Foote (ed.), *Servant of Peace*, p. 206.
2. Interview with Andrew W. Cordier, April 21, 1965.
3. Interview with Hans Engen, December 3, 1964.
4. F. P. Walters, *A History of the League of Nations*, Vol. 1 (New York: Oxford University Press, 1952), p. 90.
5. *Ibid.*, Vol. II, 617–22.
6. U. N. Doc. A/3251, November 1, 1956; U. N. Doc. S/3726, November 2, 1956.
7. Gordon Gaskill, "Timetable of a Failure," *The Virginia Quarterly Review*, XXIV (Spring 1958), 168.
8. *Ibid.*, 165–80.
9. Conor Cruise O'Brien, *To Katanga and Back* (New York: Simon and Schuster, 1962), p. 20.
10. Interview with Charles Cook, November 17, 1964.
11. Interviews.
12. Security Council, *Official Records*, 754th meeting (November 4, 1956), para. 76.
13. Security Council, *Official Records*, 751st meeting (October 31, 1956), paras. 3–4.
14. G. A. Res. 1004 (ES–II), November 4, 1956.   15. Interviews.
16. Interviews.   17. U. N. Doc. A/3485, January 5, 1957.
18. G. A. Res. 1132 (XI), January 10, 1957.
19. U. N. Doc. A/3592, June 7, 1957.
20. G. A. Res. 1133 (XI), September 14, 1957.
21. Interviews.
22. See pp. 66–69.
23. Security Council, *Official Records*, 751st meeting (October 31, 1956), para. 3.
24. U. N. Doc. S/3710, October 30, 1956.
25. Security Council, *Official Records*, 751st meeting (October 31, 1956), paras. 3–4.

26. U. N. Doc. S/3721, October 31, 1956.
27. G. A. Res. 997 (ES–I), November 2, 1956.
28. G. A. Res. 999 (ES–I), November 4, 1956.
29. Lash, *Dag Hammarskjold*, p. 84.
30. Interview with Per Lind, January 23, 1965.
31. Robertson, *Crisis: The Inside Story of the Suez Conspiracy*, p. 185.
32. Ralph J. Bunche, "The United Nations Operation in the Congo," *The Quest for Peace: The Dag Hammarskjold Memorial Lectures*, Andrew W. Cordier and Wilder Foote, eds. (New York: Columbia University Press, 1965), p. 122.
33. G. A. Res. 998 (ES–I), November 4, 1956.
34. Robertson, *Crisis: The Inside Story of the Suez Conspiracy*, pp. 214–15.
35. *Ibid.*, pp. 231 and 245; Interview with Andrew W. Cordier, April 21, 1965.
36. *Ibid.*, p. 211.
37. Interview with Andrew W. Cordier, April 21, 1965.
38. U. N. Docs. A/3293, A/3294, November 6, 1956.
39. G. A. Res. 1000 (ES–I), November 5, 1956.
40. G. A. Res. 1001 (ES–I), November 7, 1956.
41. U. N. Doc. A/3302, November 6, 1956, para. 11.
42. Laqueur, *The Soviet Union and the Middle East*, pp. 238–39.
43. E. L. M. Burns, *Between Arab and Israeli*, pp. 202–203.
44. William R. Frye, *A United Nations Peace Force* (New York: Oceana Publications, 1957), p. 84.
45. *Ibid.*, p. 28. 46. Burns, *Between Arab and Israeli*, pp. 193–200.
47. *Ibid.*, pp. 217–19; Frye, *A United Nations Peace Force*, p. 14.
48. Burns, *Between Arab and Israeli*, pp. 217–18.
49. Ernest A. Gross, *The United Nations Structures for Peace* (New York: Harper and Brothers, 1962), p. 31.
50. *Ibid.*
51. U. N. Doc. A/3375, November 20, 1956; Gross, *The United Nations Structures for Peace*, p. 33.
52. U. N. Doc. A/3511, January 23, 1957.
53. U. N. Doc. A/3512, January 24, 1957.
54. Robertson, *Crisis: The Inside Story of the Suez Conspiracy*, pp. 326–27.
55. Rosner, *The United Nations Emergency Force*, pp. 83–84.
56. Robertson, *Crisis: The Inside Story of the Suez Conspiracy*, p. 327.
57. *Ibid.*, pp. 327–328; Burns, *Between Arab and Israeli*, pp. 257–70.

58. U. N. Doc. A/3500, January 15, 1957; U. N. Doc. A/3512, January 24, 1957.
59. See statements of Western powers in General Assembly, *Official Records,* 11th year, Plenary meeting 666 (March 1, 1957) and Plenary meeting 667 (March 2, 1957).
60. Robertson, *Crisis: The Inside Story of the Suez Conspiracy,* p. 327.
61. U. N. Doc S/4882, July 22, 1961.
62. Security Council, *Official Records,* 962nd meeting (July 22, 1961), para. 2.
63. U. N. Doc. S/4885, July 23, 1961.
64. *The New York Times,* July 27, 1961, p. 3.
65. *The New York Times,* July 26, 1961, p. 4.
66. *The New York Times,* July 27, 1961, p. 3.   67. *Ibid.*
68. *New York Times,* July 29, 1961, p. 3.
69. Bunche, "The United Nations Operation in the Congo," p. 123.
70. Joseph Kraft, "The Untold Story of the UN's Congo Army," *Harper's Magazine,* CCXXI (November 1960), 76.
71. *Ibid.*   72. *Ibid.* p. 76.   73. *Ibid.,* pp. 76 and 78.
74. *Ibid.,* p. 78.
75. Ernest W. Lefever, *Crisis in the Congo: A U. N. Force in Action* (Washington, D. C.: The Brookings Institution, 1965), p. 13.
76. U. N. Doc. S/4382, July 13, 1960.
77. Colin Legum, *Congo Disaster* (Baltimore: Penguin Books, 1961), pp. 127–28.
78. Security Council, *Official Records,* 873rd meeting (July 13–14, 1960), para. 232. China also abstained on this vote.
79. Legum, *Congo Disaster,* p. 128; Kraft, "The Untold Story of the UN's Congo Army," p. 80.
80. Security Council, *Official Records,* 873rd meeting (July 13–14, 1960), para. 26.
81. *Ibid.*   82. *Ibid.,* para. 27.   83. *Ibid.,* para. 28.
84. *Ibid.,* para. 24.   85. U. N. Doc. S/4387, July 13, 1960.
86. Thomas Franck and John Carey, "The Role of the United Nations in the Congo—A Retrospective Perspective," *The Hammarskjold Forums* (New York: The Association of the Bar of the City of New York, April 30, 1962), p. 20.
87. U. N. Doc. S/4426, August 9, 1960.
88. U. N. Doc. S/4417/Add. 7, August 15, 1960.
89. Lefever, *Crisis in the Congo,* pp. 29–30.
90. U. N. Doc. S/4503, September 11, 1960.
91. Robert Good, "Congo Crisis: "The Role of the New States,"

Neutralism (Washington, D.C.: The Washington Center of Foreign Policy Research, 1961), p. 21.

92. Legum, *Congo Disaster*, pp. 154 and 154–65; O'Brien, *To Katanga and Back*, p. 96.

93. G. A. Res. 1474 (ES–IV), September 20, 1960. Guinea and the Soviet bloc states abstained.

94. Foote (ed.), *Servant of Peace*, p. 319.

95. G. A. Res. 1498 (XV), November 22, 1960.

96. Security Council, *Official Records*, 920th meeting (December 13, 1960), para. 97; General Assembly, *Official Records*, 15th year, Plenary meeting 953 (December 17, 1960), paras. 184–90.

97. G. A. Res. 1474 (ES–IV), September 20, 1960.

98. See O'Brien, *To Katanga and Back*, p. 99.

99. U. N. Doc. S/4741, February 21, 1961.

100. Foote (ed.), *Servant of Peace*, pp. 327–28.

101. For the Soviet Union's announcement that it would no longer recognize Hammarskjold as Secretary-General, see U.N. Doc. S/4704, February 14, 1961.

102. United Nations: Office of Public Information, Press Services, Press Release SG/1017, March 17, 1961.

103. U. N. Doc. S/4807/Annex I, May 17, 1961; King Gordon, *United Nations in the Congo: A Quest for Peace*, pp. 111–12.

104. *Ibid.*, pp. 112–13.   105. Interviews.

106. Ralph J. Bunche, "The United Nations Operation in the Congo," *The Quest for Peace*, Andrew W. Cordier and Wilder Foote, eds. (New York: Columbia University Press, 1965), p. 134.

107. *Ibid.*, p. 135.

108. U. N. Doc. S/4940/Add 2–3, September 14–15, 1961.

109. For additional information on this crisis, see pp. 90–93.

110. U. N. Doc. S/4023, June 11, 1958.   111. Interviews.

112. U. N. Doc. S/4052, July 17, 1958.

113. U. N. Doc. S/4114, November 14, 1958.

114. Security Council, *Official Records*, 829th meeting (July 16, 1958), paras. 10–12.

115. Security Council, *Official Records*, 835th meeting (July 21, 1958), para. 34. Another discussion of the inadvisability of a UNEF-type force in Lebanon can be found in: U. N. Doc. A/3943, October 9, 1958.

116. Security Council, *Official Records*, 873rd meeting (July 13–14), para. 24.

117. U. N. Doc. A/4800, July 1, 1961, pp. 47–57; Gordon, *United Nations in the Congo*, pp. 63–74; Harold K. Jacobson, "ONUC's

Civilian Operations: State-Preserving and State-Building,"
World Politics, XVII (October 1964), 75–107.

118. Gordon, *United Nations in the Congo*, pp. 63–64.
119. U. N. Doc. A/4800, July 1, 1961, p. 47.
120. United Nations: Office of Public Information, Press Services, Press Release SG/871, November 15, 1959.
121. Richard A. Miller, *Dag Hammarskjold and Crisis Diplomacy* (New York: Oceana Publications, 1961), pp. 251–52.
122. See pp. 75–78.   123. Lash, *Dag Hammarskjold*, p. 96.
124. G. A. Res. 1001 (ES–I), November 7, 1956.
125. U. N. Docs. A/3306 and A/3307, November 6, 1956; Lash, *Dag Hammarskjold*, pp. 96–98; Robertson, *Crisis: The Inside Story of the Suez Conspiracy*, pp. 216–20.
126. U. N. Doc. S/4409, July 22, 1960.
127. U. N. Doc. S/4482/Add. 1, September 8, 1960.
128. U. N. Doc. S/4503, September 11, 1960.
129. U. N. Doc. S/4482/Add. 2, September 9, 1960.
130. U. N. Doc. S/4503, September 11, 1960.
131. U. N. Doc. S/4482/Add. 3, September 10, 1960.   132. *Ibid.*
133. Security Council, *Official Records*, 896th meeting (September 9, 1960), para. 110.
134. G. A. Res. 1474 (ES–IV), September 20, 1960.
135. U. N. Doc. S/4557, November 2, 1960.
136. U. N. Doc. S/4741, February 22, 1961.
137. U. N. Doc. S/4752/Annex II, February 27, 1961.
138. Security Council, *Official Records*, 751st meeting (October 31, 1956), para. 4. Hammarskjold invoked this statement following the Soviet invasion of Hungary; see Security Council, *Official Records*, 754th meeting (November 4, 1956), para. 76.
139. Robertson, *Crisis: The Inside Story of the Suez Conspiracy*, p. 243.
140. *Ibid.*, p. 200.
141. Security Council, *Official Records*, 873rd meeting (July 13–14, 1960), para. 26.
142. Gordon, *United Nations in the Congo*, p. 21.   143. *Ibid.*
144. U. N. Doc. A/3322, November 6, 1956, para. 9; see also U. N. Doc. A/3943, October 9, 1958, para. 155.
145. Security Council, *Official Records*, 873rd meeting (July 13–14, 1960) para. 28.
146. Chapter VII of the Charter provides that the Members should sign agreements with the Security Council to place some of their military forces at the disposal of the Council. These

binding agreements have never been signed as a result of the political differences among the five permanent Members.

147. U. N. Doc. A/3943, October 9, 1958, para. 155.
148. U. N. Doc. A/3302, November 6, 1956, paras. 4–5. The British and French suggestions are contained in U. N. Docs. A/3293 and A/3294, November 6, 1956.
149. *Ibid.*, para. 5.   150. *Ibid.*, paras. 4–5.
151. U. N. Doc. A/3943, October 9, 1958, para. 172.
152. U. N. Doc. A/3302, November 6, 1956; see also Burns, *Between Arab and Israeli*, p. 193.
153. U. N. Doc. A/3943, October 9, 1958, para. 165.
154. "Text of Hammarskjold Memorandum on Mideast Peace Force," *The New York Times*, June 19, 1967, p. 12.
155. Ernest A. Gross, *The United Nations Structures for Peace* pp. 30–34.
156. "Text of Hammarskjold Memorandum on Mideast Peace Force," *The New York Times*, June 19, 1967, p. 12. All of the following information regarding the diplomacy surrounding the establishment of this tactical principle and Hammarskjold's views on it is taken from this memorandum.
157. U. N. Doc. A/3375, November 20, 1956. In this document both parties affirmed that they would be guided "in good faith" by their acceptance of the General Assembly resolution which established UNEF. They also agreed to the statement: ". . . in particular, the United Nations, understanding this to correspond to the wishes of the Government of Egypt, reaffirms its willingness to maintain UNEF until its task is completed."
158. G. A. Res. 1121 (XI), November 24, 1956.
159. "Text of Statement by U Thant on Hammarskjold Memorandum of 1957," *The New York Times*, June 20, 1967, p. 18.
160. Interviews.   161. U. N. Doc. S/4389/Add. 5, July 29, 1960.
162. Foote (ed.), *Servant of Peace*, pp. 246–47.
163. U. N. Doc. S/3527, February 11, 1957.
164. Security Council, *Official Records*, 835th meeting (July 21, 1958), paras. 36–37.
165. Security Council, *Official Records*, 837th meeting (July 22, 1958), paras. 10–17.
166. See Security Council, *Official Records*, 835th and 836th meetings (July 21, 1958).
167. U. N. Doc. S/4426, August 9, 1960.
168. Security Council, *Official Records*, 920th meeting (December 13, 1960), para. 97; General Assembly, *Official Records*, 15th

year, Plenary meeting 853 (December 17, 1960), paras. 184–90.

169. His plea to the Africans is contained in Foote (ed.), *Servant of Peace*, pp. 327–28. The new mandate is in U. N. Doc. S/4741, February 21, 1961.

170. U. N. Doc. A/3302, November 6, 1956, para. 12.

171. G. A. Res. 1001 (ES–I), November 7, 1956.

172. U. N. Doc. A/3943, October 9, 1958, para. 38.

173. Security Council, *Official Records*, 887th meeting (August 21, 1960), para. 36.

174. Andrew W. Cordier, "The Role of the Secretary-General," *Annual Review of United Nations Affairs, 1960–1961*, Richard N. Swift, ed. (Dobbs Ferry, New York: Oceana Publications, 1961), p. 9.

175. Security Council, *Official Records*, 887th meeting (August 21, 1960), paras. 78–82.

176. Security Council, *Official Records*, 888th meeting (August 21, 1960), para. 79.

177. Andrew W. Cordier, "The Role of the Secretary-General," *Annual Review of United Nations Affairs, 1960–1961*, Richard N. Swift, ed. (Dobbs Ferry, New York: Oceana Publications, 1961), p. 9.

178. Interview with Andrew W. Cordier, April 21, 1965. Mr. Cordier mentioned that Hammarskjold's issuance of the reports made him "the chief legislator" in the United Nations in that new mandates were usually based upon the recommendations in these reports.

179. Foote (ed.), *Servant of Peace*, p. 346.

180. U. N. Doc. A/3302, November 6, 1956, para. 8.

181. U. N. Doc. A/3943, October 9, 1958, para. 167.

182. *Ibid.*   183. U. N. Doc. A/3512, January 24, 1957, paras. 24–25.

184. *Ibid.*, paras. 5 and 13.

185. U. N. Doc. A/3563, February 25, 1957.

186. Lash, *Dag Hammarskjold*, p. 109.

187. Robertson, *Crisis: The Inside Story of the Suez Conspiracy*, p. 324.

188. Lash, *Dag Hammarskjold*, p. 110.

189. *Ibid.*, p. 109; Burns, *Between Arab and Israeli*, p. 267.

190. See pp. 143–48.

191. U. N. Doc. A/3302, November 6, 1956, para. 11.

192. *Ibid.*, para. 165.   193. Interviews. See pp. 67–74.

194. Security Council, *Official Records*, 873rd meeting (July 13–14, 1960), para. 28.

195. The Security Council gave its explicit support to the principle of nonintervention on August 9, 1960 (U. N. Doc. S/4426).

196. Security Council, *Official Records*, 887th meeting (August 21, 1960), para. 44.

197. The Soviet Union's position can be found in Security Council, *Official Records*, 885th meeting (August 8–9, 1960), paras. 217–20. Ghana's can be found in U. N. Doc. S/4420, August 6, 1960. Guinea's can be found in Security Council, *Official Records*, 888th meeting (August 21, 1960), para. 34.

198. Security Council, *Official Records*, 913th meeting (December 7, 1960), para. 39.

199. *Ibid.*   200. U. N. Doc. S/4741, February 21, 1961.

201. Security Council, *Official Records*, 917th meeting (December 10, 1960), para. 65.

202. See U. N. Doc. A/3943, October 9, 1958, para. 160.

203. He had to rescind his acceptance of combat troops from Canada for UNEF because of Egyptian opposition, but he did accept a large contingent of support personnel. In the Congo operation the Canadian contribution was also composed of support personnel.

204. Ruth B. Russell, *United Nations Experience with Military Force: Political and Legal Aspects* (Washington, D.C.: Institute for Defense Analysis, International Studies Division, 1963), p. 68.

205. Security Council, *Official Records*, 888th meeting (August 21, 1960), para. 96.

206. Rosner, *The United Nations Emergency Force*, p. 119.

207. Kraft, *"The Untold Story of the U.N.'s Congo Army,"* pp. 80, 82, and 84.

208. U. N. Doc. A/3943, October 9, 1958, para. 161.

209. Russell, *United Nations Experience with Military Force*, p. 68.

210. Rosner, *The United Nations Emergency Force*, pp. 119–20.

211. Gordon, *United Nations in the Congo*, p. 45.

212. A. G. Mezerik (ed.), *Congo and the United Nations*, Vol. I (New York: International Review Service, 1960), p. 20.

213. Burns, *Between Arab and Israeli*, p. 273.

214. *Ibid.*, p. 272.

215. Frye, *A United Nations Peace Force*, p. 15.   216. Interviews.

217. U. N. Doc. S/4940/Add. 2–3, September 14–15, 1961; U. N. Doc. S/4940/Add. 16–19, December 1–16, 1961; U. N. Doc. S/5053/Add. 14, January 11, 1963.

218. Gross, *The United Nations Structures for Peace*, p. 36. See also

Herbert G. Nicholas, *The United Nations as a Political Institution* (London: Oxford University Press, 1962), p. 331.

Notes to Chapter Five

1. Interviews.
2. Dag Hammarskjold, "The United Nations and the Major Challenges Which Face the World Community," *United Nations Review,* IV (June 1958), 29.
3. U. N. Doc. A/3936, September 30, 1958.
4. G. A. Res. 1348 (XIII), December 13, 1958.
5. Interviews.   6. G. A. Res. 1472 (XIV), December 12, 1959.
7. Interviews.   8. G. A. Res. 715 (XIII), November 28, 1953.
9. Bernard G. Bechhoefer, *Post-War Negotiations for Arms Control* (Washington, D. C.: Brookings Institution, 1961), p. 435.
10. G. A. Res. 1252 (XIII), November 4, 1958.   11. Interviews.
12. Lash, *Dag Hammarskjold,* p. 157.   13. Interviews.
14. Bechhoefer, *Postwar Negotiations for Arms Control,* p. 461.
15. *Ibid.,* p. 462.   16. Interviews.
17. G. A. Res. 1378 (XIV), November 20, 1959.
18. Security Council, *Official Records,* 815th meeting (April 29, 1958), para. 76. For his press conference statement, see United Nations: Office of Public Information, Press Services, Note No. 1779, April 8, 1958, pp. 9 and 11.
19. *Ibid.*   20. Foote (ed.), *Servant of Peace,* p. 187.
21. United Nations: Office of Public Information, Press Service Note No. 1794, May 1, 1958, pp. 7–11.
22. Security Council, *Official Records,* 816th meeting (May 2, 1958), para. 22.
23. Sven Ahman, "Mr. Hammarskjold's Not-So-Quiet Diplomacy," *The Reporter,* XIX (September 4, 1958), 12.
24. United Nations: Office of Public Information, Press Services, Press Release SG/912, April 28, 1960.
25. On November 28, 1961, the General Assembly passed a resolution (1660-XVI) creating an Eighteen-Member Disarmament Commission which included six nonaligned states. On September 20, 1961, the United States and the Soviet Union agreed in the Zorin-McCloy agreement that a future disarmament control organ would be closely integrated with the United Nations (U.N. Doc. A/4879).
26. Bechhoefer, *Postwar Negotiations for Arms Control,* p. 462.

27. United Nations: Office of Public Information, Press Services, Note No. 2082, December 11, 1959, p. 3.
28. United Nations: Office of Public Information, Press Services, Press Release SG/901, March 15, 1960.
29. Foote (ed.), *Servant of Peace*, pp. 369–70.   30. *Ibid.*, p. 370.
31. Interviews.
32. On November 28, 1961, the General Assembly passed a resolution (1660–XVI) establishing the Eighteen-Member Disarmament Commission. It included six nonaligned states along with six states from each of the two military blocs.
33. See pp. 121–24.
34. Security Council, *Official Records*, 815th meeting (April 29, 1958), para. 76. For his press conference statement, see United Nations: Office of Public Information, Press Services, Note No. 1779, April 8, 1958, pp. 9–11.
35. Emery Kelen, *Dag Hammarskjold* (New York: G. P. Putnam's Sons, 1966), p. 97.
36. Sven Ahman, "Dag Hammarskjold's Not-So-Quiet Diplomacy," *The Reporter*, XIX (September 4, 1958), 12.
37. United Nations: Office of Public Information, Press Services, Press Release, SG/912, April 28, 1960.
38. "Five Powers Present Plan for General Disarmament as Ten-Nation Disarmament Conference Convenes," *The Department of State Bulletin*, XLII (April 8, 1960), 511–15.
39. United Nations: Office of Public Information, Press Services, Press Release SG/912, April 28, 1960, p. 1.
40. United Nations: Office of Public Information, Press Services, Note No. 2148, April 8, 1960, p. 20.
41. Interviews.
42. United Nations: Office of Public Information, Press Services, Press Release SG/912, April 28, 1960, p. 2.
43. Interviews.   44. Interviews.   45. Interviews.
46. United Nations: Office of Public Information, Press Services, Note No. 2166, May 5, 1960, pp. 12–14.
47. U. N. Doc. A/4879, September 20, 1961, para. 6.

Notes to Chapter Six

1. Foote (ed.), *Servant of Peace*, p. 42.
2. U. N. Doc. A/2404, July 21, 1953, p. xii.
3. Dag Hammarskjold, "For a New Approach to International

Aid and Technical Assistance," *United Nations Review*, III (July 1956), 10.

4. Foote (ed.), *Servant of Peace*, p. 42.   5. *Ibid.*, p. 184.

6. U. N. Doc A/2404, July 21, 1953, p. xii.

7. Dag Hammarskjold, "Why the United Nations?," *United Nations Review*, V (July 1958), 17.

8. Foote (ed.), *Servant of Peace*, p. 240.   9. *Ibid.*, p. 374.

10. *Ibid.*

11. These figures are for the United Nations Expanded Program of Technical Assistance and the United Nations Special Fund.

12. Interviews.   13. U. N. Doc. A/4800, July 1, 1961, p. 136.

14. Foote (ed.), *Servant of Peace*, p. 289.   15. *Ibid.*

16. Interviews.   17. Foote (ed.), *Servant of Peace*, p. 280.

18. *Ibid.*, p. 281.

19. United Nations: Office of Public Information, Press Services, Press Release SG/758, p. 3.

20. Foote (ed.), *Servant of Peace*, p. 280.   21. Interviews.

22. Foote (ed.), *Servant of Peace*, p. 289.   23. *Ibid.*

24. U. N. Doc. A/2911, July 8, 1955, p. xi.

25. Foote (ed.), *Servant of Peace*, p. 312.   26. *Ibid.*, p. 319.

27. *Ibid.*, p. 216.

28. United Nations: Office of Public Information, Press Services, Note No. 1970, April 16, 1959, p. 6.

29. Foote (ed.), *Servant of Peace*, p. 318.   30. *Ibid.*, p. 359.

31. From 1953 to 1961 the number of African states in the United Nations increased from 4 to 28 while the total membership increased from 60 to 103.

32. Foote (ed.), *Servant of Peace*, pp. 356–57.   33. *Ibid.*, p. 121.

34. *Ibid.*   35. Interviews.

36. U. N. Doc. A/2404, July 21, 1953, p. xi.

37. On this general subject matter, see Oscar Schachter, "Dag Hammarskjold and the Relation of Law to Politics," *American Journal of International Law*, LVI (January 1962), 1–8.

38. Foote (ed.), *Servant of Peace*, p. 99.

39. Schachter, "Dag Hammarskjold and the Relation of Law to Politics," p. 7.

40. United Nations: Office of Public Information, Press Services, Press Release SG/437, August 22, 1955, p. 6.

41. United Nations: Office of Public Information, Press Services, Press Release SG/373, March 18, 1954, p. 4.

42. Andrew W. Cordier, "Motivations and Methods of Dag Hammarskjold," *Paths to World Order*, Andrew W. Cordier and

Kenneth Maxwell, eds. (New York: Columbia University Press, 1967), p. 20.

43. Foote (ed.), *Servant of Peace*, p. 89.   44. *Ibid.*, p. 111.

45. Dag Hammarskjold, "Why the United Nations?," *United Nations Review*, V (July 1958), 16.

46. Foote (ed.), *Servant of Peace*, p. 355.   47. *Ibid.*, p. 251.

48. *Ibid.*, p. 354.   49. See *Ibid.*, pp. 361–65.

50. Schachter, "Dag Hammarskjold and the Relation of Law to Politics," p. 7.

51. United Nations: Office of Public Information, Press Services, Note No. 818, March 24, 1954, p. 18.

52. Foote, *Servant of Peace*, pp. 100 and 228; United Nations: Office of Public Information, Press Services, Press Release SG/437, August 22, 1955, p. 7.

53. Interview with Andrew W. Cordier, April 21, 1965; and Interview with Oscar Schachter, October 30, 1964.

54. Foote (ed.), *Servant of Peace*, p. 97.   55. *Ibid.*

56. United Nations: Office of Public Information, Press Services, Press Release SG/373, March 18, 1954, p. 4.

57. Foote (ed.), *Servant of Peace*, p. 251.   58. *Ibid.*, p. 365.

59. *Ibid.*   60. *Ibid.*   61. *Ibid.*, p. 209.   62. *Ibid.*, p. 361.

63. *Ibid.*, pp. 363–64.   64. *Ibid.*, p. 364.   65. *Ibid.*, p. 354.

66. *Ibid.*, p. 355.   67. *Ibid.*, p. 354.   68. *Ibid.*, p. 252.

69. Dag Hammarskjold, "Why the United Nations?," *United Nations Review*, V (July 1958), 16.

70. David Mitrany, *A Working Peace System* (London: Royal Institute of World Affairs, 1946).

71. Foote (ed.), *Servant of Peace*, p. 252.   72. *Ibid.*, p. 227.

73. Adlai E. Stevenson, "From Containment to Cease-Fire and Peaceful Change," *The Quest for Peace*, Andrew W. Cordier and Wilder Foote, eds. (New York: Columbia University Press, 1965), p. 53.

74. General Assembly, *Official Records*, 15th year, Plenary meeting 869 (September 23, 1960), paras. 272–85.

75. Foote (ed.), *Servant of Peace*, p. 349.   76. *Ibid.*, p. 376.

77. *Ibid.*, p. 368.   78. *Ibid.*, p. 209.   79. *Ibid.*, pp. 227–28.

80. Jean Siotis, *Essai Sur Le Secrétariat International* (Genève: Droz, 1963), p. 249.

81. O'Brien, *To Katanga and Back*, pp. 15–16.

82. Lash, *Dag Hammarskjold*, p. 201.

83. Foote (ed.), *Servant of Peace*, p. 209.   84. *Ibid.*, p. 47.

85. *Ibid.*, pp. 200–11 and 354–75.   86. *Ibid.*, pp. 346–47.

87. *Ibid.*, p. 347.   88. *Ibid.*, p. 346.   89. *Ibid.*, p. 348.

90. See *Ibid.*, p. 369.
91. See especially G. A. Res. 1474 (ES–IV), September 20, 1960.
92. U Thant, "Looking Ahead," *The Quest for Peace*, Andrew W. Cordier and Wilder Foote, eds. (New York: Columbia University Press, 1965), pp. 39–40.
93. "Five Powers Present Plan for General Disarmament as Ten-Nation Disarmament Conference Convenes," *The Department of State Bulletin*, XLII (April 4, 1960), 511–15.
94. Foote (ed.), *Servant of Peace*, p. 257.
95. United Nations: Office of Public Information, Press Services, Press Release SG/1046, July 20, 1961, pp. 2–3.
96. Foote (ed.), *Servant of Peace*, p. 258.   97. *Ibid.*

Notes to Chapter Seven

1. Barbara Ward, "The United Nations and the Decade of Development," *The Quest for Peace*, Andrew W. Cordier and Wilder Foote, eds. (New York: Columbia University Press, 1965), p. 201.
2. Hans J. Morgenthau, "The U.N. of Dag Hammarskjold is Dead," *The New York Times*, March 14, 1965, Section VI, p. 32.
3. See pp. 243–44.
4. Quoted in Lester B. Pearson, "Keeping the Peace," *The Quest for Peace*, Andrew W. Cordier and Wilder Foote, eds. (New York: Columbia University, 1965), p. 100.
5. Peter Calvocoressi, *World Order and the New States* (New York: Frederick A. Praeger, 1962), p. 69.
6. Ward, "The United Nations and the Decade of Development," p. 201.

Bibliography

The only section of this bibliography which requires some explanation is the one entitled "Interviews." Because some of the men interviewed requested that their names not be mentioned and that information not be attributed to them, this section does not include a complete list of the interviews which the author conducted. Any information gained from these sources which is used in this study is attributed in the footnotes to "Interviews."

Books

Bailey, Sydney D. *The Secretariat of the United Nations.* New York: Frederick A. Praeger, 1964.

Barnett, A. Doak. *Communist China and Asia. A Challenge to American Policy.* New York: Vintage Books, 1961.

Bechhoefer, Bernard G. *Postwar Negotiations for Arms Control.* Washington, D. C.: Brookings Institution, 1961.

Bowett, D. W. *United Nations Forces: A Legal Study.* New York: Frederick A. Praeger, 1964.

Boyd, Andrew. *United Nations: Piety, Myth and Truth.* Harmondsworth. England: Penguin Books, 1962.

Burns, E. L. M. *Between Arab and Israeli.* New York: I. Oblensky, 1962.

Burns, Arthur Lee, and Nina Heathcoate. *Peace-keeping by U.N. Forces: From Suez to the Congo.* New York: Frederick A. Praeger, 1963.

Calvocoressi, Peter. *World Order and the New States.* New York: Frederick A. Praeger, 1962.

Campbell, John C. *Defense of the Middle East.* Revised edition. New York: Frederick A. Praeger, 1960.

Claude, Inis L., Jr. *Swords into Plowshares. The Problems and Progress of International Organization.* 2nd edition. New York: Random House, 1964.

Bibliography

Commission to Study the Organization of Peace. *The U.N. Secretary-General: His Role in World Politics.* Fourteenth Report. New York: 1962.

Cordier, Andrew W., and Wilder Foote (eds.). *The Quest for Peace. The Dag Hammarskjold Memorial Lectures.* New York: Columbia University Press, 1965.

Dallin, Alexander. *The Soviet Union at the United Nations.* New York: Frederick A. Praeger, 1962.

Eden, Anthony. *The Memoirs of Anthony Eden. Full Circle.* Boston: Houghton Mifflin Co., 1960.

Fifield, Russel H. *The Diplomacy of Southeast Asia, 1945-1958.* New York: Harper and Brothers, 1958.

Finer, Herman. *Dulles Over Suez.* Chicago: Quadrangle Books, 1964.

Foote, Wilder (ed.). *Servant of Peace. A Selection of the Speeches and Statements of Dag Hammarskjold.* New York: Harper and Row, 1962.

Frydenberg, Per. *Peace-keeping Experience and Evaluation—The Oslo Papers.* Oslo: Norwegian Institute of International Affairs, 1964.

Frye, William R. *A United Nations Peace Force.* Dobbs Ferry, New York: Oceana Publications, 1957.

Gavshon, Arthur L. *The Mysterious Death of Dag Hammarskjold.* New York: Walker and Co., 1962.

Goodrich, Leland M. *The United Nations.* New York: Thomas Y. Crowell Co., 1959.

Gordon, King. *United Nations in the Congo. A Quest for Peace.* New York: Carnegie Endowment for International Peace, 1962.

Gross, Ernest A. *The United Nations Structures for Peace.* New York: Harper and Brothers, 1962.

Hammarskjold, Dag. *Markings* (Translated from the Swedish by Leif Sjoberg and W. H. Auden; with a foreword by W. H. Auden). New York: Alfred A. Knopf Co., 1964.

Iklé, Fred Charles. *How Nations Negotiate.* New York: Frederick A. Praeger, 1964.

Kelen, Emery. *Hammarskjold.* New York: G. P. Putnam's Sons, 1966.

—— (ed.). *Hammarskjold: The Political Man.* New York: Funk and Wagnalls, 1968.

Kelly, J. B. *Eastern Arabian Frontiers.* London: Faber and Faber, 1964.

Langrod, Georges. *The International Civil Service.* Dobbs Ferry, New York: Oceana Publications, 1963.

Laqueur, Walter Z. *The Soviet Union and the Middle East.* New York: Frederick A. Praeger, 1959.

Lash, Joseph P. *Dag Hammarskjold. Custodian of the Brush-Fire Peace.* New York: Doubleday and Co., 1961.

Lefever, Ernest W. *Crisis in the Congo. A UN Force in Action.* Washington, D.C.: Brookings Institution, 1965.

Legum, Colin. *Congo Disaster.* Baltimore: Penguin Books, 1961.

Lie, Trygve. *In the Cause of Peace.* New York: Macmillan Co., 1954.

McDougal, Myres S., and Florentino P. Feliciano. *Law and Minimum World Public Order.* New Haven: Yale University Press, 1961.

Mezerik, A. G. (ed.). *Congo and the United Nations.* Vol. I. New York: International Review Service, 1960.

Miller, Richard P. *Dag Hammarskjold and Crisis Diplomacy.* Dobbs Ferry, New York: Oceana Publications, 1961.

Munro, Sir Leslie. *United Nations: Hope for a Divided World.* New York: Henry Holt and Co., 1960.

Nicholas, Herbert G. *The United Nations as a Political Institution.* London: Oxford University Press, 1962.

O'Brien, Conor Cruise. *To Katanga and Back.* New York: Simon and Schuster, 1962.

Qubain, Fahim Issa. *Crisis in Lebanon.* Washington, D.C.: Middle East Institute, 1961.

Robertson, Terence. *Crisis. The Inside Story of the Suez Conspiracy.* New York: Atheneum, 1965.

Rosner, Gabriella. *The United Nations Emergency Force.* New York: Columbia University Press, 1963.

Russell, Ruth B. *United Nations Experience with Military Force: Political and Legal Aspects.* Research Paper P–27. Washington, D.C.: Institute for Defense Analyses, International Studies Division, 1963.

Rustow, Dankwart A. *The Politics of Compromise. A Study of Cabinet Government in Sweden.* Princeton: Princeton University Press, 1955.

Schelling, Thomas C. *The Strategy of Conflict.* New York: Oxford University Press, 1963.

Schwebel, Stephen M. *The Secretary-General of the United Nations: His Political Powers and Practices.* Cambridge: Harvard University Press, 1952.

Settel, T. S. (ed.). *The Light and the Rock: The Vision of Dag Hammarskjold.* New York: E. P. Dutton and Co., 1966.

Siotis, Jean. *Essai sur le Secrétariat International.* Geneva: Droz, 1963.

Stolpe, Sven. *Dag Hammarskjold: A Spiritual Portrait.* New York: Charles Scribner's Sons, 1966.

U. S. Department of State. *United States Policy in the Middle East. September 1956–1957. Documents.* Department of State Publication 6505. Near and Middle Eastern Series 25, August 1957.

Van Dusen, Henry P. *Dag Hammarskjold: The Statesman and His Faith.* New York: Harper and Row, 1964.

Van Langenhove, Fernand. *Le Rôle Prominent du Secrétaire Général* dans *L'Opération des Nations Unies au Congo*. La Haye: Martinus Nijhoff, 1964.

Virally, Michel. *L'O.N.U. d'Hier à Demain*. Paris: Editions du Seuil, 1961.

Walters, F. P. *A History of the League of Nations*. 2 vols. New York: Oxford University Press, 1952.

Wigforss, Ernst. *Minnen*. Vol. III. Stockholm: Tidens Forlag, 1954.

Zagoria, Donald S. *The Sino-Soviet Conflict, 1956–1961*. Princeton: Princeton University Press, 1962.

Articles

Ahman, Sven. "Dag Hammarskjold," in American Swedish Historical Foundation, *Yearbook*—1962, 41–45.

———. "Mr. Hammarskjold's Not-So-Quiet Diplomacy." *The Reporter*, XIX (September 4, 1958), 9–13.

Armstrong, Hamilton Fish. "U.N. Experience in Gaza," *Foreign Affairs*, XXXV (July 1957), 600–19.

———. "U.N. on Trial," *Foreign Affairs*, XXXIX (April 1961), 381–415.

Ascoli, Max. "The Future of the U.N.—An Editorial," *The Reporter*, XXV (October 26, 1961), 21–23.

———. "The Price of Peacemongering," *The Reporter*, XV (November 29, 1956), 12.

Bailey, Sydney D. "The Troika and the Future of the United Nations, *International Conciliation*, No. 538 (1962).

Bokhari, Ahmed S. "Parliaments, Priests and Prophets," *Foreign Affairs*, XXXV (April 1957), 405–11.

Boyd, Andrew, "The Unknown United Nations," *International Journal*, XIX (Spring 1964), 202–12.

Claude, Inis L. "The UN and the Use of Force," *International Conciliation*, No. 532 (March 1961).

———. "United Nations Use of Military Force," *Journal of Conflict Resolution*, VII (June 1963), 117–29.

Cordier, Andrew W. "Motivations and Methods of Dag Hammarskjold," *Paths of World Order*, Andrew W. Cordier and Kenneth Maxwell, eds. (New York: Columbia University Press, 1967), pp. 1–21.

———. "The Role of the Secretary-General," *Annual Review of United Nations Affairs, 1960–1961*, ed., Richard N. Swift (Dobbs Ferry, New York: Oceana Publications, 1961), 1–14.

Curtis, Gerald L. "The United Nations Observation Group in Lebanon," *International Organization*, XVIII (Autumn 1964), 738–65.

Draper, Theodore, "Ordeal of the U.N.: Khrushchev, Hammarskjold and the Congo," *The New Leader*, Section 2 (November 7, 1960).

Ennis, Thomas E. "Laos: Pawn in Power Politics," *Current History* XXXVIII (February 1960), 70–75.

Finkelstein, Lawrence S. "The United Nations and Organizations for the Control of Armaments," *International Organization*, XVI (Winter 1962), 1–19.

"Five Powers Present Plan for General Disarmament as Ten-Nations Disarmament Conference Convenes," *The Department of State Bulletin*, XLII (April 4, 1960), 511–15.

Franck, Thomas, and John Garey. "The Role of the United Nations in the Congo—A Retrospective Perspective," *The Hammarskjold Forums* (New York: The Association of the Bar of the City of New York, April 30, 1962).

Gaskill, Gordon. "Timetable of a Failure," *The Virginia Quarterly Review*, XXXIV (Spring 1958), 161–91.

Good, Robert C. "Congo Crisis: The Role of the New States," *Neutralism* (Washington, D.C.: The Washington Center of Foreign Policy Research, 1961), 1–46.

Goodrich, Leland M. "The Political Role of the Secretary-General," *International Organization*, XVI (Autumn 1962), 720–35.

Hammarskjold, Dag. "Education's Stake in World Peace and Progress," *United Nations Bulletin*. XVI (February 1, 1954), 136–39.

——. "For a New Approach to International Aid and Technical Assistance," *United Nations Review*, III (July 1956), 10–13.

——. "In 'Age of Responsibility' All Can Wield Influence," *United Nations Bulletin*, XVI (February 13, 1954), 199–200.

——. "Politik och ideologi," *Tiden*, XLIV (1952), 6–17.

——. "Private Investment and International Aid," *United Nations Review* (May 1960), 24–27.

——. "Statstjanstemannen och samhallet," *Tiden*, XLIII (1951), 391–96.

——. "The Element of Privacy in Peacekeeping," *United Nations Review*, IV (March 1958), 10–33.

——. "The United Nations and the Major Challenges Which Face the World Community," *United Nations Review*, IV (June 1958), 28–31.

——. "The United Nations and Newly Independent Countries: Two Addresses by Secretary-General Dag Hammarskjold," *United Nations Review*, VI (April 1960), 10–15.

——. "The United Nations in the Modern World." *Journal of International Affairs*, IX (1955), 7–11.

——. "The Vital Role of the United Nations in a Diplomacy of Reconciliation," *United Nations Review*, IV (May 1958), 6–10.

——. "Strengthening Universal Action with Action on a Regional Level," United Nations Bulletin, XVI (March 15, 1954), 213–14.

———. "To Choose Europe," Copenhagen: United Nations, Information Center for Denmark, Iceland, Norway and Sweden. (A translation of an article which he wrote in 1952).

———. "United Nations Only Coming of Age but Confidence Already 'Voted'," *United Nations Bulletin*, XVI (June 1, 1954), 414–15.

———. "United Nations—The Way Ahead," *United Nations Bulletin*, XVI (January 1, 1954), 7–9.

———. "Why the United Nations?," *United Nations Review*, V (July 1958), 14–17.

Hoffman, Stanley. "An Evaluation of the UN," *Ohio State Law Journal*, XXII (Summer 1961), 477–94.

———. "In Search of a Thread: the U.N. in the Congo Labyrinth," *International Organization*, XVI (Spring 1962), 331–61.

———. "Sisyphus and the Avalanche: The United Nations, Egypt and Hungary," *International Organization*, XI (Summer 1957), 446–69.

Jackson, Elmore. "Constitutional Developments of the United Nations: The Growth of Executive Capacity," *Proceedings of the American Society of International Law*, LV (1961), 78–84.

———. "The Developing Role of the Secretary-General," *International Organization*, XI (Summer 1957), 431–45.

Jacobson, Harold Karan. "ONUC's Civilian Operations: State-Preserving and State-Building," *World Politics*, XVII (October 1964), 75–107.

Jordan, William M. "Concepts and Realities in International Political Organization," *International Organization*, XI (Autumn 1957), 587–96.

Kraft, Joseph. "The Untold Story of the UN's Congo Army," *Harper's Magazine*, CCXXI (November 1960), 75–76, 78, 80, and 82.

Lash, Joseph P. "Dag Hammarskjold's Conception of his Office," *International Organization*, XVI (Autumn 1962), 542–66.

Lippmann, Walter. "Dag Hammarskjold, United Nations Pioneer," *International Organization*, XV (Autumn 1961), 547–48.

Miller, E. M. "Legal Aspects of the United Nations Action in the Congo," *American Journal of International Law*. LV (January 1961), 1–28.

Morgenthau, Hans J. "The New Secretary-General," *Commentary*, January 1963, 62–65.

———. "The U.N. of Dag Hammarskjold Is Dead," *The New York Times*, March 14, 1965, Section VI, 32.

Pearson, Lester B. "Force for U.N.," *Foreign Affairs*, XXV (April 1957), 395–404.

Pyman, T. A. "The United Nations Secretary-Generalship: A Review of Its Status, Functions and Role," *Australian Outlook*, XV (1961), 240–59.

Schachter, Oscar. "Dag Hammarskjold and the Relation of Law to Politics," *American Journal of International Law*, LVI (January 1962), 1–8.

Stanton, Edwin F. "A 'Presence' in Laos," *Current History*, XXXVIII (June 1960), 337–41.

Stein, Eric. "Mr. Hammarskjold, the Charter Law and Future Role of the United Nations Secretary-General," *American Journal of International Law*, LVI (January 1962), 9–32.

Urquhart, Brian E. "United Nations Peace Forces and the Changing United Nations: An Institutional Perspective," *International Organization*, XVII (Spring 1963), 338–54.

Van Bilsen, A. A. J. "Some Aspects of the Congo Problem," *International Affairs*, XXXVIII (January 1962), 41–51.

Virally, Michel. "Le Rôle Politique de Secrétaire Général des Nations-Unies," *Annuaire Français de Droit International*, IV (1958), 369–99.

Zacher, Mark W., "The Secretary-General and the United Nations' Function of Peaceful Settlement," *International Organization*, XX (Autumn 1966), 724–49.

Documents

United Nations: General Assembly. *Official Records*.

United Nations: Security Council. *Official Records*.

United Nations: Office of Public Information, Press Services, Press Releases.

United Nations: Office of Public Information, Press Services, Notes.

Newspapers

Survey of the China Mainland Press (Hong Kong: United States Consulate General). 1954–1955.

The New York Times. 1953–1961.

Unpublished Material

Ayman [Ahman], Sven. "Impressions of Dag Hammarskjold." Unpublished Interview, Oral History Office, Columbia University, 1963.

Gross, Ernest A. "Dag Hammarskjold as Secretary-General." Unpublished Interview, Oral History Office, Columbia University, 1964.

Bibliography

Speeches

Cordier, Andrew W. "Dag Hammarskjold." Presented to the Scandinavian Society of Columbia University, December 17, 1964.
———. "The Political Role of the United Nations Secretary-General," Presented to the International Fellows Program of Columbia University, April 20, 1964.

Interviews

Ahman, Sven. United Nations Correspondent for the Stockholm Newspaper *Dagens Nyheter*, November 12, 1964.

Cook, Charles. Former Member of the United States Delegation to the United Nations, November 17, 1964.

Cordier, Andrew W. Former Executive Assistant to the Secretary-General of the United Nations, April 21, 1965, September 6, 1966.

Engen, Hans. Former Ambassador of Norway to the United Nations, December 3, 1964.

Evans, Luther. Former Director-General of the United Nations Educational, Scientific and Cultural Organization, April 23, 1965.

Foote, Wilder. Former Director of the Press and Publications Division of the United Nations' Office of Public Information, March 6, 1965.

Lind, Per. Former Assistant to Dag Hammarskjold in the Foreign Ministry of Sweden and in the United Nations, January 23, 1965.

Schachter, Oscar. Director of the General Legal Division of the United Nations, Office of Legal Affairs, October 30, 1964.

Wilcox, Francis. Former Assistant Secretary of State for International Organization Affairs, United States Department of State, April 26, 1965.

Index

Index

Israel, and conflict with Arabs in early 1956, 70-74; Mt. Scopus conflict, 83-85; passage through Suez Canal, 85-88; conflict with Syria, 115; Suez Crisis, 140-48, 187-88, 189-90; withdrawal of UNEF, 180

Jacobson, Harold, cited, 167
Japan, and Middle East conflict of 1958, 100, 182
Jenner, William, 59
Jessup, Philip, 110
Jordan, and Middle East crisis of 1958, 77-79, 83-85, 100-101, 132; Mt. Scopus conflict, 83-85; see also Arab-Israeli conflict

Kalongi, Albert, 107
Kasavubu, Joseph, 107, 108, 152, 155, 157-60, 171, 177, 191, 192
Katanga, 155, 156, 158-60, 162, 163, 170, 171, 183, 190, 195, 196
Kelen, Emery, cited, 50, 67-69, 128, 208
Kelly, J. B., cited, 97-98
Kettani, Ben Hammou, 191, 192
Khiari, Mohammed, 108
Khruschchev, Nikita, 64, 74, 134, 158, 211, 238
Knowland, William, 59
Korean Armistice Agreement, 58-59, 126
Korean War, 55, 58
Kraft, Joseph, cited, 151, 152, 194

Laotian crisis, 102-106, 167-68, 226
Laqueur, Walter, cited, 64, 144
Lash, Joseph, cited, 8, 12, 13, 17-18, 64, 70, 71, 74, 81, 86-88, 90, 91, 103, 104, 129, 131, 142, 188, 201, 241, 242
Lasswell, Harold, cited, 3

Latin American states, and Suez crisis, 147
Law of outer space, conference on, 227
Law of the sea, Conferences on, 226
League of Nations, 50, 110, 214
Leary, William, 84
Lebanon, see Middle East conflict of 1958
Lefever, Ernest, cited, 108, 153, 156
Legal powers of U.N. organs, 27-39
Legum, Colin, cited, 153, 157
Less-developed states, and international quality, 215; decision-making on economic aid, 220-22, see also Afro-Asian states and African states
Lie, Trygve, 40, 62, 126
Lind, Per, cited, 15, 46
Linnaeus, Carl, 11
Lippmann, Walter, cited, 18
Lloyd, Selwyn, 81, 88, 93, 100, 101
Lodge, Henry Cabot, 29
Lower Mekong basin, 220
Lumumba, Patrice, 108, 152, 155-59, 177, 181, 183, 190-92, 194, 195

Malaya, and Congo crisis, 159
Manila Pact Conference, 59
Markings, cited, 45, 46, 132
Marxist theory of international politics, 18-19
McCarthy, Joseph, 59
McDougal, Myres S., cited, vi, 3
Mediation by Secretary-General tactics, 113-32
Meir, Golda, 88
Membership of U.N., as basis of power, 50-51
Middle East conflict of 1958, 63-65, 76-79, 90-93, 99-102, 124, 132, 164-66
Middle East, conflicts in, 66, 67
Miller, Richard F., cited, 59, 79, 95